Classic Heathkit Computers, Calculators, and Robots

by Jeff Tranter

First Printing: February 2024.
ISBN: 978-0-9921382-2-6

This book was developed using Open Source/Free Software including the LibreOffice office suite, GIMP image manipulation program, and Ubuntu Linux desktop operating system.

Dedication

This book is dedicated to my wife Veronica, who tolerates my hobby and never complains about the many hours spent on it. At least it keeps me off the streets!

Dedication

(this page intentionally left blank)

Table of Contents

Preface

I've had a lifelong interest in computers. One of my earliest memories about computers was in grade four[1]. Each student in the class was asked to teach a lesson on a topic of their choosing. I chose to talk about computers. My entire knowledge of computers was based on the one book I had read, *The How and Why Wonder Book of Robots and Electronic Brains*[2].

Figure 1: My First Computer Book

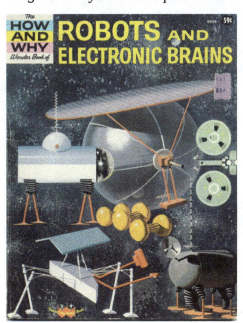

The lesson included giving the class a written quiz on the material taught, and I still remember one of the (incorrect) answers written by one of my classmates. The question was "What does IBM stand for?" and his answer was "Important Business Man".

Around the same time my father gave me a slide rule. While already becoming obsolete, it gave me a fascinating insight into numbers and how a mechanical device could perform calculations. I have a small collection of slide rules to this day.

---

1 Oddly enough, my family was living in India at the time. For more details, see my book *Letters From India: The Chronicles of a Canadian Family Living in India from 1970 to 1972*.[2]
2 A few years ago I located and purchased a copy of the book.[1]

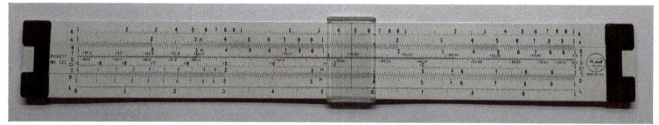

Figure 2: One of my Slide Rules

Even earlier, my father had shown me something called CARDIAC [3]. Developed by Bell Labs, it was an ingenious model of a computer processor made from paper that relied on the user to operate it. It demonstrated how a processor worked at the machine code level. I'm not sure at the time that I grasped that this was a computer. The gulf between this primitive device that could only understand ten simple operations and the computers I saw shown on television's *Star Trek* and films like *2001: A Space Odyssey* was a wide one.

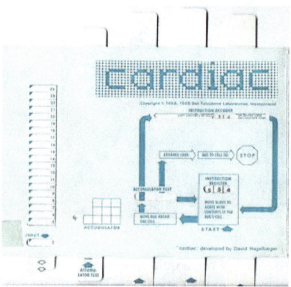

Figure 3: CARDIAC:
CARDboard Illustrative Aid
to Computing

I had some exposure to programming, in the BASIC language, in high school. By the late 1970s, computers were becoming more affordable, and in my first year of study at university I bought an Ohio Scientific Superboard II computer. As well as BASIC, I learned 6502 machine and assembly language programming. Later I worked with the Apple series, various Commodore computers, and eventually IBM PC compatibles. I ultimately made a career in computers and currently work in the field of software consulting.

For those of us who used computers at an early age, they have become a source of nostalgia. People have started collecting old computers and even building replicas, either from scratch or as kits. Vince Briel [4] [5] offered a replica of the little-known Apple 1, the first product developed by Apple

Computers in a garage in 1976 and later developed replicas of several other classic computers. As just another example, Mike Willegal [6], who also builds replicas of the Apple 1 and Apple II, has painstakingly reverse-engineered and duplicated one of the first microcomputers, the SCELBI, and is offering circuit boards to people who want to build a system.

There is a growing market for used computers on sites like eBay. Real Apple 1 computers, of which only a few dozen still exist, have sold at auction for as much as of $700,000. Apple II machines, with somewhere around six million sold, are still desirable on the used market. It is all part of the movement that is now known as *retrocomputing*.

This book is about Heathkit's computers and related products. My first exposure to Heathkit was in 1974 when my father and I built a Heathkit PT-15 Photo Timer. I went on to purchase several used Heathkits when I became interested in amateur radio and electronics. I remember seeing Heathkit's early computers when I visited the local store in Mississauga, Ontario, Canada. Years later, with the advent of the internet and eBay, it has become much easier to find and obtain Heathkits, and I've acquired some of units that I had once looked at enviously but couldn't afford when they were new. You can see videos of many of my Heathkits and other vintage equipment on my YouTube channel. [7]

Whether you are interested in collecting and restoring old Heathkit computers, or simply have nostalgia for these products, I hope this book both entertains and enlightens you.

(this page intentionally left blank)

Acknowledgments

I don't personally own most of the Heathkit computers listed here. The material was gleaned from information on the internet, mailing lists, old Heathkit catalogs, and manuals. There are undoubtedly some errors in a book of this size, and I take sole responsibility for them.

My thanks go to Lulu [8] for their print-on-demand, self-publishing, and distribution platform that I used for this and my previous books. I had the pleasure of meeting their founder and CEO Bob Young in the early days of Linux; he was the co-founder of Red Hat Linux (now part of IBM).

I welcome any corrections, suggestions for improvement, or general feedback on the book. Updated information about the book including errata and updates can be found on the book website [9].

Structure of this Book

The scope of this book is Heathkit computers, using a very wide definition of what a computer is. Chapter one presents a short history of Heathkit with particular emphasis on their computer business, which was heavily influenced by their acquisition by parent company Zenith Data Systems.

Chapter two covers Heathkit's early analog computers, devices that many people would not even consider computers by today's standards.

Chapter three covers the Heathkit electronic calculator kits that were introduced in the 1970s.

Chapter four covers the 8-bit computers, primarily the Intel 8080-based H-8, and its successors.

Chapter five covers the 16-bit H-11 and related models that were compatible with Digital Equipment Corporation's PDP-11 minicomputer.

Chapter six covers what I call 8/16-bit computers, including the H-100/Z-100, Z-110, and H-120/Z-120.

By the early 1980s, it became obvious to most computer vendors, including Heath, that IBM and compatibles were becoming the dominant architecture, and these are covered in chapter seven.

Chapter eight looks at the HERO series of Heathkit robots.

Chapter nine covers serial terminals, which were typically required to effectively use the early computers like the H-8.

Chapter 10 covers other peripherals and accessories including printers, modems, floppy and hard drives, and monitors.

Heathkit was heavily involved in education and technical training; in fact, it was their only business toward the end. Chapter 11 covers the microprocessor trainers, related educational courses, and some miscellaneous computer-related products that do not fit in any of the other categories covered in earlier chapters.

Chapter 12 looks at the various types of software offered for the Heathkit computers, including both operating systems and applications.

Chapter 13 looks at what is happening in the world of Heathkit computers today. It provides some tips on buying systems, finding parts, and restoring old hardware to working operation.

The appendix includes a comprehensive list of resources including books, websites, and other internet resources as well as a detailed product listing of over 500 Heathkit computers and accessories with selling prices and dates of manufacture. Any references listed in the text in brackets (e.g. [2]) refer to bibliographic entries given in the bibliography.

You'll also find a handy alphabetical index as well as a list of the figures in the text.

It can be quite shocking just how expensive these early computers were, especially when converted to the equivalent in today's dollars taking inflation into account. As just one example, the H-67 hard disk drive peripheral provided 11 Megabytes of storage and sold for $5,800 in 1981 - equivalent to over $15,000 in 2024. It was housed in its own case and weighed 67 pounds! At the time I write this a 16 Gigabyte USB key (providing more than a thousand times this amount of storage) can be bought for under $5. Any prices listed here are in US dollars unless otherwise indicated.

Finally, a word on terminology. Heathkit was not entirely consistent in the names of models. You'll see, for example, references to both H11 and H-11. In the case of the H-8 and H-11 series of computers and related peripherals like terminals, it appears that the addition of the dash occurred when Heath was acquired by Zenith. I've attempted to use the model names and other terminology that were used most often in Heathkit catalogs and marketing materials.

Jeff Tranter
Ottawa, Ontario, Canada.
February, 2024.

Chapter 1: A Brief History of Heathkit

The history of the Heathkit company is an interesting one, and while it has been covered in detail elsewhere, it is worth reviewing some of the highlights.

The Heath Company was originally founded as an aircraft company, the *E.B. Heath Aerial Vehicle Co.* by Edward Bayard Heath. Dealing in aircraft parts, Edward Heath also designed some airplanes. In 1926 the company offered the *Heath Parasol* airplane in kit form. It was moderately successful and can be considered the first Heathkit.

Tragically, Edward Heath was killed in the test flight of an experimental aircraft in 1931. Shortly after, the company's assets were purchased by Howard Anthony, and the business focused on selling aircraft accessories. It was at this time that the company moved to Benton Harbor, Michigan where it was to reside throughout most of its history.

After the Second World War, there was a large supply of surplus electronic parts on the market. Howard Anthony leveraged these parts to offer a kit for an oscilloscope. The O1 sold for $39.50, roughly half of what a commercially assembled unit of the time cost. It was very popular and the company expanded its product line into more kits for test equipment, and later amateur radio, Hi-Fi, and other products.

Ironically, in 1954 Howard Anthony was also killed in a plane crash. Shortly after, Heath was acquired by the Daystrom Company and continued to expand with a larger factory and distribution centers in other countries.

In 1962, Daystrom was acquired by Schlumberger Limited, and the company continued to expand through the 1960s and 70s. In 1974, the Heathkit Educational Systems division was formed to focus on the education and technical training markets.

1977 saw the introduction of Heathkit's H-8 and H-11 computers. These were immediately successful (especially the former), and attracted the interest of the Zenith Radio company, which wanted to get into the computer business. In 1979 Heathkit was acquired by Zenith, forming Zenith Data Systems (ZDS). The ownership of Zenith influenced Heathkit's direction from that point on, with an increasing focus on computers, and less on the other product lines such as test equipment and amateur radio.

In 1982, Heathkit announced the HERO (**H**eathkit **E**ducational **RO**bot), starting with the HERO 1 and later followed by the HERO Jr. and HERO 2000 models.

By 1984, most of the personal computer industry had standardized on the IBM PC, and Heathkit decided to focus on producing kits and peripherals for IBM PC compatibles.

Figure 4: Heathkit's First IBM PC Compatible Computer Kits

By this time, Heathkit had stopped developing any new amateur radio products and in 1989 Zenith Data Systems was acquired by Groupe Bull. In 1992 Heathkit officially shut down the kit business, leaving only the division focusing on educational products.

The next decade or so saw Heathkit sold to a number of different owners and investors. The stock of remaining Heathkit manuals was sold to Data Professionals (a company that sells reproduction manuals) along with the rights to sell and distribute them.

Finally, in 2012, Heathkit Educational Systems filed for bankruptcy and shut down for good. This is generally considered to be the end of Heathkit as it had been known.

In 2011, some new owners purchased the rights to the Heathkit name and announced a return to the kit business. Some proposed kits were announced which never materialized and the company went dark again.

Figure 5: A Current Heathkit Product: The Explorer TRF AM Radio

In 2013, yet another new owner of the Heathkit name announced the intention to return to the kit business. In 2015 they released the first new kit since 1992: the GR-150 Explorer TRF AM radio receiver. 2017 saw the product line expanding to include the GC-1006 Most Reliable Clock and AN-P2L Pipetenna VHF/UHF antenna kit. Also announced were preorders for their most ambitious kit, the $575 HM-1002 Precision RF Meter (still not shipping as of early 2024),

The new company is something of a mystery. Their website [10] claims "Our CEO/President, and every member of Heath Company's Board of Directors, are avid kit-builders and DIYers. Our Chief Engineer is a past Heathkit employee who designed and developed Heathkit kit products decades ago". In several interviews and sales material, the Heathkit CEO is only listed as *Andy*. For those who are curious, a search of recent patents filed by Heathkit [11] [12] lists the full names of the inventors, including one named Andrew.

It remains to be seen if the latest incarnation of Heathkit will be successful. Reviews of their initial kits have been mixed, but most enthusiasts wish them well, even if it is unlikely that they will ever return to the glory days of the past.

The table below lists some of the key milestone dates in the history of Heathkit.

Figure 6: Major Milestones for the Heath Company

1912	Heath Company founded as aircraft company by Edward Bayard Heath.
1926	Offered Heath Parasol airplane kit.
1931	Edward Heath killed in test flight.
1935	Assets purchased by Howard Anthony. Company sells aircraft accessories.
1947	Introduced O1 oscilloscope kit using war surplus parts. Focus shifts to electronic kits.
1954	Howard Anthony killed in plane crash.
1955	Heath Company acquired by Daystrom Company.
1962	Daystrom acquired by Schlumberger Limited.
1974	Heathkit Educational Systems division formed.
1977	Introduction of H-8 and H-11 computers.
1979	Acquired by Zenith Radio Company, forming Zenith Data Systems (ZDS).
1982	HERO 1 robot introduced.
1984	Computer kits focus on IBM PC compatibles.
1989	Zenith Data Systems acquired by Groupe Bull.
1992	Heathkit leaves the kit business, focuses on educational products.
1995	Heathkit sold to HIG.
1998	Sold to investment group, then to DESA International.
2008	DESA International files bankruptcy. Heathkit Educational Systems continues.
2012	Heathkit Educational Systems files for bankruptcy and shuts down.
2013	New owner of Heathkit name announces intention to return to kit business.
2015	Heathkit releases first new kit: GR-150 Explorer TRF AM radio receiver.
2017	Heathkit offers GC-1006 Most Reliable Clock and AN-P2L Pipetenna VHF/UHF antenna kit. Announces HM-1002 Precision RF Meter.

(this page intentionally left blank)

Chapter 2: Analog Computers

In this chapter, we'll take a look at the two analog computers that were offered by Heathkit, the ES series and the EC-1. Before doing that, let's take a brief look at what analog computers are.

What is an Analog Computer?

An analog computer is a device that uses some continuously variable physical phenomenon such as electrical voltage to model the problem being solved. This is in contrast to digital computers which represent quantities symbolically using discrete numerical values, usually ones and zeroes.

The slide rule and graphical nomograph are both examples of analog computers, but in the context of this book we'll focus on electronic analog computers. They were once widely used in scientific and industrial applications before the advent of digital computers made them obsolete for most purposes.

Analog computers are particularly useful for solving dynamic problems which can be expressed in the form of differential equations. There is a mathematical similarity between linear mechanical components such as springs and viscous-fluid dampers, and electrical components such as capacitors, inductors, and resistors. They can be modeled using equations of the same form.

The basic operations that can be performed by most analog electronic computers are addition, subtraction, multiplication by a constant, multiplication by -1 (inversion), and integration. They typically used DC amplifiers (also known as operational amplifiers or op-amps) as the basic building blocks. With a few external components, an op-amp can be wired to perform any of the above functions. More complex devices or circuits can also be provided, such as a function generator.

By using potentiometers and/or resistors, the coefficients for a problem can be varied. One or more variable power supplies are typically provided to set the machine variables (voltages) to the correct initial conditions.

The basic procedure for solving a problem with an analog computer is:
1. Connect suitable computing elements to simulate the problem (e.g. combinations of integration, multiplication, addition, etc.)
2. Set the machine variables (voltages) to the correct initial conditions and start operation.
3. Observe and/or record the voltage variations with respect to time, which constitute the solution of the problem.
4. Stop the machine and reset it for a new run.

Results are typically observed on a meter, DC oscilloscope, or pen chart recorder.

An oscillator driving relays can be used to cause the computer to repeat the run repetitively, allowing the operator to make changes and observe the behavior.

A typical problem, and one which was used as an example in the Heathkit manuals, is the "falling body problem". The motion of a mass under the influence of the earth's gravitational field can be modeled using the differential equation:

$$\frac{d^2y}{dt^2} = g$$

Where g is the acceleration of gravity in the earth's gravitational field and y is the distance the body falls in time t. To find the value of y, it is necessary to integrate twice. This can be done by wiring two op amps as integrators as in the diagram below:

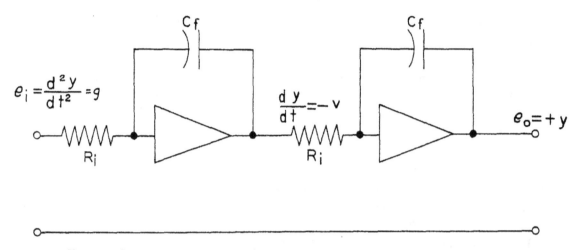

Figure 7: Falling Body Circuit (From Operation Manual for the Heath Educational Analog Computer EC-1)

The value of g can be supplied using an initial condition power supply.

To be able to run the problem repetitively, relay contacts driven by an oscillator can be connected across the capacitors in the integration circuits to discharge them at the start of a cycle. A complete circuit with component values is shown below:

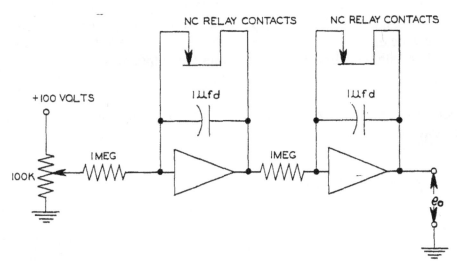

Figure 8: Complete Circuit for the Falling Body Problem (From Operation Manual for the Heath Educational Analog Computer EC-1)

When wired up on an analog computer like the Heathkit ES series or EC-1, the output can be seen on the meter or an oscilloscope. The oscilloscope will indicate position on the vertical or y axis and time on the x or horizontal axis. A typical result will appear as in the figure below:

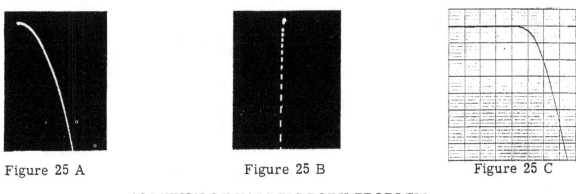

Figure 25 A   Figure 25 B   Figure 25 C

SOLUTION OF FALLING·BODY PROBLEM

(a) As observed on oscilloscope.   Body was given initial horizontal velocity.
(b) As observed on oscilloscope (no initial horizontal velocity).   The dashes represent equal time intervals, showing the increased distance traveled during each succeeding time interval.
(c) As recorded on pen recorder.

Figure 9: Solution of Falling-Body Problem (From Operation Manual for the Heath Educational Analog Computer EC-1)

The results from an analog computer are not just qualitative, they can be quantitative. By scaling the input value to voltage (for example, 1 foot equals 10 volts), and adjusting the circuit gain values according to the mathematical problem, the resulting voltage can be converted back to distance, provided that the result is within the limits of the computer (an output range of -100 to +100 volts was common).

More complex problems can be solved by wiring up suitable computing elements, within the limitations of what is available in the particular analog computer being used, such as the number of amplifiers.

The ES Series Analog Computer

Figure 10: Heathkit ES Series Analog Computer

Introduced in 1956, the ES series (shown above) was Heathkit's first Analog computer product and is generally thought to be the first commercially offered analog computer kit.

There was no model number for the computer itself as it was a modular system made up of different components that were selected based on the user's needs. It was generally called the "Heath Analog Computer" or referred to as the "ES Series Computer". As Heathkit's later computer products were often assigned an "H" series product designation (H-5, H-8, etc.) it is sometimes referred to as the H-1 but this was never used by Heathkit in any of their documentation or marketing materials. It is also sometimes mistakenly referred to as the ES-400 because this was marked on the unit, but this was only the model number of the cabinet itself.

It was a modular design where the user could pick the components needed and expand it later. It was also sold as standard bundles of modules that were less expensive to purchase than all of the individual components. They were referred to as *Group A* (typical or small configuration, typically selling for $520), *Group B* (medium configuration, selling for $760), and *Group C* (the full configuration at $945). The primary difference in the different configurations was the number of amplifiers: 5, 10, and 15 respectively.

The full ES series Group C weighed about 168 pounds, took 450 Watts of power, and at $945 in 1959 was equivalent to over $8,000 today.

A 1964 Heathkit catalog presented this description of the system and its capabilities:

"The Heathkit Modular Analog Computer Kit (ES Series) provides an advanced "slide-rule" which permits engineering and research personnel to simulate equations of physical problems electronically, thus saving many hours of costly calculation and experimentation. It offers many advantages over other commercial computers since it is available in a wide choice of component groups. It is perfect for design work and adaptable to specific problems which utilize only a portion of the items of the complete computer group.

Because it comes in kit form, and the individual components are available separately depending on your personal requirements, the cost is phenomenally low considering its many uses and applications in today's educational, scientific, and industrial worlds. And another asset obtained by building the computer yourself is the intimate knowledge you receive about the inner workings of these instruments. Construction is aided by Heath's famous "check-by-step" instructions and large pictorial reference diagrams and illustrations.

The ES-300 computer cabinet houses the power supplies, DC amplifiers and computing components. It includes an accurate dividing network which introduces voltages to a null meter with an accuracy of 1/10 of 1%. By means of a switch, a potentiometer may be connected to the meter, and its value checked. This eliminates inaccuracy due to potentiometer non-linearity, or loading. The dividing network and meter may also be used to set up initial conditions, to set diode bias, and to read any voltage which appears at the amplifier. The meter may be switched to any of the fifteen amplifiers so they will be set to give full scale deflection of +/- 2, 20 and 100 volts. The board also has the plus and minus 100 volt standard available, which is used in the dividing network. The built-in meter serves as the readout indicator or an external DC oscilloscope, pen recorder, etc. may be employed using the output terminals provided.

Some of the typical problems solved by the computer relate to mechanical vibration and oscillation, dynamic heat transfer, automotive control systems, aircraft and missile stability and control, fluid flow, simulation of nuclear reactors, rigid body dynamics, and many more complex mathematical problems.

Analyze your present computer requirements now and order the component groups you need. A free folder is available explaining the various computer groups and the function of each element in the group."

The following pages show a brochure that Heathkit offered listing the components of the ES series.

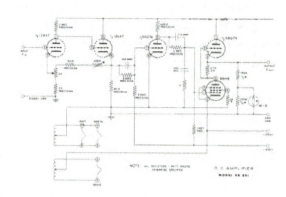

SPECIFICATIONS:

This unit will contain the following:

15 Amplifiers
30 Coefficient potentiometers
2 Auxiliary 10 turn potentiometers
6 floating initial conditions
4 dual bias diodes
1 metering circuit with dividing network
2 operational relays
1 Amplifier power supply
1 Repetitive oscillator
1 Reference power supply

Outstanding Features:

This unit is unique in its ability to calibrate for high accuracy. By means of a null meter the following functions may be accurately measured:

1—Coefficient setting
2—Overall gain from input to output of the amplifier
3—Initial Condition Set
4—Bias diode setting
5—Set up of a function generator
6—Throw voltages for operational relays

HEATH INEXPENSIVE ELECTRONIC ANALOG
computer KIT

DESCRIPTION:

This is a highly flexible and accurate analog computer, designed to fill requirements not presently met by any commercial computer. It is an instrument suitable for use as a design tool in industry and universities. An advanced "slide rule" which permits engineering or research personnel to electronically simulate equations or physical problems and save many hours of calculation or experimentation. Ideal for solving practical problems in industry, and equally valuable for research, or instructional demonstration, in colleges and universities.

Because it is a kit, and the labor and overhead costs found in present day computers are eliminated, the Heath Computer can be obtained for use in situations where a computer was ruled out in the past because of cost. Definitely not a "gadget," but a high-quality, flexible, high-accuracy device designed to work for you. Incorporates such features as:

▶ *30 coefficient potentiometers, each capable of being set to an accuracy better than 1/10 of 1%.*
▶ *One standard reference supply for amplifier DC voltages.*
▶ *A nulling meter for accurate setting of computer voltages.*
▶ *A unique patch-board panel which enables the operator to "see" his computer block layout.*

CABINET: ES-400

The computer cabinet houses power supplies, amplifiers, and computing components. It includes an accurate dividing network which introduces voltages to a null meter with an accuracy of better than 1/10 of 1%. By means of a switch, a potentiometer may be connected to the meter and read. This eliminates inaccuracy due to potentiometer nonlinearity, or loading.

The dividing network and meter may also be used to set up the initial conditions, to off-set bias diodes, and to read any voltage which appears at the amplifier. The meter may be switched to any of the 15 amplifiers so they may be set to give full scale deflection of plus or minus 2, 20 and 100 volts. The board also has the plus and minus 100-volt standard available, which is used in the dividing network.

HEATH ELECTRONIC ANALOG *computer* KIT

AMPLIFIER POWER SUPPLY — MODEL ES-2

PURPOSE: To supply power to the amplifiers and function generators.

OUTSTANDING FEATURES: The plus and minus voltages are referenced from one standard and are so interconnected as to null or cancel power supply drift to the amplifiers.

POWER OUTPUT: Plus 250 V. at 250 mills, minus 250 V. at 250 mills, minus 450 V. at 50 mills, 6.3 V.A.C. at 12 amps, and 6.3 V.A.C. at 2.5 amps.

TUBE COMPLEMENT: 1—5651, 3—12AX7, 3—6U8, 2—6080, 1—6BX7, 2—5R4GY, 1—5U4GB.

MOUNTING: This unit may be mounted in the computer cabinet or on a rack for special purpose computers.

This power supply is a highly stable unit which features voltage regulation by a single 5651 tube. It is well rated for its use.

INITIAL CONDITIONS — MODEL ES-100

PURPOSE: To supply initial condition voltage to integrators.

OUTSTANDING FEATURES: Low drift rate, ungrounded, floating supply, highly shielded.

TUBE COMPLEMENT: 2—OB2.

MOUNTING: Three of these dual initial conditions power supplies mount inside the computer cabinet. This makes a total of six floating power supplies available.

This unit contains two separate supplies both of which can be varied from zero to 100 volts. Since they are floating supplies, they may be used for offsetting amplifiers and biasing diodes.

AMPLIFIER — MODEL ES-201

PURPOSE: To provide an amplifier for integration, sign changing, addition, and multiplication by a constant.

OUTSTANDING FEATURES: This unit is a highly stable unit with low drift. It is linear from plus 100 to minus 100 volts, will deliver 10 mills, and has an open loop gain of 50,000. Its phase shift when connected as a unity inverter is less than one degree at 1200 cycles.

TUBE COMPLEMENT: 1—12AX7, 1—6BQ7A, 1—6BH6.

POWER REQUIREMENTS: Plus 250 V., minus 250 V., minus 450 V. Quiescent power is less than 5 watts.

MOUNTING: This unit may be mounted at the rear of the computer or on a standard rack mounting for special purpose computer.

This unit has a shielded chassis and makes use of printed circuits for ease of construction and uniformity. It is mounted at the top rear of the computer where it is shielded thermally and electrically from the rest of the computer.

RELAY POWER SUPPLY — MODEL ES-151

PURPOSE: To supply power to operate the functional relays.

OUTSTANDING FEATURES: Has built in voltage surge network to insure simultaneous operation of the relays.

POWER OUTPUT: Designed to supply 50 volts across four 10,000 ohm relays.

MOUNTING: This unit may be mounted in the computer cabinet or in a special purpose computer.

This unit supplies a high surge voltage for rapid simultaneous operation of the relays, then the voltage drops to that necessary to hold the relays.

REFERENCE POWER SUPPLY — MODEL ES-50

PURPOSE: To supply highly stable and accurate reference voltages.

OUTPUT: Plus 100 volts and minus 100 volts.

TUBE COMPLEMENT: 2—6X4, 2—6U8, 1—5651.

MOUNTING: This unit may be mounted in the computer cabinet or in a special purpose computer.

In this supply the positive and negative voltages are slaved together and referenced from a single 5651. When operated with the constant voltage transformer, the output ripple, jitter, and noise is negligible.

REPETITIVE OSCILLATOR — MODEL ES-505

PURPOSE: To provide repetitive operation of the functional relays.

OUTSTANDING FEATURES: Has an adjustable repetition rate of 0.6 to 6.0 times per second.

TUBE COMPLEMENT: 1—6J6.

MOUNTING: This unit may be mounted in the front of the computer cabinet or in a special purpose computer.

The repetitive oscillator allows problem solutions to be displayed on an oscilloscope.

HEATH ELECTRONIC ANALOG computer KIT

price list

SMALL COMPUTER—GROUP A $495

GROUP CONTAINS:

One ES 2   Amplifier power supply kit
One ES 100   Initial condition power supply kit.
One ES 151   Relay power supply kit
Five ES 201   Operational amplifier kits
One ES 400   Cabinet kit
One ES 405   Patch cord kit

MEDIUM COMPUTER—GROUP B $775

GROUP CONTAINS:

One ES 2   Amplifier power supply kit
One ES 50   Reference power supply kit
Two ES 100   Initial condition power supply kits
One ES 151   Relay power supply kit
Ten ES 201   Operational amplifier kits
One ES 400   Cabinet kit
One ES 401   Voltage regulator transformer kit
Two ES 405   Patch cord kits
One ES 447   Coefficient potentiometer kit
One ES 505   Repetitive oscillator kit

FULL COMPUTER—GROUP C $945

GROUP CONTAINS:

One   ES 2   Amplifier power supply kit
One   ES 50   Reference power supply kit
Three   ES 100   Initial condition power supply kits
One   ES 151   Relay power supply kit
Fifteen ES 201   Operational amplifier kits
One   ES 400   Cabinet kit
One   ES 401   Voltage regulator transformer kit
Three   ES 405   Patch cord kits
Two   ES 447   Coefficient potentiometer kits
One   ES 450   Auxiliary coefficient potentiometer kit
One   ES 505   Repetitive oscillator kit

FUNCTION GENERATOR
Model ES-600

PURPOSE:

To provide a function of "X" for any input of "X".

Power Requirements: +250 volts at 16 ma.
                                    −250 volts at 16 ma.
                                    117 volts AC at 100 ma.

Input: . . . . A voltage which varies with
                                    respect to time.

Output: . . . . Approximation of functions
                                    by straight line segments.

OUTSTANDING FEATURES:

Variable breakpoint voltages.
High static accuracy (.5%).

TUBE COMPLEMENT:

    5-6AL5   2-OB2

MOUNTING:

This unit is in a separate portable cabinet and is connected to the computer by means of varicon connectors.
   This unit approximates curves or functions by straight line segments. The unit has a total of ten segments, five in the plus X direction and five in the minus X direction. The break voltage and slope of the segments are set by controls on the front panel.
   The break voltages may be varied from zero to 100. The maximum slope per breakpoint is approximately one to one. The output voltage F(x) has a range of ± 100v.

INDIVIDUAL COMPONENT PARTS LIST

Model No.	Description	Price
ES 2	Amplifier power supply kit	$132.95
ES 50	Reference power supply kit	22.95
ES 100	Initial condition power supply kit	19.95
ES 151	Relay power supply kit	11.95
ES 201	Operational amplifier kit	14.95
ES 400	Cabinet kit	247.95
ES 401	Voltage regulator transformer kit	96.95
ES 405	Patch cord kit (contains 12 patch cords)	16.95
ES 447	Coefficient potentiometer kit	26.95
ES 450	Auxiliary coefficient potentiometer kit	36.95
ES 505	Repetitive oscillator kit	16.95
ES 600	Function generator	69.95

HEATH COMPANY *a subsidiary of Daystrom, Incorporated* **BENTON HARBOR, MICHIGAN**

Here is a description of all of the modules that I could identify as being offered for the ES series:

The **ES-600** Function Generator was sold from 1956 to 1962 for $72.95 and weighed 6.5 pounds. It used seven tubes: two 0B2 and five 6AL5. The module can generate a function (waveform) by approximating it as a series of ten points, each specified as a break voltage and slope. It has 10 controls or knobs. It accepts an input voltage and performs the function on it, specified by straight line segments. It is a standalone unit that does not install in the ES-400 cabinet but takes its power (+/- 250 VDC) from it. A full manual for it can be found on the internet. It is an interesting precursor to the much more sophisticated function generators and arbitrary waveform generators that are still offered as test equipment today.

The **ES-400** cabinet and front panel was sold from 1956 to 1962 and weighed 70 pounds. It has a sloping front panel and cabinet with switches, a meter, and a patch board. A required component for an ES series computer, it contained no tubes or other active components but housed the power supplies, amplifiers, and computing components. The meter may be switched to any of the up to 15 amplifiers.

The **ES-401** was a Voltage Regulator Transformer.

The **ES-405** Patch Cord Kit provided 32 patch cords for programming problems.

The **ES-447** was a Coefficient Potentiometer Kit and the **ES-450** was an Auxiliary Coefficient Potentiometer Kit.

The **ES-447** (weighing three pounds) and **ES-450** (weighing one pound) were parts of the cabinet.

The **ES-1** Amplifier Power Supply was an early version of the ES-2, described below.

The **ES-2** Amplifier Power Supply, at 42.5 pounds, ran on an input voltage of 105-125 VAC and consumed 80 Watts of power. It provided the following output voltages: +250 VDC @250 mA, -250 VDC @250 mA, -450 VDC @50 mA, 6.3 VAC @12 A, and 6.3 VAC @2.5 A. It incorporated 13 tubes: three 5U4GA, two 6AS7G, two 12AX7, two 0A2, one 6BX7, one 6AU6, one 0B1, and one 5651. It supplied power to the amplifier, diodes, and function generator and served as a reference standard when extreme accuracy was not required. Installed inside an ES-400 cabinet or on a rack for special-purpose computers, it was a required module for the system. The ES-2 replaced the earlier ES-1 version with similar features that is listed in early catalogs.

The **ES-200** DC Amplifier was an earlier version of the ES-201, described below.

The **ES-201** DC Amplifier was powered by the ES-2 and cabinet, taking three Watts of power and weighing one pound. It made use of three tubes: one 12AX7, one 6BQ7A, and one 6BH6. It installed on the top rear of an ES-400 cabinet or on a standard rack and was shielded from the rest of the computer. A key part of the analog computer, a complete system would typically use 5 to 15 of these units. The output voltage range is +/-100 VDC @10 mA and it provided an open loop gain of 50,000 with a frequency response from DC to 2 kHz (unity gain). It provided an amplifier for integration, sign changing, addition, and multiplication by a constant. It replaced the earlier ES-200 model which had similar features but used different tubes.

The **ES-50** Reference Power Supply was powered from the cabinet (using 117VAC at 20 Watts) and produced outputs of -90 to -110 VDC and +90 to +110 VDC. Utilizing five tubes (two 6X4, two 6U8, one 5651) it weighed 5 pounds and installed inside the cabinet. It provided the +100 and -100 VDC reference voltages for the rest of the computer.

The **ES-100** Initial Condition Power Supply weighed three pounds and ran on 117VAC at 23 Watts, taken from the cabinet where it would be installed. It supplies initial conditions to the integrators, producing two floating variable output voltages from 0 to +/-108 VDC @10mA. It utilized two 0B2 tubes. Up to three units could be mounted inside the cabinet for a total of six supplies.

The **ES-505** Repetitive Oscillator ran on 105 to 125VAC at 8 Watts, weighed two pounds, and was installed in the cabinet. It provided output via a switched relay with an adjustable frequency from 0.6 to 6 Hertz (or pulses per second). The frequency was controlled by knobs on the front of the cabinet. It used one 6J6 tube in a multivibrator circuit.

The **ES-151** Relay Power Supply, running on 105 to 125 VAC at 2 Watts and weighing two pounds, produced an output of 50 VDC across a 50 Kilohm load. Installed in the cabinet, it supplied power for the functional relays of the computer.

The Full Component Group C configuration included these modules:
- one ES-2,
- one ES-50,
- one ES-100,
- one ES-151,
- fifteen ES-201,
- one ES-400,
- one ES-401,
- three ES-405,
- two ES-447,
- one ES-450, and
- one ES-505.

This provided it with the following building blocks:
- fifteen amplifiers,
- thirty coefficient potentiometers,
- two auxiliary 10-turn potentiometers,
- six floating initial conditions,
- four dual bias diodes,
- four multipliers,
- two function generators,
- 22 external connectors,
- one metering circuit with dividing network, and
- two operational relays.

As far as I can determine, full manuals for the ES series are not available on the internet but there are schematics for most modules and a complete manual for the ES-600 Function Generator.

The ES series was offered from 1956 until 1964. It was less popular than the later EC-1 model and is quite rare. The cost was beyond most hobbyists (it's doubtful there even was a hobbyist market for analog computers at that time) and was mostly marketed at research labs and educational institutions.

I have not seen a complete unit show up on eBay or other sources. There are some surviving units in private collections and museums including the Computer History Museum at NASA's Ames Research Center and the Computer History Museum in Mountain View, California.

The EC-1 Educational Analog Computer

Educational electronic ANALOG COMPUTER

✳ **Ideal for schools, colleges, industry**
✳ **9 DC operational amplifiers**
✳ **3 initial condition supplies**
✳ **Built-in repetitive oscillator**
✳ **5 coefficient potentiometers**

The Heathkit model EC-1, lowest cost analog computer of its quality on the market, puts advanced engineering techniques within the reach of everyone! Used widely in industry, the EC-1 is capable of solving a multitude of complex mechanical and mathematical problems with swift electronic accuracy. Many concerns are using the EC-1 to train computer operators and engineers in setting up problems. Schools and colleges find the EC-1 ideal for teaching engineering, physics and math classes the basic principles of analog computer application and design. Featured are: 9 DC operational amplifiers with provision for balancing without removing problem setup; 3 initial condition power supplies; repetitive oscillator and 5 coefficient potentiometers with terminals on the panel. Comprehensive operational manual gives basic computer theory and operating procedures. Housed in rugged steel case with convenient access hatch. Measures 19¾″ W x 11½″ H x 15″ D. 43 lbs.

Kit EC-1...$27.15 dn., $23 mo...$271.50

SPECIFICATIONS—Amplifiers: Open loop gain approximately 1000. Output —60 +60 volts at .7 ma. **Power supplies:** ±300 volts at 25 ma electronically regulated; variable from +250 to +350 by control with meter reference for setting +300 volts. Negative 150 volts at 40 ma regulated by VR tube. **Repetitive operation:** Multivibrator cycles a relay at adjustable rates (.1 to 15 cps), to repeat the solution any number of times; permits observation of effect on solution of changing parameters. **Meter:** 50-0-50 ua movement. **Power requirements:** 105-125 volts, 50 /60 cycles, 100 watts

Figure 11: The EC-1 Educational Analog Computer

Introduced in 1959, the EC-1 Educational Analog Computer was a smaller and lower-cost computer (as compared to the ES series) aimed at the educational market. It was sold as a kit and was a self-contained unit with no options or accessories.

The unit featured nine operational amplifiers having an open loop gain of approximately 1,000 and an output voltage range of +/- 60 volts from DC to 600 Hz. There were two input and output connections for each amplifier. The user had to wire external components to determine the amplifier function, i.e. adding, multiplying, or integrating. It used crystal-style plugs on which standard parts could be mounted. It provided a center zero 100 uA meter with ranges for 1-0-1, 10-0-10, and 100-0-100 Volts. The meter could be switched to read power supply voltages, initial condition voltages, amplifier balance, and output.

Three floating zero to 100 Volt initial condition power supplies could provide positive or negative voltages that were regulated. A relay with four sets of contacts was provided for supplying initial conditions and resetting problems. A multivibrator oscillator supported repetitive operation from 0.1 to 15 Hertz. The main power supply provided +330 VDC at 25 mA, and -150 VDC at 40 mA regulated power. Five coefficient potentiometers were provided on the front panel. The unit came with precision resistors, capacitors, and patch cords for setting up problems.

It used 10 vacuum tubes: one 6AQ5, one 6BH6, two 6U8, one 0A2, four 0B2, and one 12BH7. It was housed in a 19-inch wide cabinet (the same as that used by some Heathkit amateur radio equipment of the time) or it could be mounted in a standard 19-inch instrument rack. It weighed 37-1/2 pounds and ran on 105-125 VAC 50-60 Hz, with a power consumption of 100 Watts.

It was estimated to take about 25 to 30 hours to assemble the kit depending on the experience of the builder.

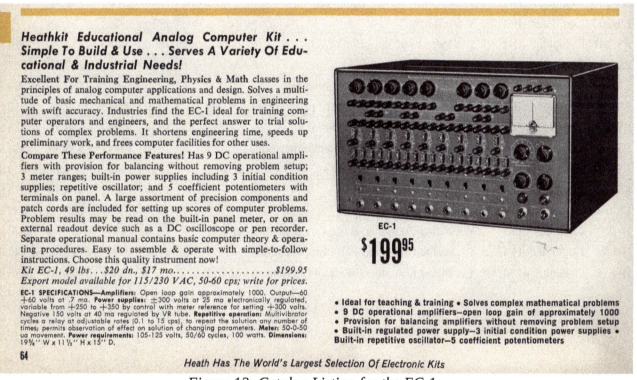

Figure 12: Catalog Listing for the EC-1

Aimed at the educational market, it was more popular than the ES series. It came with an Assembly Manual and Operation Manual (both of which can be found on the internet). The Operation Manual described some sample computing problems.

The EC-1 was offered by Heathkit until 1971. While they are not particularly common, they do show up periodically on sources like eBay and you can find some videos of units operating on YouTube.

Product Listing

The table below summarizes the Heathkit analog computer components that I have been able to identify.

Figure 13: List of ES Series Components

Model	Category	Series	Kit	Description	First Year	Last Year	Lowest Price	Highest Price
EC-1	Computer	EC-1	Y	Educational Analog Computer Kit	1961	1971	$199.95	$243.95
ES-1	Computer	H-1	Y	Amplifier power supply kit	1956	1956		
ES-100	Computer	H-1	Y	Initial condition power supply kit	1956	1964	$19.95	$19.95
ES-151	Computer	H-1	Y	Relay power supply kit	1956	1964	$11.95	$11.95
ES-2	Computer	H-1	Y	Amplifier power supply kit	1956	1964	$132.95	$132.95
ES-200	Computer	H-1	Y	Amplifier	1956	1956		
ES-201	Computer	H-1	Y	Operational amplifier kit	1956	1964	$14.95	$14.95
ES-400	Computer	H-1	Y	Cabinet kit	1956	1964	$247.95	$247.95
ES-401	Computer	H-1	Y	Voltage regulator transformer kit	1956	1964	$96.95	$96.95
ES-405	Computer	H-1	Y	Patch cord kit (contains 12 patch cords)	1956	1964	$16.95	$16.95
ES-447	Computer	H-1	Y	Coefficient potentiometer kit	1956	1964	$26.95	$26.95
ES-450	Computer	H-1	Y	Auxiliary coefficient potentiometer kit	1956	1964	$36.95	$36.95
ES-50	Computer	H-1	Y	Reference power supply kit	1956	1964	$22.95	$22.95
ES-505	Computer	H-1	Y	Repetitive oscillator kit	1956	1964	$16.95	$16.95
ES-600	Computer	H-1	Y	Function generator	1956	1964	$69.95	$69.95
H-1	Computer	H-1	Y	Analog Computer, Basic Component Group A	1956	1959	$495.00	$520.00
H-1	Computer	H-1	Y	Analog Computer, Full Component Group C	1956	1964	$945.00	$1,445.00
H-1	Computer	H-1	Y	Analog Computer, Medium Component Group B	1956	1959	$760.00	$775.00

Chapter 3: Electronic Calculators

In the late 1960s, LSI (large-scale integration) technology allowed increasingly complex electronic circuits to be built into a single integrated circuit "chip". In 1969, Intel developed the first single-chip microprocessor, the 4004, for a contract with Japanese company Busicom for use in a desktop electronic calculator. The 4004 became the first in a line of microprocessors that directly led to the Intel x86-based CPUs used in many computers today.

By 1970 the first battery-operated hand-held calculators were introduced by companies such as Sharp, Canon, and Sanyo at prices of $300 to $400. By 1972, many companies entered the growing market, and the now pocket-sized calculators dropped in price below $100.

Seeing this growing market, in 1973 Heathkit added calculators to its product line, following its usual business model of offering them as kits that the user would assemble. The April 1973 issues of Popular Science and Popular Mechanics magazines included advertisements for these new calculator kits.

Figure 14: Catalog Entry for the IC-2009 Calculator

A typical model was the Heathkit IC-2006 introduced in 1973 at $69.95, dropping to $39.95 by the Christmas 1974 catalog. By 1976, the last year it was offered, it was selling for $29.95.

Heathkit calculators were a short-lived product line lasting only a few years. By 1975, industry prices for basic four-function calculators had dropped below $20, and many companies left the business due to increasing competition and low profit margins.

It no longer made economic sense to build a calculator from a kit. By 1977, calculators were gone Heathkit's catalogs and the company was concentrating on the much more lucrative computer business and their new H-8 and H-11 computers.

One exception was a specialized calculator that continued to be offered, the OC-1401 Aircraft

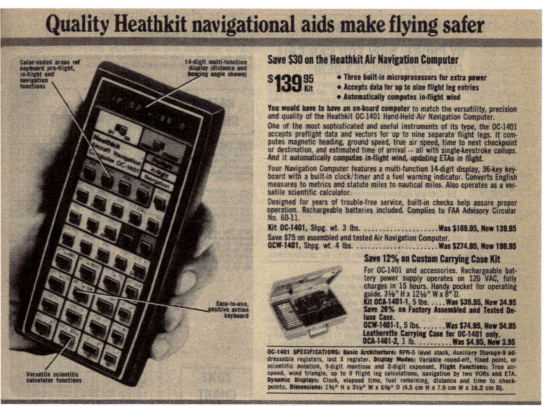

Figure 15: Catalog Entry for the OC-1401 Aircraft Navigation Computer

Navigation Computer. Introduced in 1978, it was an RPN (Reverse Polish Notation) entry scientific calculator that could make aircraft navigation calculations using preflight data and vectors for up to nine flight legs.

It was offered either as a kit (OC-1401) or assembled (OCW-1401). The OC-1401 was sold through 1981 (one of my 1981 catalogs lists it as "price cut 33%").

It was part of a small line of aircraft-related products that also included a strobe light/beacon (OL-1155) and aircraft clock/timer (OI-1154). Both of the latter products, to comply with FAA regulations, needed to be returned and inspected at a Heathkit store or the factory before they could be used in an aircraft.

It seems appropriate that Heathkit dabbled in aircraft products, given that it originally started as an aircraft company.

Product Listing

The following table lists some of the models of calculators that Heathkit offered, followed by some relevant catalog pages.

Figure 16: List of Calculator Products

Model	Category	Series	Kit	Description	First Year	Last Year	Lowest Price	Highest Price
IC-2006	Calculator	n/a	Y	Four-function pocket calculator kit. 1/8" high LED 8-digit display. 9V battery. Optional GRA-43-1 AC adapter.	1973	1976	$29.95	$69.95
IC-2008	Calculator	n/a	Y	Desktop calculator kit. 8-digit gas discharge display 4-function plus constant. Fixed and floating point modes.	1972	1972	$139.95	$139.95
IC-2008A	Calculator	n/a	Y	Desktop calculator kit. 8-digit gas discharge display. 4-function plus constant. Fixed and floating point modes. Replaced IC-2008.	1973	1973	$139.95	$139.95
IC-2009	Calculator	n/a	Y	Four-function pocket calculator kit. 8-digit LED display. Auto power-off. Internal rechargeable NiCd batteries. Optional desk set with charger, pen and pad holder. Optional carrying case.	1973	1974	$74.95	$99.50
IC-2100	Calculator	n/a	Y	Electronic Slide Rule Desktop calculator kit. 4 function plus square, square root, log and trig functions in degrees and radians. 1/2" 8-digit gas discharge display. Memory register. Line powered.	1974	1976	$79.95	$119.95
IC-2108	Calculator	n/a	Y	Desktop calculator kit. 4-function plus constant. Fixed and floating point modes. 1/2" 8-digit gas discharge display. Line powered.	1973	1976	$29.95	$69.95
ICL-2009	Calculator	n/a	Y	IC-2009 calculator with carrying case and desk set	1974	1976	$49.95	$74.95
OC-1401	Calculator	n/a	Y	OC-1401 Aircraft Navigation Computer. Flight calculations based on air speed, wind triangle, VOR, up to 9 flight legs. Internal rechargeable batteries. Optional hard and soft carrying cases.	1978	1981	$99.95	$169.95
OCW-1401	Calculator	n/a	Y	Assembled version of OC-1401	1978	1981	$149.95	$199.95

A new Electronic Slide Rule joins

NEW Heathkit IC-2100 offers full slide-rule capability in a convenient, easy-to-operate desktop calculator

- *Duplicates classical slide rule functions with greater accuracy and keeps the decimal point!*
- *Performs logarithmic & trigonometric functions with a single keystroke — eliminates the need to refer to tables*
- *Computes trig functions in degrees or radians*
- *Accumulating memory*
- *Extra-large, easily read display with legible, easy-to-operate keys — easier to use than pocket slide rule calculators*

The new Heathkit IC-2100 Electronic Slide Rule is the perfect Christmas gift for the engineer, mathematician, teacher, or any math-using professional. It will perform all classical slide rule functions, with greater accuracy. Its desk top size makes it easier to use and its big ½" Beckman displays make it easier to read. It displays up to eight digits and automatically positions the decimal point throughout its entire calculating range.

Versatile operation. In addition to the four standard arithmetic functions (with chain operation in all modes), the IC-2100 will also perform the following functions:

Trigonometric: sin x, arc sin x; cos x, arc cos x, tan x, arc tan x.
Logarithmic: e^x, ln x, log x.
Other functions: A^x, $\sqrt{x}$, 1/x, π.

Squares, square roots and reciprocals are computed with a single keystroke. The Degree/Radian switch allows you to compute in radians as well as degrees. Through a combination of keys you can calculate typical sine, cosine and tangent functions and solve complex equations with ease. Problems can be entered in algebraic form and it's not necessary to clear registers before entering a new problem.

The group of twelve upper/lower keys at the center of the keyboard are dual function keys which can be operated in the normal arithmetic mode or a transcendental function mode. In the function mode, the lower function indicated on the key is entered when the key is depressed. After entering a function, the IC-2100 automatically returns to the normal mode.

A separate memory register with full accumulation ability is provided for storage and retrieval of constants or intermediate answers while performing complex calculations. Two register exchange keys allow the display register to be interchanged with the working register or the memory register. This feature can be used to change incorrect entries, examine the contents of the working or memory register or to place a displayed number into the working or memory register.

The keyboard is color-coded for easy operation — white keys enter numerals and control transcendental functions, blue keys control the arithmetic functions and red keys control memory operations. The bright, easy-to-read display is mounted on a sloped surface to reduce glare. The display shows all numerals, floating decimal, negative signs, calculation overflow and error indications. And the low profile case allows it to be taken anywhere — it will even fit in an attache case. Calculator measures 2¼" H x 7" W x 9⅝" D.

The IC-2100 is easy to build. The "flat-pack" IC mounts in a special socket and requires no internal adjustments. Can be wired for 120/240 VAC.

Kit IC-2100, 4 lbs., mailable **119.95**

A) Heathkit Pocket Calculator — the perfect gift at a new low price . . . only 39.95

Less than 1" thin, and ready to go anywhere under its own 9V battery power or with an optional AC Converter. The IC-2006 features a sophisticated integrated circuit "brain" that performs all mathematical operations, including addition, subtraction, multiplication and division wth computer-like speed and accuracy. A constant (K) can be entered to speed repetitive calculations in multiplication and division.

Other top-flight features include a 17-key keyboard and an 8-digit easy-to-read ⅛" high LED display with no distorting "magnifier." Complete operations manual thoroughly explains operation and gives examples and valuable reference tables for many applications. Operates on inexpensive, easily obtainable 9-volt batteries (not supplied) or with the optional AC converter (below) for continuous operation from any 120 VAC source. Fits in pocket, purse or briefcase — makes a great "energy-saver" for the businessman on the go, the shopping housewife and the student away at school. And, like all Heathkit calculators, it's designed for easy assembly, even for beginning kit builders. Measures 5" L x $2\frac{13}{16}$" W x $\frac{15}{16}$" D, and weighs in at a featherweight 7 oz. (less battery). The Heathkit IC-2006 is a perfect Christmas gift for practically everyone.

Kit IC-2006, 2 lbs.,
mailable .... **Was $59.95, Now Only 39.95**

GRA-43-1 AC Converter, 1 lb., mailable **3.95**

B) The Heathkit Desktop Calculator is a gift the whole family will appreciate . . . 69.95

Sleek, low-profile case fits easily in an attache case — has bright ½"-high Beckman planar gas-discharge tubes in an easy-to-read 8-digit display — and the large color-coded keyboard is conveniently sloped to let you rest your entire arm while operating the calculator. The full-function IC-2108 is loaded with features that make addition, subtraction, multiplication and division operations even easier. A constant key (K) simplifies repetitive problem solving. The separate equal key (=) permits entering computations as you would write them out, totaling up as you go, or working in a chain manner. The display has individual lighted indicators for entry and result overflow. A negative number sign gives the credit-balance capability. Reciprocals (1/x) are quickly found using the constant, divide and equal keys. A rocker switch places the decimal in either the floating mode or in a single fixed position, preselected during kit assembly. And there's no warm-up delay in the IC-2108. Turn it on and the display lights up instantly. The kit is easy to build, with the single LSI mounting in a socket, and related circuitry going on 3 single-sided printed circuit boards. Can be wired for 120/240 VAC. Measures 2¼" H x 7" W x 9⅝" D.

Kit IC-2108, 4 lbs., mailable **69.95**

C) Our rechargeable Pocket Calculator now reduced to only 74.95

Put this 11 oz. "electronic brain" in your pocket, purse, or brief case and carry it with you for instant battery-powered calculations wherever you travel. Or order the optional Executive Desk set (below) along with the calculator for battery-saving plug-in desk top use with built-in pen and note pad.

In portable use, an internal nickel-cadmium battery delivers four to eight hours of use before recharging. Or leave it connected to the charger supplied with the kit for indefinite operation. The charger can be wired for either 120 or 240 VAC operation.

The "brain" of the IC-2009 is an MOS large scale integrated circuit that performs all functions — addition, subtraction, multiplication and division with computer-like speed and accuracy. Operational features include full floating decimal point that protects most significant digits in event of overflow; chain operations without subtotaling; credit balance capability with plus and minus results; constant key (K) for repetitive multiplication or division; bright 8-digit LED display.

A special battery-saver circuit turns off the lighted digital display after 15 seconds pass without entries. Meantime, the calculator retains all information, and the display is instantly reactivated by depressing the display recall key (D), or by entering a new number or operation. And another Heathkit exclusive — the calculator can be serviced by you. The keyboard and display board are plug-in modules, making both assembly and self-service a breeze. Plus, the assembly manual contains a complete trouble-shooting section as well. Calculator measures 5½" H x 3¾" W x 1¾" D. Charger measures 2½" L x 1⅞" H x 2½" W. Nickel-cadmium battery supplied.

Kit IC-2009, 3 lbs., mailable, was 89.95 **NOW ONLY 74.95**

ICS-2009, calculator & desk set, 6 lbs., mailable .... **NOW 79.95**

ICA-2009-1, carrying case, 1 lb., mailable **3.95**

14

You can build any Heathkit product with no prior knowledge or experience. We won't let you fail

the Heathkit calculator line-up.

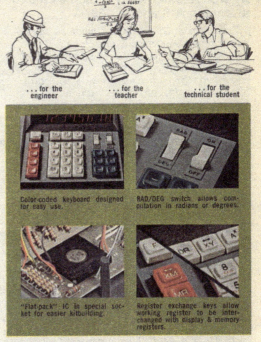

... for the engineer

... for the teacher

... for the technical student

Color-coded keyboard designed for easy use.

RAD/DEG switch allows computation in radians or degrees.

"Flat-pack" IC in special socket for easier kitbuilding.

Register exchange keys allow working register to be interchanged with display & memory registers.

A)

SAVE $20
NOW ONLY $39.95

Great Christmas gift and at a new low price! Complete calculator capability in shirt pocket-size. Just right for home work, shopping, even the office. Buy now and save!

SAVE $15

C)

B)

Executive Calculator Desk Set for your IC-2009 only 7.95

The built-in battery charger keeps your calculator fully charged, ready for use. Includes Schaeffer Pen, 3" x 6" pad, engravable nameplate. Can be wired for 120/240 VAC. 2⅜" H x 8½" W x 8¾" D. Order with the IC-2009 and save (see C above). For use with IC-2009 Calculator only. Kit ICA-2009-2, 3 lbs., mailable ... 7.95

(this page intentionally left blank)

Chapter 4: The 8-Bit Computers

Introduction

Thanks to Moore's law, the cost of microprocessors and other electronic components such as memory continued to come down to the point where a digital computer became affordable for early adopter hobbyists. In 1974 a small company called MITS introduced the Intel 8080-based Altair 8800 computer. Despite being limited in features (the user interface was a front panel with binary LEDs and toggle switches and only 256 bytes of memory were included in the base unit) and relatively expensive ($439 in 1974, equivalent to over $2,500 today) it was a runaway success with thousands of orders in the first month.

Based on the success of the Altair a number of companies got into the market, offering compatible systems. The Altair used a design with a backplane and card cage supporting expansion boards that used a 100-pin edge connector that became a de facto standard known as the S-100 bus. Most Altair compatible systems used the S-100 bus and many manufacturers started offering boards for this market, such as memory, input/output devices, and floppy disk controllers.

The other area of standardization around these Intel 8080 (and later Zilog Z80) S-100 systems was the use of the floppy disk-based CP/M operating system. The introduction of CP/M added file storage, printing, and a large selection of software applications that dramatically improved the capabilities of these early microcomputers, making them a useful tool for hobbyists and businesses.

By the end of the 1970s, prices would come down even further with the introduction of microcomputers from companies such as Apple, Commodore, and Radio Shack. The hobbyist market for computers would expand at an even greater rate, although in some ways it was a step backward from the days of S-100 and CP/M, as the new microcomputers were largely incompatible with each other, something that would later change with the introduction of the IBM Personal Computer.

H-8/WH-8

No doubt inspired by the success of the Altair and similar systems, Heathkit decided to enter the microcomputer market, introducing the H-8 in 1977, sold as a kit at a price of $379.

The system consisted of a main unit with a cabinet containing a power supply, front panel, and expansion card slots. It utilized an Intel 8080A CPU running at 2.048 MHz.

A 16-key front panel with eight 7-segment red LEDs and four discrete LEDs could display addresses and registers and allow the system to be programmed. This was easier to use than systems like the Altair that had binary switches. The LEDs displayed continuously while programs were executing and a monitor program in ROM could load and dump programs (via paper tape. a serial port, or cassette tape) without requiring the user to first enter a boot loader program by hand on each power up.

The card cage accepted up to nine cards. It used a backplane with a 50-pin buffered bus, similar to but not compatible with the S-100 bus. The lack of compatibility with S-100 boards was a notable design

THE HEATHKIT H8 COMPUTER

$499.95 Kit

The powerful, easy-to-use personal computer with the "intelligent" front panel featuring octal entry keyboard and digital readout — plus a fully wired and tested 8080A CPU and system software (BASIC, assembler, editor and debug) at no extra cost!

Requires at least one H8 memory board to operate

6 EVENING KIT Fast, Easy Assembly

The Heathkit H8 Computer is a powerful 8-bit machine based on the 8080A CPU. It's combination of unique features and low cost makes it an outstanding value among general purpose computers. Because of its expansion capabilities, its a computer system you can stay with. Unlike many of the so-called low-priced "all-in-one" packaged systems, the H8 lets you add memory and peripherals to increase its power and versatility as you increase your programming prowess.

The 16-key front panel keyboard provides octal data entry giving you direct access to registers and memory, one-button program load and dump, and I/O keys for direct communication with any port. Because of this intelligent front panel, the H8 and a simple 4K of memory makes an ideal computer trainer.

The 9-digit octal readout gives you far more information than conventional computers. Memory, register and I/O port displays are continuously updated even while your programs are executing for direct monitoring of program activity.

Memory Display

Register Display

I/O Port Display

Complete front panel functions include display and alter of memory locations, display and alter of registers, dynamic monitoring of memory locations or registers, program execution control, automatic tape load and store through a built-in routine that permits one-button program loading or dumping, and write or read any I/O port.

The H8 is supplied with complete systems software in 1200 baud audio cassette form to get you up and running fast. Benton Harbor BASIC, HASL-8 2-pass absolute assembler, TED-8 line-oriented text editor, and BUG-8 terminal console debug program let you begin communicating with the H8 right away. See next page for a rundown of this powerful software.

Complete systems software included!

Other features of the H8 include: exclusive Heath-designed 50-pin fully buffered bus; mother board with positions for up to 9 plug-in circuit boards that accept the CPU, front panel memory, I/O and other accessory cards; built-in convection cooled power supply; built-in speaker for audible feedback and special effects; front panel status lights and more. The CPU board is fully wired and tested for easy system setup and kit assembly. The H8 is housed in a heavy-duty metal cabinet with modern, high-impact structural foam side panels. 16¼" W x 6½" H x 17" D. Switch-selected 120/240 VAC, 50/60 Hz. **Requires at least one H8-1 memory board to operate.**

Kit H8, Shpg. wt. 30 lbs. **499.95**

72

SAVE!

H8-1 Memory Board. 8Kx8 memory card supplied with 4K memory, plugs directly into H8 bus. Features maximum storage capacity of 8192 8-bit words. Uses modern 4Kx1 static memory IC chips for easy assembly and service. Access time, less than 450 nS. With on-board regulators, heat sinks and full buffering. Expandable to 8K memory with H8-3 chip set below.
Kit H8-1, Shpg. wt. 2 lbs.
Was 249.95 . . . . . Now 229.95

H8-3 Chip Set. Kit of eight 4K static memory IC's. Expands H8-1 to full 8K storage. With sockets.
Kit H8-3, Shpg. wt. 1 lb. .... **Was 179.95 Now 159.95**

H8-2 Parallel Interface. Connects H8 to any parallel device such as a paper tape reader/punch (required for H10, page 77) or line printer. Has three independent parallel ports, each with 8 bits input and 8 bits output and universal handshaking capability. Compatible with all Heath software. 390 mS maximum transfer time. With diode-clamped inputs, buffered outputs and full interrupt capability.
Kit H8-2, Shpg. wt. 3 lbs. **259.95**

H8-5 Serial I/O and Cassette Interface. Connects the H8 to serial devices such as the H9 video terminal (page 76) or the H36 DEC Writer II (page 78). Features jumper selectable data rate from 110 to 9600 baud, plus common input/output interfaces including 20 mA current loop and EIA RS-232C compatible levels. The cassette recorder interface permits use with the Heathkit ECP-3801, page 78. Uses the popular Byte/Manchester recording format but runs at 1200 baud.

Has control lines for remote start and stop of two cassette units to allow separate record and playback for easy program or file editing. Also has full interrupt capability. LED test circuit for easy board setup and overall system servicing. Fully compatible with all Heath software.
Kit H8-5, Shpg. wt. 3 lbs. **189.95**

NOTE: Proper operation of the H8-5 is assured only if you use the Heath ECP-3801 cassette player/recorder and Heath-recommended recording tape (ECP-3802, page 78). Heath is not responsible for improper operation associated with other cassette units.

Extended Benton Harbor BASIC: An enhanced and more powerful version of the BASIC supplied with the H8 (see next page for description). It provides even faster operation and includes character strings, additional convenience commands and math functions, dynamic storage allocation, access to real time clock, keyboard interrupt processing, expanded error messages and recovery ability, LED display control and key pad support. A minimum of 12K memory is required to run this BASIC, 16K is preferred if full use is to be made of its capabilities.

HC-8-13 (1200 baud audio cassette). Includes file capabilities which allow saving data generated by BASIC programs to permit multiple programs to work on the same data base, or a single program to work on several data bases. Shpg. wt. 1 lb. **13.95**
H8-14 (fan-fold paper tape) No file capability. 1 lb. **13.95**

Paper Tape Systems Software: A paper tape version of the systems software supplied with the H8 computer. It consists of four fan fold paper tapes, one each for Benton Harbor BASIC, HASL-8 assembler, TED-8 editor, and BUG-8 debug. For use with the H10 paper tape reader/punch or other paper tape I/O equipment. See next page for complete software description.
H8-15, Shpg. wt. 1 lb. **26.95**

The H8 software is the "heart" of your computer system

The software supplied with the H8 computer has a number of features that make it easier to use and more practical than other systems. Automatic "command completion" simplifies typing; dynamic syntax checking instantly alerts you to errors and a special user configuration lets you really personalize your system. H8 software is memory efficient to give you more computing power for your memory dollar, has modular design for easy expansion, and is thoroughly documented for easy programming and maximum effectiveness.

Software supplied with the H8 computer includes:

PANEL MONITOR (PAM-8). This ROM program monitor controls the front panel and permits you to load, execute and debug programs written in 8080 machine language. It provides memory contents display and alteration, register contents display and alteration, program execution control, self-contained bootstraps for one-button program loading and dumping, and port input and output routines.

BENTON HARBOR BASIC. This conversational programming language uses simple English statements and familiar algebraic equations to perform operations and solve problems. It is compact enough to run in the Heathkit H8 with limited memory, yet powerful enough to satisfy most problem-solving requirements. Requires a minimum of 8K memory. Extended Benton Harbor BASIC is also available, order from page 72.

ASSEMBLY LANGUAGE (HASL-8). This two-pass absolute assembler lets you create source programs using letters, numbers and symbols to generate efficient machine language code. It assembles the source program into a listing and an object program in binary format executable by the H8. A minimum of 8K memory is required.

TEXT EDITOR (TED-8). Converts the H8 computer and terminal into a powerful typewriter for generating text and editing. It prepares the source code for H8 assembly language, BASIC and other languages, and can be used to prepare reports, write letters and edit manuscripts. Requires a minimum of 8K memory.

CONSOLE DEBUGGER (BUG-8). This enhanced and extended version of the front panel monitor allows entry and debugging of user machine language programs via an external terminal. It features single or multiple stepping through programs, breakpointing, load and dump from tape storage. It requires 3K memory plus user program.

Buy a complete computer system and SAVE!

You can choose a complete computer system consisting of the H8 computer, one major peripheral, plus memory and accessories, and deduct 5% from the purchase price (excluding shipping and handling charges). Choose one of the Heath-recommended systems below (which already have the discount calculated for you), or "roll your own" with system components you select!

H8 System One: The minimum recommended H8 system. Includes H8 computer, one H8-1 4K memory, H8-3 4K Chip Set, H8-5 Serial I/O and Cassette Interface, H9 Video Terminal and ECP-3801 Cassette Recorder/Player. If purchased separately, $2049.70. **Heath System Price is $1945.00.**

H8 System Two: A deluxe H8 System. Includes H8 Computer, Two H8-1 4K Memories, Two H8-3 4K Chip Sets, H8-5 Serial I/O and Cassette Interface, H9 Video Terminal, ECP-3801 Cassette Player/Recorder and H8-13 Extended BASIC in Cassette Form. If purchased separately, $2453.55. **Heath System Price is $2300.00.**

HM-800 Manual Set. Here's your chance to LOOK before you buy, and with no risk! The HM-800 manual set includes the complete assembly and operations manuals for the H8 Digital Computer, H8-1 memory card, H8-2 parallel interface; H8-3 4K Expansion Chip Set; H8-5 Serial I/O and Cassette Interface; H9 Video Terminal and H10 Paper Tape Reader/Punch. The complete H8 software documentation is also included! All in handsome 3-ring binder that's handy for reference and additional information. You can deduct the price of the manual set when you buy your H8.

HM-800, Shpg. wt. 11 lbs. 30.00

73

decision. Heathkit claimed it was done to improve on some of the design flaws of the S-100 bus, but it was also a way to lock users into buying their peripheral cards. The cabinet included a built-in convection cooled (fanless) power supply and a speaker that could produce a beep.

While it came with a fully wired and tested CPU card, the system was offered as a kit and the user had to assemble the power supply and front panel circuit boards, internal wiring, and mechanical components of the case. It was estimated to take six evenings to assemble.

Initially selling for $379.95, the basic system needed some additional accessories to run: at minimum, at least one H8-1 memory board with 4K of RAM. The board came with 4K but could be expanded to 8K by adding eight more memory ICs (bought from Heath or off the shelf) and you could install up to four memory cards subject to the number of free slots.

Serial I/O and cassette tape storage required the H8-5 Serial I/O and Cassette Interface board. Typically the system was controlled using a serial terminal like the Heathkit H-9 video terminal or H-36 DEC Writer II printing terminal that Heath offered. Cassette storage ran at 1200 baud and could use any tape deck, although Heathkit only guaranteed proper operation using their ECP-3801 unit (an assembled General Electric model) and Heathkit recording tape ECP-3802.

The H8-2 Parallel Interface allowed the H-8 to connect to a paper tape reader/punch like the H-10, or to a parallel printer. The interface had three 8-bit parallel ports.

Also offered was a bundle that could be purchased at a discount over the individual components. The minimum recommended system (System One) consisted of:
- H-8 system main unit
- 4K Memory board with additional 4K RAM chips (total of 8K RAM)
- H8-5 Serial I/O and Cassette Interface
- H-9 Video Terminal
- ECP-3801 Cassette recorder

The "deluxe system" or System Two consisted of:
- H-8 system main unit
- Two 4K Memory boards with additional 4K RAM chips (total of 16K RAM)
- H8-5 Serial I/O and Cassette Interface
- H-9 Video Terminal
- ECP-3801 Cassette recorder
- Extended Benton Harbor BASIC

Potential buyers could purchase a complete set of all the manuals to review before buying, and then deduct the cost if they bought a system.

Included with the purchase of an H-8 was the following software, supplied on cassette tape and requiring at least 8K of RAM (except for the ROM monitor):

1. Panel Monitor ROM that allowed entering, loading, saving, and running 8080 machine language programs. It could display and change memory and register contents (displayed in octal on the 7-segment LEDs).
2. Benton Harbor BASIC: Heathkit's version of the popular BASIC programming language. Benton Harbor, of course, was the location of Heathkit's headquarters and was a nod to the name of the original BASIC dialect, sometimes referred to as Dartmouth BASIC. Extended Benton Harbor BASIC was an enhanced version that offered additional commands and features and was available for purchase at an additional cost.
3. Assembly Language: HAL-8 was a two-pass absolute assembler for 8080A assembly language. It assembled into object or binary formats.
4. Text Editor: TED-8 was provided for editing of assembly language source code, BASIC programs, and text files.
5. Console Debugger: BUG-8 was an extended version of the front panel monitor that allowed entering and debugging programs from an external terminal and supported such features as single step, breakpoints, and loading and saving to tape. It used 3K of RAM.

If you owned an H-10 or similar paper tape reader/punch, at an additional cost you could purchase the above software on paper tape.

To accommodate users who were unwilling or unable to build the H-8 in kit form, they also offered a factory assembled version of the system, known as the WH-8, at a higher cost.

Floppy and Hard Drives

Using an H-8 with cassette tape or paper tape was slow and tedious. You had to first spend several minutes loading the application (e.g. BASIC) and then load your BASIC program from tape. In 1978 the H-17 floppy drive was introduced. A factory assembled version of the drive was offered as the WH-17.

It was a standalone unit that included one drive but could accommodate up to two (and later, three). With a built-in power supply, it included a controller card that installed into the H-8 card cage. The disk format was 40 tracks, 10 sectors per track, hard sectored, and provided 102 kilobytes of storage on each 5.25" disk. The drive itself was a WANGCO/Siemens model 82.

The software included was essentially floppy-based versions of the same assembler, text editor, and debugger as offered on cassette, as well as the Extended Benton Harbor BASIC and some utilities.

The floppy drive was supported by the Heath-written HDOS operating system as well as CP/M and required at least 16K of RAM. It should be noted that running CP/M on early H-8 machines required either a special version of CP/M that was loaded at 8K rather than at zero, or making a small hardware modification and installing an updated ROM. At additional cost you could purchase the source code for HDOS and for the ROMs for the H-17 floppy system. Heath later also offered other operating systems including UCSD Pascal (software is covered in more detail in chapter 12).

To accommodate higher-end business users who needed more mass storage, Heathkit later offered the H-47 eight-inch floppy disk system and the WH-67 10 MB hard drive.

H-88 and H-89

The H-8 required a serial terminal if the user wanted to program it using more than the front panel, and the H-9 video terminal offered for the H-8 was quite limited: it could only display uppercase characters as twelve 80-character lines or 48 20-character lines in four columns. It didn't even make use of a microprocessor. In 1978 they introduced the H-19 terminal which offered a higher-quality display with 23 80-character lines with upper and lower case and graphics characters and DEC VT52 compatibility. The keyboard featured 80 keys including 12 function keys and a numeric keypad. It was controlled by a Z80 microprocessor (chapter 9 covers terminals in more detail).

At the same time, the trend in microcomputers was moving away from units with separate serial terminals and peripherals, and moving to integrated units with a main unit, keyboard, display, and floppy drives (one example being the Radio Shack TRS-80).

Leveraging the H-19 terminal. Heathkit offered the H-89 "All-In-One Computer" which was essentially an H-8 computer and dual floppy drive integrated into an H-19 terminal.

It was also upgraded to use the Z80 CPU-based controller card that had previously been offered as an optional upgrade for the H-8, so the system now had two 2.048 MHz Z80 CPUs (one for the main processor and one for the terminal). It also came with 16K of RAM and could be expanded to 48K by plugging additional RAM chips onto the CPU board.

The H-89 came with one 100K 5.25" floppy drive. A less expensive model, the H-88, was identical but shipped without a floppy drive and controller and included an interface for cassette tape storage.

The H-89 only had room for one internal drive. The H-77 was an external dual floppy drive that allowed expanding the system up to a total of three drives.

The H-88 and H-89 were fully software compatible with the H-8. Both the H-88 and H-89 were offered in factory assembled versions, the WH-88 and WH-89 respectively.

Z-89/Z-90

The Z-89 was a Zenith-branded version of the H-89, sold only in assembled form. The Z-90 was a lower cost version that lacked a floppy drive. It used a non-glare green CRT, and could be purchased in different models with varying amounts of RAM and floppy drives. It came standard with the CP/M operating system rather than HDOS.

One accessory was the Z-67 external drive, which offered an 11MB Winchester hard drive and an 8-inch floppy drive. My 1982 catalog lists it at $8,9995.50 - equivalent to over $25,000 today!

H-89A

An updated model, the H-89A, expanded the standard RAM to 48K (supporting up to 64K), offered anti-glare white or green CRTs, and came with three serial ports. It also included the hardware modifications needed to run standard CP/M. A double-density floppy disk controller was offered that stored 160KB versus the 100K of the standard drives. External floppies were supported by a new H-37 dual floppy drive unit. This drive supported using single-density 100 KB drives and dual-density 160 KB (both hard-sectored), or double-density soft-sectored floppies which could store 640 KB. They even offered a Winchester hard drive for it.

Current Status

The H-89 computer was discontinued in 1983. By then, Heath had introduced their next generation of systems based on the H-100 (covered in chapter 6).

Today, the H-8 and H-89 are probably the most popular Heathkit computer systems among the retrocomputing community. Many people have systems that have been restored, and running applications under CP/M or HDOS on these old systems can be a lot of fun.

Systems and accessories can be found on sites like eBay, although prices have gone up dramatically in the last few years as interest has increased. There is an active community of websites and forums devoted to the H-8 series. Manuals and software are available, and some users have even designed new circuit boards!

If you just want to get a feel for how these systems worked, you can watch YouTube videos or even try running an emulator on a modern PC [13].

Product Listing

The following table lists all of the models related to the H-8 series that I have been able to glean from various Heathkit catalogs and other sources (more peripherals and accessories are covered in Chapter 10).

Figure 17: List of 8-Bit Computer Products

Model	Category	Series	Kit	Description	First Year	Last Year	Lowest Price	Highest Price
ECP-3801	Accessory	H-8	N	Heath-recommended cassette recorder for use with H-8	1978	1978	$69.95	$69.95
ECP-3802	Accessory	H-8	N	Heath-recommended audio recording tape (3 pack)	1978	1978	$8.95	$8.95
H-10	Accessory	H-8/H-11	Y	Paper Tape Reader/Punch	1978	1978	$499.95	$499.95
H-10-2	Accessory	H-10	N	Three Rolls Blank paper tape	1978	1978	$15.95	$15.95
H-10-3	Accessory	H-10	N	Three Boxes Fan-Fold Paper Tape	1978	1978	$15.95	$15.95
H-17	Disk	H-8	Y	Floppy Disk System	1980	1982	$575.00	$975.00
H-17-1	Disk	H-89	N	Single-Sided Floppy Disk Drive for H-77/Z-77 Disk Systems	1978	1984	$295.00	$425.00
H-17-3	Accessory	H-8	Y	Three Drive Modification Kit	1981	1982	$85.00	$139.95
H-17-4	Disk	H-89	N	Single-Sided Floppy Disk Drive for H-37/Z-37 Disk Systems	1982	1983	$550.00	$795.00
H-17-5	Disk	H-89	N	Double-Sided Floppy Disk Drive for H-77/Z-77 Disk Systems	1984	1984	$550.00	$550.00
H-47	Disk	H-8	Y	8-Inch Dual-Drive Floppy Disk System	1981	1981	$2,995.00	$2,995.00

Model	Category	Series	Kit	Description	First Year	Last Year	Lowest Price	Highest Price
H-77	Disk	H-88	Y	One 5.25" disk drive	1980	1981	$595.00	$625.00
H-8	Computer	H-8	Y	H-8 Computer	1978	1983	$299.00	$559.95
H-8-1	Accessory	H-8	N	8K Memory Board, includes 4K	1978	1978	$249.95	$249.95
H-8-10	Accessory	H-8	Y	Wire Wrapping Board	1980	1983	$29.95	$49.95
H-8-13	Accessory	H-8	N	Extended Benton Harbor BASIC (1200 baud audio cassette)	1978	1978	$13.95	$13.95
H-8-14	Accessory	H-8	N	Extended Benton Harbor BASIC (fan fold paper tape)	1978	1978	$13.95	$13.95
H-8-15	Accessory	H-8	N	H-8 Systems Software on Paper Tape	1978	1978	$26.95	$26.95
H-8-19	Accessory	H-8	N	Z80 Replacement ROM and Front Panel Key Caps	1983	1983	$20.00	$20.00
H-8-2	Accessory	H-8	Y	Parallel Interface	1978	1982	$150.00	$249.95
H-8-3	Accessory	H-8	N	4K Memory Expansion Chip Set	1978	1978	$179.95	$179.95
H-8-4	Accessory	H-8	Y	4-Port RS-232C Serial Interface	1981	1983	$195.00	$279.95
H-8-5	Accessory	H-8	Y	Serial Cassette Interface	1978	1983	$95.00	$169.95
H-8-7	Accessory	H-8	Y	Circuit Design Breadboard Card	1980	1983	$79.00	$169.95
H-8-9	Accessory	H-8	Y	PAMGO ROM, Allows 1 or 3-button boot-up instead of 10	1980	1983	$20.00	$29.95
H-87	Disk	H-88	Y	Two 5.25" disk drives	1981	1981	$895.00	$895.00
H-88	Computer	H-88	Y	All-In-One Computer, without floppy, includes H-88-5 audio cassette interface	1980	1980	$1,295.00	$1,295.00
H-88-1	Accessory	H-89	N	Hard-Sectored Disk Controller Board for H/Z-89 Computers	1982	1984	$150.00	$229.95
H-88-10	Accessory	H-89	N	Wire Wrapping Board with Bus Connectors	1980	1984	$30.00	$49.00
H-88-18	Accessory	H-89	N	All-In-One Cassette Operating System	1982	1982	$40.00	$40.00
H-88-2	Accessory	H-89	N	16K Random Access Memory (RAM) Expansion Set	1980	1983	$29.00	$95.00
H-88-3	Accessory	H-89	N	3-Port Serial Interface for Older H-89s	1980	1984	$100.00	$150.00
H-88-4	Accessory	H-88	N	Floppy Disk Drive and Controller for H-88	1980	1981	$450.00	$490.00
H-88-5	Accessory	H-89	N	Cassette Interface (not used with CP/M)	1980	1984	$49.00	$165.00
H-88-6	Accessory	H-89	N	Backplate Modification Kit	1980	1982	$50.00	$79.50
H-88-7	Accessory	H-89	Y	Replacement ROM Kit	1981	1981	$55.00	$55.00
H-88-9	Accessory	H-89	N	High Capacity Drive Installation Kit	1984	1984	$50.00	$50.00
H-89	Computer	n/a	Y	All-In-One Computer, 16K RAM, floppy	1980	1980	$1,695.00	$1,695.00
HA-8-1	Accessory	H-8	N	Extender Board	1980	1982	$40.00	$69.95
HA-8-16	Accessory	H-8	N	16K Byte RAM Chip Expansion Set for WH-8-64	1982	1983	$89.95	$89.95
HA-8-2	Accessory	H-8	N	Music Synthesizer System	1980	1983	$159.00	$295.00
HA-8-3	Accessory	H-8	N	Color Graphics Board	1981	1983	$295.00	$799.95
HA-8-6	Accessory	H-8	N	Z80 CPU Card for H-8	1981	1983	$199.00	$269.95
HA-8-8	Accessory	H-8	N	Extended Configuration Option	1981	1983	$65.00	$99.95

Model	Category	Series	Kit	Description	First Year	Last Year	Lowest Price	Highest Price
HA-88-3	Accessory	H-89	N	3-Port Serial Interface for older H-89s	1981	1984	$120.00	$165.00
HCA-3	Accessory	H-89	N	Plastic Anti-Glare Filter, Clear	1980	1981	$8.95	$12.95
HCA-5-8	Accessory	H-8	N	Dust Cover for H-8	1981	1983	$14.00	$19.95
HCA-5-89	Accessory	H-89	N	Dust Cover for H/Z-89, Z-90, H/Z-19	1982	1984	$14.00	$24.95
HCA-6	Accessory	H-89	Y	Wire Wrapping Kit	1980	1983	$12.95	$21.95
HCA-7	Accessory	H-89	N	Wire Wrapping Socket Kit	1980	1984	$29.95	$49.95
HKS-82	Computer	H-8	N	Complete Advanced H-8 Computer System	1980	1980	$1,995.00	$1,995.00
HKS-89-1	Computer	H-89	Y	H-89 All-In-One Computer with non-glare white CRT, floppy drive	1981	1981	$1,725.00	$1,725.00
HKS-89-2	Computer	H-89	Y	H-89 All-In-One Computer with non-glare green CRT, floppy drive	1981	1981	$1,725.00	$1,725.00
HKS-89-3	Computer	H-89	Y	H-89 All-In-One Computer with standard white CRT, floppy drive	1981	1981	$1,695.00	$1,695.00
HM-800	Accessory	H-8	N	H-8 Manual Set	1978	1981	$30.00	$30.00
HS-19-10	Computer	H/Z-19	N	H/Z-19 Conversion System to convert to H-89 All-In-One Computer	1983	1983	$995.00	$995.00
HS-37-1	Disk	H/Z-89, Z-90	Y	Floppy drive, 5.25", single-sided, external, single	1982	1984	$795.00	$1,195.00
HS-37-2	Disk	H/Z-89, Z-90	Y	Floppy drive, 5.25", single-sided, external, dual	1982	1984	$1,295.00	$1,895.00
HS-77-1	Disk	H/Z-89, Z-90	Y	Floppy drive, 5.25", single-sided, external, single	1982	1984	$499.00	$825.00
HS-77-2	Disk	H/Z-89, Z-90	Y	Floppy drive, 5.25", single-sided, external, dual	1982	1984	$769.00	$1,125.00
HS-88-1	Computer	H-88	Y	H-89 All-In-One Computer with non-glare white CRT, no floppy drive	1981	1981	$1,325.00	$1,325.00
HS-88-2	Computer	H-88	Y	H-89 All-In-One Computer with non-glare green CRT, no floppy drive	1981	1981	$1,325.00	$1,325.00
HS-88-3	Computer	H-88	Y	H-89 All-In-One Computer with standard white CRT, no floppy drive	1981	1981	$1,295.00	$1,295.00
HS-89-1	Computer	H-89	Y	All-In-One Computer with anti-glare white CRT	1982	1982	$2,795.00	$2,795.00
HS-89-2	Computer	H-89	Y	All-In-One Computer with anti-glare green CRT	1983	1984	$1,049.95	$2,795.00
HS-89-3	Computer	H-89	Y	All-In-One Computer with standard white CRT	1983	1984	$999.95	$2,750.00
WH-13	Accessory	H-8	N	Acoustic Modem	1980	1980	$175.00	$175.00
WH-17	Disk	H-8	N	Floppy Disk System	1978	1982	$645.00	$1,095.00
WH-8	Computer	H-8	N	Factory Assembled and Tested H-8 Computer	1980	1980	$399.00	$399.00
WH-8-16	Accessory	H-8	N	16K RAM Wired Memory Board	1980	1981	$299.00	$299.00
WH-8-37	Accessory	H-8	N	Soft-Sectored Floppy Disk Controller Board	1983	1983	$249.00	$395.00
WH-8-4	Accessory	H-8	N	4-Port RS-232C Serial Interface	1980	1981	$250.00	$250.00
WH-8-41	Accessory	H-8	N	Serial adapter cable	1980	1983	$15.00	$31.95

Model	Category	Series	Kit	Description	First Year	Last Year	Lowest Price	Highest Price
WH-8-47	Disk	H-8	N	Wired H-8 to H-47 Interface, with two RS-232C Serial Ports	1981	1981	$235.00	$235.00
WH-8-5	Accessory	H-8	Y	Serial Cassette Interface	1980	1981	$20.00	$145.00
WH-8-51	Accessory	H-8	N	Serial adapter cable	1980	1983	$15.00	$32.95
WH-8-64	Accessory	H-8	N	64K Wired Memory Board	1982	1983	$599.95	$599.95
WH-87	Disk	H-89	N	Assembled Dual-Drive Floppy Disk System	1980	1980	$1,195.00	$1,195.00
WH-88-16	Accessory	H-89	N	64K RAM Expansion Kit	1981	1984	$115.00	$174.95
WH-88-47	Accessory	H-8	N	Wired All-In-One to H-47 Interface	1981	1981	$195.00	$195.00
WH-89-CA	Computer	H-89	N	Fully Assembled All-In-One Computer, 48K RAM, floppy, serial i/o	1980	1980	$2,895.00	$2,895.00
Z-87-89	Disk	H/Z-89	N	Floppy drive, 5.25", single-sided, external, dual	1984	1984	$769.00	$769.00
Z-87-90	Disk	Z-90	N	Floppy drive, 5.25", single-sided, external, dual	1983	1984	$769.00	$999.00
Z-89-11	Accessory	H-89	N	Multi-Mode Interface Card	1982	1982	$225.00	$225.00
Z-89-37	Accessory	H-89	N	Soft-Sectored Disk Controller Board for H/Z-89 Computers	1982	1984	$299.00	$495.00
Z-89-67	Accessory	H-89	N	Interface, Required to interface Z-67 to H/Z-89 All-In-One Computer	1981	1982	$195.00	$255.00
Z-89-81	Computer	H-89	N	Assembled and tested H-89 with 48K bytes of RAM, built-in floppy disk drive 100K bytes of data storage and three serial I/O ports	1982	1983	$3,745.00	$3,995.00
Z-89-FA	Computer	Z-89	N	Assembled Z-89 Computer with 48K RAM, 5.25" Floppy	1981	1981	$2,895.00	$2,895.00
Z-90-80	Computer	H-89	N	Assembled with 64K bytes of RAM, Z-89-37 Double-Density Disk Controller Board, no internal disk storage and three serial I/O ports	1982	1983	$3,745.00	$3,995.00
Z-90-82	Computer	H-89	N	Assembled with 64K bytes of RAM, the Z-89-37 Controller Board, built-in floppy disk drive for 160K bytes of data storage and three serial I/O ports	1982	1983	$4,145.00	$4,395.00
Z-90-90	Computer	H-89	N	Assembled and tested H-89 with Z-89-37 Controller Board, 64K RAM, less disk drive	1984	1984	$2,499.00	$2,499.00
Z-90-92	Computer	H-89	N	Assembled and tested H-89 with Z-89-37 Controller Board, 64K RAM, 48 TPI disk drive	1984	1984	$2,799.00	$2,799.00
ZC-37	Disk	H/Z-90, Z-90	N	Floppy drive, 5.25", double-sided, external, dual	1984	1984	$1,699.00	$1,699.00

(this page intentionally left blank)

Chapter 5: The 16-Bit Computers

Introduction

In the 1960s through 1980s there was a clear division in classes of computers. On the low end were microcomputers, small inexpensive systems based on microprocessors, with limited memory and often built on one circuit board. These appeared in the late 1970s, typically sold for under $1,000, and were aimed at hobbyists. On the high end were the mainframes: large expensive computers that took up rooms of equipment, costing as much as millions of dollars, and were typically used by government and large businesses. IBM was the leader in this market.

In between the two was the minicomputer, with a size, cost, and computing power somewhere between micros and mainframes. They typically sold for less than $25,000 (circa 1970) and were used for control and instrumentation purposes for single users or small numbers of users, offering programming languages like BASIC and FORTRAN as well as assembly language.

At the peak of the minicomputer era, over one hundred companies produced systems, many of them in the New England region of the USA. The leader in this market was Digital Equipment Corporation (DEC). They developed several minicomputers, but their PDP-11 series was the most popular, likely the most popular minicomputer ever sold, shipping around 600,000 units from 1970 into the 1990s.

The PDP-11 [14] had a CPU with a powerful and flexible instruction set and a standard bus for accessing a wide variety of peripherals. It was used both for general-purpose computing as well as real-time applications like robotics. The design inspired later, more powerful microprocessors including the Intel x86 and Motorola 68000. It was also the first machine to run the Unix operating system which used the C programming language.

In 1975, the LSI-11/03 or PDP-11/03 model was introduced that utilized a CPU contained in four Large Scale Integration (LSI) chips manufactured by Western Digital. It standardized on a bus for peripheral cards called Q-bus. This allowed the system to be made physically smaller and lower in cost than earlier models.

By the 1980s, the IBM PC and its clones as well as Apple computers had started to take over the small computer market. The falling cost of microprocessors and other hardware eliminated the cost advantages of the PDP-11 and other minicomputers. DEC attempted to build a line of personal computers around the PDP-11 but was not successful. By the 1990s, the minicomputer had been squeezed out of the market. DEC was acquired by Compaq in 1998, and subsequently merged with Hewlett-Packard (HP) in 2002.

The Opportunity

How is this relevant to Heathkit and the H-11? When they decided to get into the computer market, the Heath Company understood the clear division between microcomputers and minicomputers. In a bold move, they simultaneously introduced product offerings in both segments. The H-8 and its successors, discussed in Chapter 4, covered the 8-bit microcomputer market. The H-11 addressed the 16-bit minicomputer segment.

The minicomputer market was a large one, and developing a new product from scratch was beyond the resources and time frames available to Heathkit. They made the wise decision to partner with Digital Equipment Corporation to offer a version of the existing PDP-11/03 in kit form.

This allowed Heathkit to get into the market sooner with a proven computer platform: the most popular minicomputer on the market. The selling proposition was that, by assembling it yourself, you could acquire a minicomputer at a significantly lower cost, and know how to maintain and service it. Previously a minicomputer was beyond the range of what was affordable to the hobbyist or small business.

What did DEC get out of this? You might think they would be concerned that Heathkit would undercut sales of their systems by offering them at a lower price. But Heathkit likely argued that the market of hobbyists and educational users who were willing to build a system from a kit was primarily a new market segment that would not have bought an assembled PDP-11/03. DEC also manufactured the CPU boards in the H-11 and licensed the operating system, so they profited from the sale of each Heathkit system. When purchasing a system, buyers had to sign a Heath/DEC software license agreement that only allowed the software to be run on a single CPU, limiting software piracy.

Product Introduction

Heath introduced the H-11 (most early catalogs and advertisements referred to it as the H11) in 1977 at a retail price of $1295. The basic system included the following features:

- KD11F (LSI-11) 2.5 MHz CPU board with 4K words (8 KB) of RAM and 8K words (16 KB) of ROM.
- Case with card cage and power supply.
- Backplane with seven Q-bus slots for peripheral cards.

The system was a kit. The CPU board was a factory-assembled KD11F board manufactured by DEC. The user had to solder and assemble the circuit boards for the front panel and power supply, assemble the case and backplane, and make the wiring interconnections.

Heath also offered a factory-assembled version of the system, the WH-11, and assembled versions of the peripheral cards.

Unlike the H-8, the system did not have a front panel other than power and run/halt switches. To do anything useful you needed a serial terminal and paper tape reader. Heathkit offered the H-9 Video Terminal and H-10 Paper Tape Reader/Punch. Connecting to the terminal required the HT11-5 Serial Interface board and the paper tape reader required the HT11-2 Parallel Interface.

You also needed to expand the built-in 4K words of memory to at least 8K to run any significant software. Memory could be expanded with the HT11-1 4K Memory Expansion module, up to a total of 32K words (64 KB). A 16K memory card was later introduced.

THE HEATHKIT/DIGITAL H11 COMPUTER

Two of the finest names in modern electronics, Heath and Digital Equipment Corporation (DEC) combine to bring you one of the world's first 16-bit computers priced within reach of the general public! Equivalent commercial versions of this powerful computer would cost $1000's of dollars more!

New lower memory prices! $2195.00 Kit

The Heath/DEC H11 combines the advanced, performance-proven hardware and software of the LSI-11 with Heath's expertise in kit design and documentation to bring you a personal computer of almost incredible power and versatility. Together with its total-system peripherals and complete systems software, you have a computing machine that will provide you with years of practical and effective service.

The H11 features an electrically superior bus with 38 high-speed lines for data, address, control and synchronization. Data and control lines are bidirectional, asynchronous, open-collector lines capable of providing a maximum data transfer rate of 833K words per second under direct memory access operation.

The fully assembled and tested KD11F board contains the LSI-11 CPU, a 4096 x 16 read/write MOS semiconductor memory, DMA operation; and it executes the PDP-11/40 instruction set with over 400 powerful instructions. Additional memory cards can be added to expand memory capacity up to 20K in the H11 cabinet (32K words total).

Has single-level, vectored automatic priority interrupt, real-time clock input signal line, ODT/ASCII console routine/bootstrap resident in microcode. The backplane card guide assembly holds the microcomputer and up to six I/O and memory modules. The backplane/card guides are fully compatible with all standard DEC LSI-11 accessories.

The H11 is supplied with versatile PDP-11 software (see next page for full description). This software is supplied in paper tape format and requires a minimum of 8K memory, with 12K to 16K total memory recommended for maximum capability. See software license agreement, next page. Rugged metal cabinet with high-impact plastic sides measures 19" W x 6½" H x 17" D. For 110/220 VAC, 50/60 Hz.
Kit H11, Shpg. wt. 34 lbs. 2195.00

H11-1 4K Memory Expansion Module: Plugs into H11 backplane, adds 4K x 16-bit word capacity to H11 memory. Uses high-reliability 1Kx4 static MOS RAM chips. Access time is less than 500 nS. Has decode circuitry for operation on 4K address boundaries. Handle for easy removal and insertion. Compatible with PDP 11/03 and other LSI-11 backplane machines.
Kit H11-1, Shpg. wt. 2 lbs. . . . . **Was 459.95 Now 399.95**

NOTE: DEC, DIGITAL, FOCAL AND PDP ARE REGISTERED TRADEMARKS OF DIGITAL EQUIPMENT CORPORATION.

H11-2 Parallel Interface: General-purpose parallel interface featuring 16 diode-clamped latched data input lines, 16 latched output lines, 16-bit word or 8-bit byte data transfers. Has LSI-11 bus interface and control logic for interrupt processing and vectored addressing; control status registers compatible with PDP-11 software routines. Four control lines for output data ready, output data accepted, input data ready and input data accepted logic operations. Maximum data transfer rate, 90K words per second under program control. Maximum drive capability, 25-ft. cable. Plugs into H11 backplane, can be used with DEC PDP-11/03 and other LSI-11

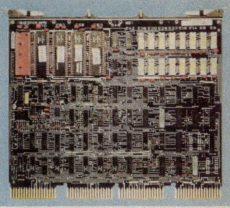

Fully Assembled and tested KD11F board

backplane machines. Also compatible with TTL or DTL logic devices. The H11-2 is required for interfacing the H11 to the H10 Paper Tape Reader/Punch.
Kit H11-2, Shpg. wt. 2 lbs. 179.95

H11-5 Serial Interface: Universal asynchronous receiver/transmitter serial interface module for use between LSI-11 bus and serial devices such as the Heathkit H9 video terminal (page 76) or LA36 teleprinter (page 78). Has optically isolated 20 mA current loop and EIA interfaces; selectable baud rates of 50, 75, 110, 134.5, 150, 200, 300, 600, 1200, 1800, 2400, 4800 and 9600. Plugs into H11 backplane, fully compatible with PDP 11/03 and other LSI-11 backplane machines. With all mating connectors.
Kit H11-5,
Shpg. wt. 2 lbs. . . .179.95

H11-6 Extended Arithmetic Chip: Adds powerful arithmetic instructions to the LSI-11, including fixed point multiply, divide and extended shifts plus full floating point add, subtract, multiply and divide. Helps minimize or eliminate arithmetic sub-routines, speeds up program execution and eases program development. Saves memory space too. 40-pin dual-inline package IC plugs into socket on KD11F board.
H11-6, Shpg. wt. 1 lb. 299.95

Manual Set for H11 Computer: Includes complete assembly and operation manuals for the H11 Digital Computer, H11-1 4K memory board, H11-2 parallel interface, H11-5 serial interface, H9 CRT terminal, and H10 paper tape reader/punch. Also includes complete software documentation — monitor, editor, assembler, linker, BASIC, FOCAL and related software. In handsome 3-ring binder.
HM-1100 Manual Set, Shpg. wt. 12 lbs. 30.00

NOTE: The price of the manual set can be deducted when you order an H11. Manuals are included with each kit.

74

H11 Dual Floppy Disk! Coming Soon See page 78

POWERFUL HEATH/DEC PDP-11 SOFTWARE AT NO EXTRA COST!

The H11 includes a sophisticated software package that lets you get your computer up and running with practical programming capabilities. This paper tape based software would cost over $1200 if purchased separately. A minimum of 8K memory is required to run the software. The programs include:

ED-11. Assists you in the creation and modification of ASCII source tapes, also used to write assembly language programs and for general text editing or word processing functions.

PAL-11S. Relocatable assembler converts ASCII source tapes into relocatable binary modules. This lets you create programs in small, modular segments for easier coding and debugging. These binary modules serve as inputs to LINK-11S.

LINK-11S. Link editor which links the modules created by the PAL-11S into a load module ready for execution on the H-11. The module is loaded into the H-11 via the Absolute Loader.

Absolute Loader. Loads absolute binary tapes into the H11 memory for execution.

ODT-11X. Lets you debug the programs which you have created. Permits modifying and controlling program execution "on the fly" for quick, efficient debugging.

IOX. I/O executive program permits I/O programming without developing device-driving programs. Links to your programs using the LINK-11S. For use with high speed paper tape reader/punch and line printer.

DUMP-AB and DUMP-R. Lets you dump absolute binary contents of memory to the paper tape punch.

BASIC. DEC's powerful version of standard Dartmouth BASIC interpreter uses English-type statements and mathematical symbols to perform operations. Immediately translates, stores and executes the program. Includes string capability.

FOCAL™. DEC's own interpretive computer language which combines simplicity with computing power. Ideal for most scientific, engineering and math applications. FOCAL™ programs can be written and executed easily. Both 4K and 8K versions are included.

Buy a complete H11 system and SAVE! You can choose a complete computer system consisting of the H11 computer, one major peripheral, plus memory and accessories, and deduct 5% from the total price (excluding shipping and handling charges). See the Heath recommended systems below or "roll your own" with components YOU select!

HS-11-1 System: The minimum recommended H11 System. Includes H11 Computer, H11-1 4K Memory (for a total of 8K memory), H11-2 Parallel Interface, H11-5 Serial Interface, H9 Video Terminal and H10 Paper Tape Reader/Punch. If purchased separately, $4354.75. **Heath System Price is $4137.00.**

H11 SPECIAL SYSTEM OFFER! A deluxe H11 system discounted even MORE than 5% to really save you money! Consists of H11 Computer, H11-1 4K Memory (for a total of 8K memory), H11-2 Parallel Interface, H11-5 Serial Interface, H10 Paper Tape Reader/Punch and H36 LA36 DEC Writer II. If purchased separately, $5649.80.

YOU SAVE $399.80!   **Special System Price is $5250.00**

HS-11 Computer System. Shpg. wt. 78 lbs. 5250.00

75

The serial and parallel interface cards and memory expansion boards were kits that the user had to fully assemble. These were Heathkit designs, but are believed to be based on the designs for DEC boards and were software compatible with them.

You could buy a system bundle and get a discount on the price of the individual components. The HS-11-1 system bundle included:

- H-11 Computer
- H11-1 4K Memory
- H11-2 Parallel Interface
- H11-5 Serial Interface
- H-9 Video Terminal
- H-10 Paper Tape Reader/Punch

This typically retailed for about $2500. A deluxe system that included an LA36 Dec Writer II printing terminal rather than the H-9 video terminal was $3350.

Heathkit provided full assembly, operation, and software manuals for the system and peripherals, with their typical high level of quality and detail. While manuals were included with the purchase of an H-11, they could be ordered separately by customers who wanted to review the manuals before buying or to have a spare set. If you bought the manuals first, you could deduct them from your H-11 purchase.

The software included with the system included the following (developed by DEC):

- ED-11 Editor
- PAL-11S Relocatable assembler
- LINK-11S Linker
- Absolute Loader (for loading tapes into memory)
- ODT-11X Debugger
- IOX I/O Executive
- DUMP-AB and DUMP-R (dumps memory to paper tape punch)
- BASIC (DEC's version of the Dartmouth BASIC programming language)
- FOCAL (DEC's interpretive programming language)

The above came on paper tape and some (like the full version of FOCAL) required at least 8K of memory.

This software gave the user the ability to develop and write programs in assembly language, BASIC, or FOCAL. The H-11 was also compatible with most software written for the PDP-11 series of computers, particularly the PDP-11/03.

Floppy Support

The basic system was pretty limited and tedious to use. You needed to load BASIC or FOCAL from paper tape, then load your program from tape, all of which was slow (50 characters per second), taking

Shown with optional
830-35 LTC Switch

H-27 Floppy Disk gives much faster access to data and information

$1995.00 Kit

- Full compatibility with DEC RX01 (PDP-11V03) system
- Z-80 microprocessor-based controller
- Dual-drive system for more on-line storage — up to ½ Meg bytes
- Fast 6 mS head step time
- Uses larger 8" floppy disks with greater capacity

The **Heathkit H-27 Floppy Disk System** gives you dual-drive versatility, with a total of ½ Meg bytes of on-line program and data storage area — enough room for most of your general-purpose application needs. The H-27 stores data and information on 8-inch floppy disks, which are compatible with equipment using the IBM 3740 format.

The **Z-80 microprocessor-based disk controller** in the Heathkit H-27 Floppy Disk System provides an average data access time of 250 milliseconds. This means you will have very fast access to data.

You get full compatibility with DEC and RXV11 RX01 (PDP-11/03 and PDP-11V03) hardware and software when you use the Heathkit H-27 Floppy Disk System. This gives you the capability of using the hundreds of application programs written by users of the DEC PDP-11, one of the most popular microcomputers. Performance-proven hardware and software bases, including the Heathkit H-11A Computer, provide outstanding computer power.

See the full line of software for the H11A Computer, including the FORTRAN language, on pages 45, 46 and 47.

While compatible with the DEC systems, the H-27 Floppy Disk System gives you even more. A built-in self-test diagnostic, which operates during power-up, protects existing programs on your disks. A mechanical interlock prevents accidental damage to data and information — if the floppy disk is not seated properly, the door will not close and the H-27 Floppy Disk System will not operate. A write-protect function protects important files and programs from being inadvertently written over. And a reformatting procedure gives you the capability of initializing a diskette with the standard IBM 3740 format.

A **single-board bootstrap/interface circuit** uses just one backplane slot on the Heathkit H-11A Computer, leaving more space for memory and I/O additions to your Heathkit H-11A Computer System. The H-27 Floppy Disk System measures 7.75" H x 18" W x 20" D. It operates on 120 or 240 VAC, 60 Hz power, and draws a maximum of 240 watts. To use the full capabilities of the HT-11 Operating Systems Software, which is designed for used with the Heathkit H-27 Floppy Disk System, you need a Heathkit H-11A Computer with at least 16K words of memory.

Kit H-27, Shpg. wt. 93 lbs., Motor Freight . . 1995.00

Assembled WH-27 Dual-Drive Floppy Disk System. WH-27, Shpg. wt. 69 lbs., Motor Freight . . . 2595.00

Package of 5 Blank 8-Inch Floppy Disks for the Heathkit H-27 Floppy Disk System, supplied in standard IBM 3740 format.
H-27-2, Shpg. wt. 2 lbs. 25.00

H-27/WH-27 SPECIFICATIONS: Diskette: 8-inch. **Capacity** (8-bit bytes, IBM 3740 format): 256,256 bytes per diskette; 3,328 bytes per track; 128 bytes per sector. **Recording Surfaces Per Diskette:** One. **Tracks Per Diskette:** 77 (0-76 or 0-114[8]). **Sectors Per Track:** 26 (1-26 or 1-32[8]). **Bit Density:** 3200 bpi at inner track. **Track Density:** 48 tracks per inch. **Recording Technique:** Double frequency. **Data Transfer Rate: Diskette to Controller Buffer:** 4 μS/data bit (250k bps). **Track-To-Track Move:** 6 mS/track maximum. **Head Settle Time:** 15 mS maximum. **Rotational Speed:** 360 rpm, ±2.5%; 166 mS/revolution nominal. **Average Access:** 250 mS, calculated as follows: Seek (77 tracks/8.3) x Settle (3 mS + 15 mS) + Rotate (166 mS/2) = Total (250 mS). **Temperature: Operating:** 59 deg. F to 90 deg. F (15 deg. C to 32 deg. C) ambient. **Maximum Temperature Gradient:** 20 deg. F/hr (11.1 deg. C/hr). **Non-Operating:** −30 deg. F to +140 deg. F (−35 deg. C to +60 deg. C). **Diskette Non-Operating:** −30 deg. F to +125 deg. F (−35 deg. C to +52 deg. C). **Humidity: Operating:** 77 deg. F (25 deg. C) maximum wet bulb; 36 deg. F (2 deg. C) minimum dew point, 20 to 80% relative humidity. **Non-Operating:** 5 to 98% relative humidity (no condensation). **Diskette Non-Operating:** 10 to 80% relative humidity. **Power Requirement:** 120/240 VAC, 60 Hz, 240 watts maximum. **Interface Module Power Requirement:** 5 VDC, 1 amp typical, 1.5 amps maximum. **Dimensions:** 7.75" H x 18" W x 20.75" D (20.32 x 45.72 x 52.71 cm). **Net Weight:** 61 lbs. (27.67 kilograms).

Alaska, Hawaii and Michigan Residents: Call 616-982-3411

COMPUTERS/39

several minutes. Saving programs was also to paper type, which was slower than reading (10 characters per second). There was no file system or operating system as such.

Within a year, Heath introduced the H-27 floppy drive. This was a dual 8-inch floppy drive, providing 256KB of storage per disk (for a whopping half a megabyte of total online storage!). It used the IBM 3740 storage format and was compatible with DEC's RX01 system.

It was controlled by a card that was installed in the card cage, which utilized a Z80 microprocessor. The system needed at least 16K words of memory to use the floppy drive.

The floppy allowed the user to run the HT-11 operating system, which avoided the need to use paper tape and was much more powerful. It was sold separately at a typical cost of $350. HT-11 was a modified version of the RT-11 real-time operating system from DEC, and offered compatibility with programs written for RT-11. The disk-based system could run additional software including a FORTRAN language compiler.

The Pascal-based UCSD P-System was also offered as an alternative operating system. More information about the software offered for the H-11 is covered in Chapter 12.

The H-11A

In 1980, an updated version of the H-11, the H-11A was introduced. It featured a new CPU card, the DEC KD11-HA (LSI-11/2), which was half the size of the earlier KD11F and freed up an additional backplane slot. Unlike the H-11, the new board had no on-board RAM, and so required additional memory to be installed. By this time Heathkit was offering a 16K word memory board, and memory prices had come down since 1977. There were no other significant differences between the H-11 and H-11A.

End Of The Era

The H-11 was significantly more expensive than the H-8 and other competing microcomputer systems and beyond the reach of most hobbyists. This limited its popularity.

While it offered compatibility with DEC's RT-11 OS and applications written for it, Heathkit only had a limited offering of software available. Some PDP-11 software would not run on the H-11 due to its limited memory. Perusing catalogs of the time demonstrates that much more software was available for the H-8 series.

Heathkit decided to discontinue the product, and the Spring/Summer 1982 Heathkit catalog was the last time the system appeared. This was inevitable, as the entire minicomputer market was ultimately squeezed out by microcomputers. Heathkit focused on the microcomputer market, with the H-8, H-89, H-100, and succeeding systems.

Buying and Restoration Tips

H-11 systems are quite rare (certainly less common than the H-8) but do show up on eBay and other sources. They are not considered highly collectible due to the limited amount of software available.

If looking for systems on auction sites, it should be noted the Heathkit H-8 (described in Chapter 4) appears similar to the H-11 but is an entirely different and incompatible system. The H-11 can be easily distinguished from an H-8 by the lack of a front panel display and keypad.

As well as an H-11 or H-11A unit with CPU, you will need serial and parallel interface cards, a paper tape reader/punch, and a serial terminal or computer with a serial port running a terminal emulator. You'll also need at least 8K words of memory, meaning one or two memory modules depending on the model of the computer.

The CPU boards were either a KD11-HA or KD11F made by DEC and could potentially be taken from a PDP-11 or LSI-11 system.

Realistically you would want a floppy drive and controller to run a disk-based system.

Some of the manuals can be found on the internet. I'm aware of assembly manuals for the H-11, serial board, parallel board, and memory expansion boards, as well as the operation manual for the H-11. Some PDP-11/03 documents should be relevant too.

Finding the software is even more challenging. It would be a daunting task to get a unit working unless you are fortunate enough to get one with all the hardware and software. I'm not aware of anyone who currently has a fully working H-11A with floppy drives and an HT-11 operating system.

Product Listing

The table below lists the different models of H-11 systems, peripherals, and accessories.

Figure 18: List of 16-Bit Computer Products

Model	Category	Series	Kit	Description	First Year	Last Year	Lowest Price	Highest Price
830-35	Accessory	H-11	Y	Line Time Clock Switch Modification Kit	1980	1982	$53.50	$93.50
H-11	Computer	H-11	Y	Digital H-11 Computer	1978	1978	$2,195.00	$2,195.00
H-11-1	Accessory	H-11	Y	4K Memory Expansion Module	1978	1982	$275.00	$275.00
H-11-10	Accessory	H-11	N	Wire Wrapping Board	1981	1981	$35.00	$35.00
H-11-19	Accessory	H-11	Y	Wire Wrapping Board	1982	1982	$44.95	$44.95
H-11-2	Accessory	H-11	Y	Parallel Interface	1978	1981	$95.00	$130.00
H-11-2	Accessory	H-11	Y	Parallel Interface	1982	1982	$95.00	$95.00
H-11-5	Accessory	H-11	Y	Serial Interface	1980	1981	$105.00	$135.00
H-11-5	Accessory	H-11	Y	Serial Interface	1978	1982	$95.00	$95.00
H-11-6	Accessory	H-11	N	Extended Arithmetic Chip	1978	1981	$190.00	$190.00
H-11-6	Accessory	H-11	Y	Extended Arithmetic Chip	1982	1982	$159.00	$159.00
H-11A	Computer	H-11	Y	DEC-compatible 16-Bit Computer	1980	1982	$1,195.00	$2,195.00
H-27	Disk	H-11	Y	8" Disk System Kit with 2 drives	1980	1981	$1,995.00	$2,195.00
HKS-11	Computer	H-11	N	Complete H-11A 16-Bit Microcomputer System	1981	1982	$3,995.00	$5,494.90

Model	Category	Series	Kit	Description	First Year	Last Year	Lowest Price	Highest Price
HM-1100	Accessory	H-11	N	H11 Manual Set	1978	1981	$25.00	$30.00
HS-11	Computer	H-11	N	H11 Computer System with 8K, parallel interface, serial interface, paper tape reader/punch, DEC Writer terminal	1978	1978	$3,350.00	$3,350.00
HT-11	Software	H-11	N	BASIC Interpreter	1981	1982	$350.00	$490.00
HT-11-1	Software	H-11	N	FORTRAN Language	1981	1982	$250.00	$350.00
WH-11-1	Accessory	H-11	N	Assembled 4K Memory Expansion Module	1980	1980	$95.00	$95.00
WH-11-2	Accessory	H-11	N	Parallel Interface	1980	1981	$150.00	$160.00
WH-11-5	Accessory	H-11	N	Serial Interface	1980	1981	$150.00	$160.00
WH-11-51	Accessory	H-11	N	Adapter Cable for H-11-5 Serial Interface	1980	1981	$15.00	$15.00
WH-11-UL	Computer	H-11	N	Assembled/UL-approved Computer	1981	1981	$2,100.00	$2,100.00
WH-11A	Computer	H-11	N	Assembled H-11A Computer	1980	1982	$1,995.00	$2,995.00
WH-27	Disk	H-11	N	Assembled H-27 Dual-Drive Floppy Disk System	1980	1982	$2,595.00	$3,995.00
WHA-11-16	Accessory	H-11	N	32K Byte (16K Word) Memory Expansion Module	1981	1981	$495.00	$495.00
WHA-11-5	Accessory	H-11	N	Printer to H-11A Serial Interface Board	1980	1981	$150.00	$150.00
WHA-11-6	Accessory	H-11	N	16K Word (32K Byte) Memory Expansion Module	1980	1982	$480.00	$795.00

(this page intentionally left blank)

Chapter 6: The 8/16-Bit Computers

As outlined in Chapter 1, in 1979 the Zenith Radio Company acquired Heathkit from Schlumberger, forming Zenith Data Systems. They realized that the H-11 had a limited market due to its high price and minicomputer operating system, and the H-8 and its successors like the H-89A were at a disadvantage due to the proprietary HDOS (although they could also run CP/M) and proprietary bus for expansion cards. The Z80 was also no longer state of the art with new 16-bit microprocessors coming out. They were also limited by the terminal-based interface with no graphics capability except with a separate video card driving a television.

The next generation of systems Heathkit introduced was an interesting hybrid featuring an 8085 CPU that could run CP/M and an 8088 CPU that could run an OEM version of MS-DOS. They featured a standard S-100 bus that could accept S-100 peripheral cards.

The H-100 was offered in two models: an "All-In-One" unit with an integral display and a "Low-Profile" system with an external display. They featured built-in 5.25" floppy drives and serial and parallel ports.

They were sold both as kits under the Heathkit name as well as factory-assembled machines branded as Zenith. The Z-110 was the Zenith-branded assembled version of the H-100 Low-Profile model and the Z-120 was the same for the All-in-one model.

The main CPU board was factory assembled. For the Heathkit versions, the user had to assemble the power supply and video board, and perform the mechanical assembly and wiring.

The 8088 CPU initially ran at 5 MHz and was later upgraded to 8 MHz. RAM started at 128 KB and could be expanded up to 768 KB.

The systems had a 96-key integral keyboard with a numeric keypad and offered two serial ports and one Centronics type parallel port.

There was support for color and monochrome video with 640x225 resolution graphics. The internal monitor was 12-inch monochrome with amber, green, and white phosphors available. A color monitor had to be external.

The disk format was soft-sectored, double-sided, double-density storing 320K. The system came with one drive with the option to add a second internally. You could also optionally add an internal 11 MB hard drive or an optional external 8-inch floppy drive.

The system had five IEEE-696/S-100 slots, one of which was taken by the controller card, leaving four available.

The system could run CP/M or Z-DOS, which was Heath/Zenith's OEM version of Microsoft's MS-DOS. At the time, MS-DOS was licensed by Microsoft in many OEM versions to run on different hardware.

HSG-1121-22 All-In-One Computer with two 5.25" DSDD disk drives

The Advanced H-100* All-In-One Desktop Computer

As low as

$2149⁰⁰

- Dual microprocessors to run both 8/16-bit software
- Standard 128 KB RAM expandable to 768 KB
- High-capacity 320 KB single disk drive storage
- Built-in monochrome monitor with choice of CRTs
- Standard parallel and dual serial output ports
- Highly detailed graphics in monochrome or color
- MS-DOS operating system included

Dual 16- and 8-bit microprocessors offer the best of both worlds. The 8088 microprocessor provides for significantly improved performance from the H-100 Computer by allowing use of sophisticated 16-bit applications software. Run programs faster, up to 10 times faster than 8-bit software, and manipulate more information, or both. The H-100 also uses an 8-bit 8085 microprocessor that allows you to run most 8-bit CP/M* software programs.

A standard 128K byte RAM memory in the H-100 provides the capacity to handle most all software programs. For larger, more comprehensive business programs, memory can be easily expanded to 192K bytes right on the motherboard. For even larger programs, memory can be expanded up to 768K bytes via S-100 expansion slots. Optional Z-205 RAM memory board lets you add 256K to memory.

Designed for expansion, the H-100 features four open expansion slots. These are industry standard S-100 slots that can be filled with memory and peripheral devices as you need them. This add-on capability protects your computer investment by being able to take advantage of advancing future technology.

Excellent high-resolution graphics is made possible on the H-100 through bit-mapping. With individual dot (pixel) control of a 640 by 225 pixel area, you can create highly detailed drawings and graphs. Thirty-three special graphic characters are available through the keyboard for use in less detailed graphics. Install two

HS-1101-22 Low-Profile with optional HVM-122A

Modular H-100 Low-Profile Desktop Computer

As low as

$1999⁰⁰

- Features all the advantages of the All-In-One less the built-in monochrome video display
- Offers you the option of selecting either a monochrome or high-resolution color video display
- Expandable memory and high-capacity disk drives
- Three ports for extensive communications access
- MS-DOS operating system included

Offering all the features of the H-100 All-In-One, the Low-Profile version also provides a modular alternative to a complete computer. Select either an RGB color monitor or a high-resolution monochrome display at additional cost. Then place your Low-Profile H-100 where you like to work and the monitor where you choose.

Power, performance and flexibility marks the Low-Profile Computer like the All-In-One. An advanced 8088 microprocessor provides 16-bit computing power while an 8085 microprocessor runs 8-bit software faster than ever before...both processors run at 5 MHz. Enjoy the benefits of 16-bit software and retain access to the huge base of 8-bit CP/M software.

For easy access to information, the Low-Profile Computer features one or two 5.25-inch floppy disk drives. Each double-sided double-density drive can store up to 320K bytes of data. Support for an external 8-inch drive (HS-207 on page 89) for up to 2.5 megabytes of data storage is standard.

128 kilobytes of RAM is standard and an additional 64K bytes can be added to the main board for up to 192K of memory on the motherboard. And that can be expanded up to 768K bytes with the addition of two 256K RAM Upgrade boards.

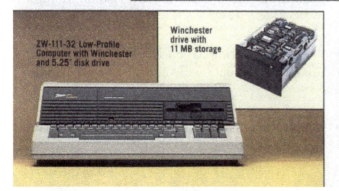

ZW-111-32 Low-Profile Computer with Winchester and 5.25" disk drive

Winchester drive with 11 MB storage

Assembled Low-Profile Computer with Winchester

Huge on-line data storage, that's what you get with an H-100 that has a built-in 11 megabyte Winchester hard disk drive. It allows you to conveniently store data that would otherwise require several dozen floppy diskettes. With a Winchester drive you can easily handle those large amounts of data encountered with lists of accounts and large inventories.

For serious computer users, a Winchester disk drive can be an economical data storage alternative to a 5.25-inch floppy disk system. Especially when many disk drives, costing more than a Winchester drive, are required to put all needed information "on-line" at the same time.

Dramatically decreasing seek time over floppy disk drives, a Low-Profile Computer with a Winchester drive can be finished retrieving information while a 5.25-inch correct disk system is just getting started. This high speed access to information is ten to twenty times faster than systems using 5.25-inch floppy disk

Despite running MS-DOS, it was not hardware compatible with the IBM PC in that it could not accept IBM peripheral cards. It did support cards for the S-100 bus, and there were many third-party S-100 cards on the market. Generic MS-DOS programs would run on the H-100 series, but most commercial IBM PC software used IBM BIOS extensions that were not present and would fail. Several companies offered hardware or software solutions to permit unmodified IBM PC programs to work on the Z-100.

Product Listing

The table below lists some of the different models of systems, peripherals, and accessories for the 8/16-Bit computers.

Figure 19: List of 8/16-Bit Computer Products

Model	Category	Series	Kit	Description	First Year	Last Year	Lowest Price	Highest Price
H-19-2	Accessory	H-19	Y	Conversion kit, convert H-19 to H-88 All-In-One Computer	1981	1982	$695.00	$995.00
H-19-3	Accessory	H-19	Y	Conversion kit, convert H-19A to H-88 All-In-One Computer	1982	1982	$995.00	$995.00
HA-108	Accessory	H-100	Y	8 MHz and 256K RAM Conversion Kit for H-100	1985	1985	$249.95	$249.95
HDC-100	Accessory	H-100	N	Dust Cover for Low-Profile Computer	1983	1985	$16.00	$16.00
HDC-120	Accessory	H-100	N	Dust Cover for All-In-One Computer	1983	1985	$16.00	$16.00
HDC-207	Accessory	H-100	N	Dust Cover for the HS/Z-207	1984	1984	$16.00	$16.00
HS-100-21	Computer	Z-100	Y	Low Profile, monochrome graphics, 128 KB RAM, one 5.25" drive	1983	1983	$2,199.00	$3,299.95
HS-1100-21	Computer	H-100	Y	Low-Profile Computer, Monochrome graphics, 128KB RAM, one 320KB 5.25" floppy	1983	1983	$1,999.00	$1,999.00
HS-1101-21	Computer	H-100	Y	Low Profile, monochrome graphics, 128 KB RAM, one 320 KB 5.25" drive, Z-DOS	1984	1984	$1,999.00	$1,999.00
HS-1101-22	Computer	H-100	Y	Low Profile, monochrome graphics, 128 KB RAM, two 320 KB 5.25" drives, Z-DOS	1984	1984	$2,299.00	$2,299.00
HS-1108-41	Computer	H-100	Y	H-100 Low-Profile Computer, 256K RAM, MS-DOS	1986	1986	$999.00	$999.00
HS-1108-41	Computer	H-100	Y	Low-Profile with 256K RAM, one 5.25" drive, 8 MHz operation, and MS-DOS	1985	1985	$1,599.00	$1,599.00
HS-1108-42	Computer	H-100	Y	Low-Profile with 256K RAM, two 5.25" drives, 8 MHz operation, and MS-DOS	1985	1985	$1,799.00	$1,799.00
HS-207-41	Disk	H-100	Y	Eight-inch Floppy Disk System with one disk drive and capable of storing 1.25 megabytes (MB) of data on a double-sided double-density 8" diskette	1984	1984	$999.00	$999.00
HS-207-42	Disk	H-100	Y	Eight-inch Floppy Disk System with two 8" disk drives, 2.5MB of data storage	1984	1984	$1,599.00	$1,599.00
HS-217	Disk	H-100	Y	Winchester upgrade kit for H-100, for models with full-height drives	1984	1985	$999.00	$1,799.00
HS-217A	Disk	H-100	Y	Winchester upgrade kit for H-100, for models with half-height drives	1984	1985	$999.00	$1,799.00

Model	Category	Series	Kit	Description	First Year	Last Year	Lowest Price	Highest Price
HSA-1120-21	Computer	H-100	Y	All-In-One Z/Z-100 series computer, non-glare amber CRT	1983	1983	$2,149.00	$3,499.95
HSA-1121-21	Computer	H-100	Y	Monochrome graphics, non-glare amber CRT, 128 KB RAM, one 320 KB 5.25" drive, Z-DOS	1984	1984	$2,149.00	$2,149.00
HSA-1121-22	Computer	H-100	Y	Monochrome graphics, non-glare amber CRT, 128 KB RAM, two 320 KB 5.25" drives, Z-DOS	1984	1984	$2,449.00	$2,449.00
HSA-1128-41	Computer	H-100	Y	All-In-One with monochrome graphics, non-glare amber CRT, 256K RAM, one 5.25" drive, 8 MHz operation, and MS-DOS	1985	1985	$1,699.00	$1,699.00
HSA-1128-42	Computer	H-100	Y	All-In-One with monochrome graphics, non-glare amber CRT, 256K RAM, two 5.25" drives, 8 MHz operation, and MS-DOS	1985	1985	$1,899.00	$1,899.00
HSG-1120-21	Computer	H-100	Y	Monochrome graphics, non-glare green CRT, 128 KB RAM, one 320 KB 5.25" drive, Z-DOS	1984	1984	$2,149.00	$2,149.00
HSG-1121-21	Computer	H-100	Y	Monochrome graphics, non-glare green CRT, 128 KB RAM, one 320 KB 5.25" drive, Z-DOS	1984	1984	$2,149.00	$2,149.00
HSG-1121-22	Computer	H-100	Y	Monochrome graphics, non-glare green CRT, 128 KB RAM, two 320 KB 5.25" drives, Z-DOS	1984	1984	$2,449.00	$2,449.00
HSG-1128-41	Computer	H-100	Y	All-In-One with monochrome graphics, non-glare green CRT, 256K RAM, one 5.25" drive, 8 MHz operation, and MS-DOS	1985	1985	$1,699.00	$1,699.00
HSG-1128-42	Computer	H-100	Y	All-In-One with monochrome graphics, non-glare green CRT, 256K RAM, two 5.25" drives, 8 MHz operation, and MS-DOS	1985	1985	$1,899.00	$1,899.00
HSG-120-21	Computer	H-100	Y	All-In-One Z/Z-100 series computer, non-glare green CRT	1983	1983	$2,349.00	$3,499.95
HSW-1120-21	Computer	H-100	Y	Monochrome graphics, non-glare white CRT, 128 KB RAM, one 320 KB 5.25" drive, Z-DOS	1983	1983	$2,149.00	$2,149.00
HSW-1121-21	Computer	H-100	Y	Monochrome graphics, non-glare white CRT, 128 KB RAM, one 320 KB 5.25" drive, Z-DOS	1984	1984	$2,149.00	$2,149.00
HSW-1121-22	Computer	H-100	Y	Monochrome graphics, non-glare white CRT, 128 KB RAM, two 320 KB 5.25" drives, Z-DOS	1984	1984	$2,449.00	$2,449.00
HSW-1128-41	Computer	H-100	Y	All-In-One with monochrome graphics, non-glare white CRT, 256K RAM, one 5.25" drive, 8 MHz operation, and MS-DOS	1985	1985	$1,699.00	$1,699.00
HSW-1128-42	Computer	H-100	Y	All-In-One with monochrome graphics, non-glare white CRT, 256K RAM, two 5.25" drives, 8 MHz operation, and MS-DOS	1985	1985	$1,899.00	$1,899.00
HSW-120-21	Computer	H-100	Y	All-In-One Z/Z-100 series computer, non-glare white CRT	1983	1983	$2,349.00	$3,499.95
TM-100	Accessory	H-100	N	H/Z-100 Technical Manuals	1983	1985	$55.00	$110.00
TM-240	Accessory	Z-200	N	Technical Manual for the Z-200	1985	1985	$49.00	$49.00
Z-204	Accessory	H-100	N	Assembled H/Z-100 Multiport Input/Output Card (serial and parallel)	1985	1985	$395.00	$395.00
Z-205	Accessory	H-100	N	256 KB RAM Upgrade Circuit Board	1983	1985	$599.00	$999.00
Z-205-1	Accessory	H-100	N	64 KB RAM Memory Expansion Set	1983	1985	$79.99	$180.00
Z-205-4	Accessory	Z-200	N	256K RAM Chip Set	1985	1985	$199.00	$199.00

Model	Category	Series	Kit	Description	First Year	Last Year	Lowest Price	Highest Price
Z-205-4	Accessory	H-100	N	256K RAM Chip Set	1985	1985	$199.00	$199.00
Z-207-3	Disk	H-100	N	Second Disk Drive for kits and ZF-100-21	1983	1983	$99.95	$395.00
Z-207-41	Disk	H-100	N	Assembled and tested Eight-inch Floppy Disk System with one disk drive and 1.25MB storage	1983	1984	$1,599.00	$1,599.00
Z-207-42	Disk	H-100	N	Assembled and tested Eight-inch Floppy Disk System with two disk drives and 2.5MB storage	1983	1984	$2,299.00	$2,299.00
Z-207-6	Disk	H-100	N	Assembled and tested second Half-Height Eight-Inch Disk Drive, 1.25MB double-sided, double-density storage	1984	1984	$699.00	$699.00
Z-216-8	Accessory	H-100	N	8087 Numeric Coprocessor for H/Z-100 Computers	1985	1985	$429.00	$429.00
Z-219-1	Accessory	H-100	N	Color Video RAM Chip Set	1983	1985	$74.99	$160.00
ZA-100-4	Accessory	H-100	N	S-100 Extender Board, allows easy maintenance and troubleshooting of accessory boards that fit into S-100 slots	1984	1985	$59.00	$79.00
ZF-100-21	Computer	Z-100	N	Assembled Low-Profile Computer with monochrome graphics and one 5.25" floppy disk drive	1982	1983	$2,899.00	$4,895.00
ZF-101-31	Computer	Z-100	N	Assembled, Low Profile, monochrome graphics, 192 KB RAM, one 320 KB 5.25" drive, Z-DOS	1984	1984	$3,029.00	$3,029.00
ZF-110-22	Computer	Z-100	N	Assembled Low-Profile Computer with color graphics capability and two 5.25" floppy disk drives	1982	1985	$3,499.00	$5,995.00
ZF-111-22	Computer	Z-100	N	Assembled, Low Profile, color graphics, 192 KB RAM, two 320 KB 5.25" drives, Z-DOS	1984	1984	$3,499.00	$3,499.00
ZF-118-42	Computer	H-100	N	Assembled Low-Profile with monochrome graphics, 256K RAM, two 5.25" drives, 8 MHz operation, MS-DOS and LOTUS 1-2-3	1985	1985	$2,399.00	$2,399.00
ZF-120-22	Computer	Z-100	N	Assembled All-In-One H-100, 12" green CRT, 128 KB RAM, two 320 KB 5.25" drives	1983	1985	$3,499.95	$4,099.00
ZFG-121-32	Computer	H-100	N	Assembled H-100 with non-glare green CRT, 192K RAM, two 5.25" drives, 8 MHz operation, MS-DOS and LOTUS 1-2-3	1985	1985	$2,499.00	$2,499.00
ZW-110-32	Computer	Z-100	N	Assembled Low-Profile Computer with color graphics capability, 192KB RAM, one 320KB 5.25" floppy disk drive and an internal 11MB Winchester disk drive	1983	1983	$5,499.00	$5,799.00
ZW-111-32	Computer	Z-100	N	Assembled and tested Low-Profile Desktop Computer with internal 11 MB Winchester disk drive, one 320 kilobyte 5.25-inch floppy disk drive, 192 kilobytes of RAM, color graphics capability	1984	1984	$5,499.00	$5,499.00
ZW-118-42	Computer	H-100	N	Assembled Low-Profile with internal 11MB Winchester, one 5.25" drive, 256K RAM, 8 MHz operation, MS-DOS and LOTUS 1-2-3	1985	1985	$3,399.00	$3,399.00

Model	Category	Series	Kit	Description	First Year	Last Year	Lowest Price	Highest Price
ZW-120-32	Computer	Z-100	N	Assembled and tested Low-Profile Desktop Computer with non-glare green CRT, 192 KB RAM, one 320 KB 5.25" disk drive and an internal 11 MB Winchester disk drive	1983	1983	$5,599.00	$5,899.00
ZW-121-32	Computer	Z-100	N	Assembled and tested All-In-One Desktop Computer with internal 11 MB Winchester disk drive, one 320 kilobyte 5.25-inch floppy disk drive, 192 kilobytes of RAM, non-glare green CRT	1984	1984	$5,599.00	$5,599.00
ZWG-121-32	Computer	H-100	N	Assembled All-In-One with internal 11MB Winchester, one 5.25" drive, 192K RAM, 5 MHz operation, MS-DOS and LOTUS 1-2-3	1985	1985	$3,499.00	$3,499.00

Chapter 7: The IBM Compatible Era

By 1984 it had become clear that the PC wars were over and the largest market was for IBM PC compatibles or "clones" of which many manufacturers had competing products. Apple still had a relatively small niche market with the last of the Apple II series and short-lived Apple ///, Lisa, and eventually Macintosh systems which were not cloned. On the low end, there were also proprietary computers primarily used for gaming from companies like Commodore and Atari.

It was also clear that CP/M was dead and MS-DOS (but not yet Microsoft Windows) was the operating system of choice for PCs. Heathkit still had an opportunity to offer what no one else did: sell IBM-compatible PCs in kit form, and that is what they focused on.

This strategy started in 1984 with the offering of the HS-151 and HS-161 models.

Heathkit introduces the first kit computers that are compatible with the IBM-PC...the HS-151 Personal Computer and the HS-161 Portable Computer

The HS-151 was essentially an IBM PC clone offered in kit form as well as an assembled Zenith branded version. It featured an 8088 CPU, 128K of RAM, and up to two optional floppy drives in IBM 360K format, and an optional hard drive. It had a detached keyboard, monochrome and color video output, two serial ports and one parallel port, and four IBM-compatible slots. It ran standard MS-DOS. It was featured in the October 1984 issue of PC Magazine. The kit version was quite challenging as you had to solder and assemble all circuit boards including the motherboard. Unlike a standard IBM PC, it featured built-in diagnostics and on-board LEDs to show status with power-up self-tests in ROM and additional diagnostics on floppy disk. Given that it was a kit, these features were needed to diagnose problems and confirm that it was correctly working after assembly.

The HS-161 was a "portable", often called a luggable. While it was a single unit with a handle, it weighed 39 pounds! This was pretty typical of such systems of the time and it competed with units like the Compaq Portable and IBM Portable PC.

Through the 1980s PC technology advanced quickly, and Heathkit introduced models to keep up with the latest advancements. They followed the progress of the industry, with memory moving to 640KB and beyond, processors progressing from Intel 8088 to 286 and 386, floppies increasing in density as they moved from 5.25" to 3.5", and internal hard drives becoming affordable. Video progressed from monochrome to color, with various graphics standards including EGA, CGA, and VGA. Eventually, Heathkit introduced some laptop computers. Typically they offered models offered as kits as well as factory-assembled under the Zenith name.

Heathkit's offering of PCs in kit form ended in 1992 when the company left the kit business although they continued to sell some assembled computers under the Zenith brand. The next few pages show some representative models taken from Heathkit catalogs.

Introducing Heath/Zenith solutions to your computing needs...the HS-151 Personal Computer

HS-151 Personal Computer features Heathkit quality and IBM compatibility

Low-Profile for as low as

$1899.00

Kit Price

- Takes advantage of IBM software and hardware
- Standard 128 KB memory expandable to 640 KB
- Available with one or two 5.25-inch floppy disk drives or optional Winchester*

Heath/Zenith proudly offers a new and exciting personal computer...the HS-151 Desktop Personal Computer...with the enhanced features that you are looking for. A quality personal computer, the HS-151 PC provides Heathkit excellence in design and workmanship along with access to the wealth of available IBM software and hardware.

Using the advanced 16-bit 8088 microprocessor, the HS-151 PC gains a great deal of high speed computing power along with the ability to run sophisticated and high quality 16-bit software. In addition, the 8088 supports the MS*-DOS operating system. This allows you to select software from the full range developed for the IBM Personal Computer and run it on the Desktop PC.

A standard 128 kilobytes (KB) of RAM user memory, with internal parity checking, is available on all models of the HS-151. For larger programs where additional memory is needed or desired, 64 KB increments can be added to the main memory board for up to 320 KB of RAM. For the user's convenience, a very useful debugger is permanently stored in ROM along with a pre-set auto-boot routine which can be disabled.

Optional single or dual 5.25-inch floppy disk drives supply the HS-151 PC with high-capacity auxiliary storage. These double-sided, double-density drives are IBM formatted and each stores up to 360 KB of data. An optional hard disk drive* provides an extensive 10.6 megabytes (MB) of added storage for those larger, more comprehensive business and scientific programs.

Four open IBM compatible slots are provided for your future expansion. Use one of these slots to expand memory up to 640 kilobytes, or use one for a Winchester controller card,* or both. By being able to accept most peripheral boards designed for the IBM-PC, the HS-151 PC provides unlimited off-the-shelf flexibility in hardware configurations. With more hardware choices available, you can choose from a wider variety of software programs and peripherals to meet your ever-changing and expanding computer needs.

Two video outputs on the rear panel of the Desktop PC provide connections for either a color or monochrome video display monitor. Connect an RGB monitor to the standard nine-pin D connector and enjoy the benefits of a full color presentation. In the character mode, see a colorful 80 character by 25 line display in a selectable one of eight background colors and 1 of 16 foreground colors. In the graphics mode, each pixel of a 320 x 200 area can be painted in one of four colors selected from 1 of 2 color pallets. For easier viewing of word processing and accounting programs, a standard phono type connector allows the use of monochrome video display monitors. On a monochrome monitor, color displays are represented by a corresponding gray level.

A detached low-profile keyboard adds to the HS-151 Personal Computer's ease of use. The user-friendly keyboard is clearly labeled and has color-coded keypads that permit rapid key identification. It is laid out in the standard typewriter format, even the shift and return keys are where they belong. Ten programmable function keys, and separate plus and minus keys increase the HS-151 PC's accurate data entry capability. A calculator-style keypad, with enter key, allows rapid entry of large groups of numbers. LED indicators on the keyboard give instant operating status notice at a glance. An audible click is sounded at each keypress to signal successful key entry. This lightweight keyboard connects to the main unit by a coiled cord that expands up to six feet and plastic legs swing out for two levels of keyboard adjustment.

Three communication ports provide the HS-151 PC with the flexibility to expand. Available are two IBM compatible serial ports and a parallel port that can be used with peripherals such as a matrix or letter quality printer or a modem. The two serial I/O ports are standard EIA HS-232 DTE connectors capable of baud rates between 110 and 9600 operating in asynchronous full or half duplex. The parallel interface is a Centronics compatible printer port using a 25 pin D connector.

Three separate testing procedures allow you to check your Desktop PC's hardware accuracy and adds to your data entry protection. These three levels of diagnostics include: power-on checks with their results indicated on eight internal LEDs; a ROM-based user-implemented screen diagnostic; and, optionally, an extensive disk-based set of diagnostics. The diagnostic floppy disk is included with the HS-151 PC and provides an easy and broad range of diagnostic tests to ensure your computer is operating at peak efficiency.

Many editing capabilities are provided with the HS-151 Desktop PC to aid you in your program writing. With the HS-151, you can insert and delete characters and lines; erase a line; erase to the beginning of a line, to the end of a line, or to the end of the page. Control the cursor with up, down, left, right, and home controls. Scroll through your programs with options such as a jump or smooth scroll, or a scroll that's ROM or software selected.

Filled with important extras, the HS-151 PC lets you enjoy using a computer. Enjoy such features as a ready-to-use computer three to four seconds after applying power, easy hardware configuration with a menu- and diagram- driven program, booting from any drive, smooth scroll search, flickerless video and much more.

In the office or in the home, the HS-151 Desktop Personal Computer is ready to provide even more ways to help you be more productive and creative. One way is with the MS-DOS operating system that's included with the computer. It'll start you on the way to using software packages like those found on pages 45 and 46.

An all-metal chassis with decorative bezels blends strength and superior styling into the HS-151 PC. It measures 16" wide by 6½" high and 6½" deep, excluding the keyboard. The computer operates on 120/240 volts AC at 50/60 Hz and uses 300 watts (maximum) of power.

Heathkit Kit HS-151-21, Low-Profile Personal Computer, 128K RAM, one 5.25" disk drive with 360 KB storage 64 lbs. 1899.00

Heathkit Kit HS-151-22, Low-Profile Personal Computer, 128K RAM, two 5.25" disk drives with 720 KB storage 73 lbs. 2199.00

Zenith data systems ZF-151-21, Assembled Low-Profile Personal Computer, 128K RAM, one 5.25" disk drive with 360 KB storage, 38 lbs. 2699.00

Zenith data systems ZF-151-22, Assembled Low-Profile Personal Computer, 128K RAM, two 5.25" disk drives with 720 KB storage. 41 lbs. 3099.00

Zenith data systems ZW-151-22, Assembled Low-Profile Personal Computer, 128K RAM, 10.68 Mbyte 5.25" rigid disk, one 5.25" disk drive with 360 KB total storage, Shpg. wt. 42 lbs. 4799.00

*Watch the July catalog for further Winchester upgrade information. MS is a registered trademark of Microsoft, Inc.

30/COMPUTERS

 Use your Visa or MasterCard credit cards to purchase your kit!

and the HS-161 Portable Personal Computer...new total-performance 16-bit kit computers

HS-161 Portable Personal Computer with Heathkit capability and IBM compatibility

Assembled and tested

$2899⁰⁰

Computer

- Designed for a computer user to be more productive while on-the-go
- Takes advantage of IBM software and hardware
- Standard 128 KB memory with single or dual 5.25" drives

For those who need a computer to go, Heath/Zenith introduces the HS-161 Portable Personal Computer. It does everything a personal computer can do, perhaps a bit more, and it can do it on the go. Designed-in are Heathkit quality and performance with the added plus of IBM compatibility. Move it from the office, to meetings, to the hotel room, and to your home. Use the computer at your convenience and be able to take advantage of virtually all IBM programs and hardware without changing any computer hardware. With the HS-161 PC, you get problem-solving power, portability and flexibility...a powerful combination.

Extensive memory and storage capacity are two advantages of the new HS-161 Portable. A standard 128 kilobytes (KB) of RAM is available on all models which can be expanded on the main board to 320 KB. For auxiliary storage, the portable computer is available with one or two high-capacity 5.25-inch floppy disk drives. Each drive stores data in the standard IBM format on double-sided, double-density disks for a total capacity of 360 KB. When not in use or during transit, the disk drive section can be lowered into the computer.

For future expansion, four open slots are available for almost any off-the-shelf IBM compatible accessory boards. This allows you access to hundreds of software and hardware alternatives to meet your ever-changing computer needs.

A 9-inch amber phosphor video display monitor is built into the HS-161 PC with full business graphics capability. The amber monitor is most preferred by users for easy-on-the-eyes viewing during long periods of use. A "gray scale" feature allows color intensities to be programmed for easier viewing of color programs on a monochrome screen. As an option, an RGB color monitor can be used with the portable for a more exciting graphics display.

A detached 84-key keyboard connects to the main unit by a coiled cable. This allows the user to located the keyboard at a convenient working position. The keyboard is laid out like a standard typewriter. Keypads are clearly marked and color coded for easy identification. Ten programmable function keys can be user defined for special software applications. Separate plus and minus keys and an L-shaped return key increase the portable's ease of operation. LED indicators, for caps lock and numeric lock, give instant notice of operating status. When moved, the keyboard safely locks into the front of the computer.

Utilize the three input/output ports of the HS-161 and expand the usefulness of this portable computer. A parallel port and two IBM compatible serial ports are available on the rear panel for use with dot matrix or letter quality printers, modems and other computer-expanding peripherals.

Protect your data entries by using three separate testing procedures to check the HS-161 Portable's hardware accuracy. One test is automatically conducted when the portable computer is powered up. Eight internal LEDs indicate the results of this test. Access the ROM or monitor diagnostic which is displayed on the CRT. Or, use the diagnostic disk that's included with the computer for an extensive check of the HS-161 PC's operation.

Featuring many extras, the HS-161 Portable offers a quick 3–4 second start-up time from turn on, booting from either drive and a friendly configuration program including menus and diagrams. The computer also features a smooth video display without the flicker as seen in other models, high-density diskette formatting on floppy drives, plus many other advantages.

Your access to a wealth of software, is another plus feature of the HS-161 Portable Computer. Included with the HS-161 PC is the powerful MS-DOS operating system (page 45) that allows you to use all the applications software developed for the IBM-PC. Several of these software packages can be found on pages 45 and 46. These programs will help you become more productive and creative.

Keyboard and drives nest safely and neatly inside computer during transit.

Kit HS-161-21, Portable Personal Computer with non-glare 9" amber CRT, 128 KB RAM, 4 open IBM compatible expansion slots, one 5.25" disk drive, with 360 KB of storage. ...... **AVAILABLE IN JULY CATALOG.**

Kit HS-161-22, Portable Personal Computer with non-glare 9" amber CRT, 128 KB RAM, 4 open IBM compatible expansion slots, two 5.25" disk drives, with 720 KB of storage capacity. .... **AVAILABLE IN JULY CATALOG.**

ZFA-161-21, Assembled Portable Computer with non-glare 9" amber CRT, 128 KB RAM, 4 open IBM compatible expansion slots, one 5.25" disk drive, with 360 KB of storage capacity, 55 lbs. **2799.00**

ZFA-161-22, Assembled Portable Computer with non-glare 9" amber CRT, 128 KB RAM, 4 open IBM compatible expansion slots, & two 5.25" disk drives, with 720 KB of storage capacity, 55 lbs. **3199.00**

Z-205-1, 64 KB RAM Memory Expansion Set, nine chip set installs onto main board. of Personal and Portable Computers. Three sets required for 320 KB limit, Shpg. wt. 1 lb. .... **EACH 165.00**

Second Optional Drive, available by visiting your local Heathkit Electronics Center or calling 800-253-7057 from 8 AM to 6 PM EST Mon.-Fri.

HS-151 and HS-161 SPECIFICATIONS: Processor: Intel 16-bit 8088. **Clock:** 4.77 MHz. **On-Board Memory:** 128 KB standard expandable to 320 KB on main board, up to 640 KB total memory via expansion slot. **VIDEO DISPLAY: CRT (HS-161 only):** Non-glare 9-inch diagonal, amber phosphor. **Display Format:** 25 lines of 80 characters. **Display Size:** 5.0" high x 7.0" wide. **Character Size:** 0.165" high x 0.075" wide. **Character Type:** 8 x 8 dot matrix. **Dot Resolution:** 640 horizontal x 200 vertical. **Colors:** Characters: 1 of 8 background colors with 1 of 16 foreground colors. Graphics: Each pixel can be 1 of 4 colors selected from 1 of 2 color pallets. **Gray Scale:** Eight levels on a monochrome display. **Video Outputs:** RGB with intensity control and composite monochrome. **Cursor:** Blinking underline or reverse video or off. **Cursor Controls:** Up, down, left, right, home. **Cursor Addressing:** Relative and direct. **Tab:** 8 columns. **Refresh Rate:** 60 Hz, 50 Hz. **Edit Functions:** Insert and delete characters or lines. **Erase Functions:** Erase line, erase to beginning of line, erase to end of line, erase to end of page. **Bell:** Audible alarm in receipt of ASCII BEL command. **BUS STRUCTURE: Type:** IBM compatible. **Slots:** 8, 4 available for expansion. **KEYBOARD: Type:** 84 keys, 57 alphanumeric and 10 special function plus 17 keypad keys including separate numeric keypad. **Key Click:** Yes. **DISK SYSTEM: Drives:** single or dual 5.25-inch double-sided double-density 48 TPI floppy disk drive. **Capacity:** IBM formatted for 360 KB each. **Winchester Drive:** Optional internal 5.25-inch rigid disk drive with single 5.25-inch floppy disk drive. Capacity: 12.76 unformatted, 10.68 formatted. **INPUT/OUTPUT: Serial I/O:** Dual DTE RS-232C ports. Baud Rate: 110-9600. **Operation:** Asynchronous full or half duplex. **Parallel I/O:** Centronics compatible. **Power Supply:** 120/240, 50/60 Hz, 300 watts (maximum). **Dimensions:** HS-151: 16" W x 6¼" H x 16½" D (40.6 x 15.9 x 42 cm). HS-161: 19½" W x 8⅜" H x 19⅛" D (20.9 x 49.5 x 48.6 cm). **Weight:** HS-151: Approximately 42 lbs. with keyboard and two disk drives. HS-161: 39 lbs.

 Discover the fun of kitbuilding at your Heathkit Electronic Center.

COMPUTERS/31

Special $1299
Lowest price ever!

There's no better buy than Heath's 386SX computer, now with Zenith FTM monitor

Built to the same exacting standards as the famous Zenith Data Systems compact desktop computer, the popular Heath HS-5100 is priced to beat the competition! With its compact size (6" H x 14" W x 15" D), this easy-to-assemble kit computer leaves more room on your desk and fits into even the smallest workspace. Heath Sales Advisors are ready to help you customize your HS-5100 with a wide range of floppy and hard drives, coprocessors, additional memory and more. Call 1-800-253-0570 8:00 am - 4:30 pm EST, Monday-Friday. **Limited Quantities**

Kit HS-5100-SX includes 386SX processor board, 3.5" floppy drive, 1 MB memory, software (Diagnostix, MS-DOS, MS-Windows 3.0), 40MB Winchester drive and Zenith's best Flat Tension Mask VGA color monitor. (40 lbs.) List $3304 **Special $1299**

Special $999
Reduced $450!

No other laptop provides this much value for the price

The Heath 286 laptop you build from an easy-to-assemble kit offers the performance of a desktop PC at a remarkable price! At less than 15 lbs., it has enough power to double as your laptop on the road and your desktop in the office. The HS-2862-A offers full PC compatibility and AT computing power, and comes packed with 1MB of standard RAM, enough for those long spreadsheets and databases. Its 640 x 480 Page White VGA display is easy on your eyes. Kit includes 4.0 A/hr. battery, 20MB Hard Drive, MS-DOS and Diagnostix. Call 1-800-253-0570 for custom hardware configurations, including additional floppy drives, coprocessors, memory and more.

Kit HS-2862-A (29 lbs.) Was $1449 **Now $999**
HFM-9600 Internal Fax/Modem with software (for all Heathkit laptops and ZDS equivalents) operates as 9600 baud fax or 2400 baud modem with MNP5.
Limited Quantities (2 lbs.) List $329 **Special $149**

Heath's high-intensity 80 MB 386 computer at bargain price

Heath's most powerful computer offers a 32-bit, 25 MHz 80386 processor and zero wait state technology to speed through the most demanding programs. It's perfect for windowing operations, desktop publishing, software development, CAD/CAM, large spreadsheets and networking. Discover the ease of computing with 386 power and the simplicity of assembling this extraordinary computer value yourself. Computer kit includes 2MB RAM, 16K cache memory, two 40MB 28MS Winchester hard drives, 1.4MB 3.5" floppy drive and HVB-550 video card. Software: MS-DOS, MS Works, Diagnostix and MS-Windows 3.0. **Limited Quantities**

Kit HS-3629-B (46 lbs.) Was $2393 **Now $1795**

Special $1795

*HS-3629 Desktop Computer
with 25MHz clock speed*

Includes Integrated 7+. This menu-driven applications package contains a spreadsheet as easy as 1-2-3, a word processor, relational database manager, database merging, graphics, terminal emulation and PC-to-PC communications. A super value!

16MHz 386 Desktop Computer: Equipped with 1MB RAM, dual port video card and 1.4MB 3.5″ disk drive. Includes MS-DOS, Diagnostix, Integrated 7+ software, MS-Windows and a printer cable.
Kit HS-386-C (62 lbs.) .... *Was* $2999.00 *Now* **$2699.00**
Accessories:

3.5″ 1.4MB Disk Drive. Requires ZCA-14 (below).
Assembled ZD-14 (3 lbs.) **$219.00**

ZCA-14 Cable. Includes mounting hardware.
Assembled ZCA-14 (1 lb.) **$29.00**

5.25″ 1.2MB Disk Drive
Assembled ZD-12 (5 lbs.) **$250.00**

5.25″ 360K Disk Drive
Assembled Z-207-7 (5 lbs.) **$199.00**

Winchester Upgrade Kit. Allows installation of an optional 20MB 65ms hard disk drive. Disk has plated recording media for maximum durability and data integrity, plus automatic head lifters to prevent head damage. Includes all installation cables.
Assembled HWD-20-AT (3 lbs.) **$239.00**

80MB Winchester Hard Drive. Requires Z-417-2 cable when installing in floppy-only models. Formats at 72MB.
Assembled ZD-800 (1 lb.) **$1999.00**

40MB 28ms Winchester Hard Drive. Includes all installation cables and formats at 44MB.
Assembled HWD-4028 (4 lbs.) **$659.95**

Winchester Hard Drive Cable. Required for the installation of the first Zenith Winchester hard disk drive.
Assembled Z-417-2 (1 lb.) **$20.00**

80386 Upgrade. For Z-248 computers.
Assembled ZUS-386 (12 lbs.) **$2999.00**

High-Speed Cache Memory Card. Includes 64K RAM.
Assembled Z-525 (3 lbs.) **$599.00**

1MB Memory Expansion Board. Fully populated, with enable/disable EMS memory.
Assembled Z-505 (3 lbs.) **$799.00**

4MB Memory Expansion Board. Fully populated, with enable/disable EMS memory.
Assembled Z-515 (3 lbs.) ...... *Was* $2999.00 *Now* **$1999.00**

80287 10 MHz Numeric Co-Processor
Assembled Z-416-2 (1 lb.) **$525.00**

80387 16 MHz Numeric Co-Processor
Assembled Z-516 (1 lb.) **$1199.00**

Color Video Card. Contains two ports and automatic video switching between MDA, CGA, VGA, EGA and Hercules graphics. Allows you to run VGA/EGA/CGA software on the new FTM monitor. For IBM and compatible computers.
Assembled HVB-550 (1 lb.) ...... *Was* $599.00 *Now* **$329.95**

new HS-3629 desktop computer: the most powerful computer kit ever

SKILL LEVEL 3 This 32-bit, 25MHz 80386-based computer, with superb high-resolution graphics, includes bonuses like MS-DOS, MS-Windows, Diagnostix and Integrated 7+ software. High reliability is ensured, because every 80386 microprocessor in our 386s is 100 percent tested for all functions.

The HS-3629 is perfect for windowing operations, software development, CAD/CAM, desktop publishing, large spreadsheets and networking. In addition, you can run most PC and AT compatible software, and at 25 MHz, you'll blaze through all your favorite applications.

You get a dual port video card capable of operating your VGA, EGA, CGA, TTL or Zenith's new FTM monitor. You also get a dual disk controller card that operates two 5.25″ or 3.5″ floppy drives and two hard disk drives.

The HS-3629 comes with zero wait state technology, 2MB RAM expandable to 32MB, serial and parallel communication ports for printers and modems, plus a deluxe keyboard. The HS-3629 uses 115/230 VAC, 50/60 Hz. An alternate AC line cord is required for 230 VAC operation. Dimensions are 6″H x 21″W x 17″D.

Configurations:

25MHz 386 Desktop Computer: Equipped with 2MB RAM, 64K cache memory, HVB-550 video card and 1.4MB 3.5″ disk drive. Includes MS-DOS, Diagnostix, Integrated 7+ software and MS-Windows.
Kit HS-3629 (62 lbs.) **$3999.00**

48

Product Listing

A partial list of IBM-compatible computers that were offered is listed in the table below. The list is incomplete and does not include some models that were only sold under the Zenith name.

Figure 20: List of IBM-Compatible Computers

Model	Category	Series	Kit	Description	First Year	Last Year	Lowest Price	Highest Price
HS-1151-21	Computer	HS-151	Y	Low-Profile Personal Computer, 128K RAM, one 5.25" disk drive with 360KB storage	1985	1985	$1,299.00	$1,299.00
HS-1151-22	Computer	HS-151	Y	Low-Profile Personal Computer, 128K RAM, two 5.25" disk drives with 720KB storage	1985	1985	$1,499.00	$1,499.00
HS-148-41	Computer	H-148	Y	Compact Personal Computer with one 5.25" disk drive	1985	1985	$999.00	$999.00
HS-151-21	Computer	HS-151	Y	Low-Profile Personal Computer, 128K RAM, one 5.25" disk drive with 360KB storage	1984	1984	$1,899.00	$1,899.00
HS-151-22	Computer	HS-151	Y	Low-Profile Personal Computer, 128K RAM, two 5.25" disk drives with 720KB storage	1984	1984	$2,199.00	$2,199.00
HS-158-41	Computer	H-158	Y	Expandable Personal Computer with one 5.25" disk drive	1985	1985	$1,599.00	$1,599.00
HS-158-42	Computer	H-158	Y	Expandable Personal Computer with two 5.25" disk drives	1985	1985	$1,799.00	$1,799.00
HS-161-21	Computer	HS-161	Y	Portable Personal Computer with non-glare 9" amber CRT, 128 KB RAM, 4 open IBM compatible expansion slots, one 5.25" disk drive, with 360 KB of storage	1984	1984	$1,699.00	$1,699.00
HS-161-22	Computer	HS-161	Y	Portable Personal Computer with non-glare 9" amber CRT, 128 KB RAM, 4 open IBM compatible expansion slots, two 5.25" disk drives, with 720 KB of storage	1984	1984	$1,999.00	$1,999.00
HS-248	Computer	n/a	Y	IBM compatible, 286, 512KB RAM, one 5.25" floppy	1986	1986	$2,499.00	$2,499.00
HS-2526	Computer	IBM PC	Y	IBM compatible, 286 processor, 12 MHz CPU, 1MB RAM, one 3.5" floppy drive	1988	1988	$2,199.00	$2,199.00
HS-2526-A	Computer	IBM PC	Y	IBM compatible, 286 processor, 12 MHz CPU, 1MB RAM, one 3.5" floppy drive	1989	1989	$1,899.00	$1,899.00
HS-2860	Computer	IBM PC	Y	Laptop, 286 CPU, 1MB RAM, one 3.5" floppy drive	1988	1989	$2,599.00	$2,999.00
HS-2862	Computer	IBM PC	Y	IBM compatible laptop, 286, 1MB RAM, one 3.5" floppy	1990	1990	Call	Call
HS-2862-A	Computer	IBM PC	Y	IBM compatible laptop, 286, 1MB RAM, 20MB hard drive, 640x480 video.	1992	1992	$999.00	$1,449.00
HS-3286	Computer	n/a	Y	IBM compatible laptop, 16 MHz 386SX CPU, 3 MB RAM	1990	1990	Call	Call

Model	Category	Series	Kit	Description	First Year	Last Year	Lowest Price	Highest Price
HS-3629	Computer	n/a	Y	IBM compatible, 386, 2MB RAM, one 3.5" floppy	1989	1989	$3,999.00	$3,999.00
HS-3629-A	Computer	IBM PC	Y	IBM compatible, 386, 2MB RAM	1990	1990	Call	Call
HS-3629-B	Computer	IBM PC	Y	IBM compatible, 386, 2MB RAM, 2x40MB hard drive, 3.5" floppy	1992	1992	$1,795.00	$2,393.00
HS-386-A	Computer	IBM PC	Y	16 MHz 386 Desktop Computer, 1MB RAM, 5.25" floppy drive	1987	1987	$3,349.95	$3,349.95
HS-386-C	Computer	IBM PC	Y	16 MHz 386 Desktop Computer, 1MB RAM, 3.5" floppy drive	1988	1989	$2,699.00	$3,349.00
HS-3860	Computer	IBM PC	Y	IBM compatible laptop, 386, 2MB RAM, one 3.5" floppy, 40MB hard drive	1989	1989	$4,369.00	$4,369.00
HS-40	Computer	IBM PC	Y	IBM compatible, 8 MHz 286, 1MB RAM, two 3.5" floppies	1988	1988	$1,699.00	$1,699.00
HS-40A	Computer	IBM PC	Y	IBM compatible, 8 MHz 286, 1MB RAM, two 3.5" floppies	1989	1989	$1,599.00	$1,599.00
HS-42	Computer	IBM PC	Y	IBM compatible, 12 MHz 286, 1MB RAM, two 3.5" floppies	1989	1989	$1,799.00	$1,799.00
HS-5100	Computer	IBM PC	Y	IBM compatible, 1MB RAM	1990	1990	Call	Call
HS-5100-A	Computer	IBM PC	Y	IBM compatible, 1MB RAM, 286 processor	1990	1990	Call	Call
HS-5100-SX	Computer	IBM PC	Y	IBM compatible, 386SX, 1MB RAM, 3.5" floppy, 40MB hard drive, Zenith FTM VGA monitor.	1992	1992	$1,299.00	$3,304.00
HS-5100-X	Computer	IBM PC	Y	IBM compatible, 1MB RAM, 386SX processor	1990	1990	Call	Call
HSA-2161-21	Computer	HS-161	Y	Portable PC with amber CRT and single 5.25" disk drive	1985	1985	$1,299.00	$1,299.00
HSA-2161-22	Computer	HS-161	Y	Portable PC with amber CRT and dual 5.25" disk drives	1985	1985	$1,499.00	$1,499.00
HSG-2161-21	Computer	HS-161	Y	Portable PC with green CRT and single 5.25" disk drive	1985	1985	$1,299.00	$1,299.00
HSG-2161-22	Computer	HS-161	Y	Portable PC with green CRT and dual 5.25" disk drives	1985	1985	$1,499.00	$1,499.00
PBS-101	Computer	IBM PC	Y	Portable Workstation,laptop, 20MB hard drive, printer	1988	1988	$3,399.00	$3,399.00
PBS-202	Computer	IBM PC	Y	High-Performance Compact Workstation, two 3.5" floppies, 20MB hard drive, monitor, printer, software	1988	1988	$2,799.00	$2,799.00
PBS-4	Computer	IBM PC	N	Affordable Student Workstation, 20MB hard drive, printer	1988	1988	$999.00	$999.00
PBS-502	Computer	IBM PC	Y	Desktop Publishing Workstation, 1 3.5" floppy drive, 20 MB hard drive, laser printer, mouse, UPS	1988	1988	$5,599.00	$5,599.00
PBS-602	Computer	IBM PC	Y	Complete Office Manager Workstation, 2 3.5" floppy drives, 20MB hard drive, printer, fax machine	1988	1988	$6,299.00	$6,299.00

Model	Category	Series	Kit	Description	First Year	Last Year	Lowest Price	Highest Price
PBS-702	Computer	IBM PC	Y	Computer-Aided Design Workstation, 386 CPU, 387 processor, 80MB hard drive	1988	1988	$13,499.00	$13,499.00
PBS-801	Computer	IBM PC	N	Computer-Based Instrument Workstation, 286 CPU, digital scope, industrial monitor, printer, UPS	1988	1988	$5,999.00	$5,999.00
ZA-138-42	Computer	n/a	N	Z-138 Portable Computer, IBM PC compatible	1985	1986	$1,999.00	$1,999.00
ZDH-1211-DE	Computer	IBM PC	N	Z-159 Model 2 Computer with 640K RAM, two 5.25" floppies	1988	1988	$1,599.00	$1,599.00
ZDH-1217-DE	Computer	IBM PC	N	Z-159 Model 2 Computer with 640K RAM, one 5.25" floppy, one 20MB hard drive	1988	1988	$2,199.00	$2,199.00
ZF-148-41	Computer	H-148	N	Assembled Compact Personal Computer with one 5.25" disk drive	1985	1985	$1,499.00	$1,499.00
ZF-148-42	Computer	H-148	N	Assembled Compact Personal Computer with two 5.25" disk drives	1985	1985	$1,799.00	$1,799.00
ZF-151-21	Computer	HS-151	N	Assembled Low-Profile Personal Computer, 128K RAM, one 5.25" disk drive with 360 KB storage	1984	1984	$2,699.00	$2,699.00
ZF-151-22	Computer	HS-151	N	Assembled Low-Profile Personal Computer, 128K RAM, two 5.25" disk drives with 720 KB storage	1984	1984	$3,099.00	$3,099.00
ZF-158-41	Computer	H-158	N	Assembled Expandable Personal Computer with one 5.25" disk drive	1985	1985	$2,199.00	$2,199.00
ZF-158-42	Computer	H-158	N	Assembled Expandable Personal Computer with two 5.25" disk drives	1985	1985	$2,499.00	$2,499.00
ZF-171-42	Computer	n/a	N	Z-171 Portable PC, 256K RAM, two 5.25" floppy drives	1985	1986	$2,399.00	$2,699.00
ZF-241-81	Computer	Z-200	N	Assembled Z-200 with 512K RAM and one 1.2MB floppy drive	1985	1985	$3,999.00	$3,999.00
ZFA-161-21	Computer	IBM PC	N	Assembled Portable Personal Computer with non-glare 9" amber CRT, 128 KB RAM, 4 open IBM compatible expansion slots, one 5.25" disk drive, with 360 KB of storage	1984	1985	$2,150.00	$2,799.00
ZFA-161-25	Computer	IBM PC	N	Assembled Portable Personal Computer with non-glare 9" amber CRT, 128 KB RAM, 4 open IBM compatible expansion slots, two 5.25" disk drives, with 720 KB of storage	1984	1985	$2,599.00	$3,199.00
ZFL-171-42	Computer	IBM PC	N	Assembled Portable Z-171 Computer with 256K RAM, two 5.25" drives, LCD display	1986	1986	$2,699.00	$2,699.00
ZFL-181-92	Computer	IBM PC	N	Z-180 Laptop, 640K RAM, two 3.5" floppies	1986	1986	$2,399.00	$2,399.00
ZFL-181-93	Computer	IBM PC	N	Z-181 Laptop, 640K RAM, two 3.5" floppies	1987	1987	$2,399.00	$2,399.00
ZP-150	Computer	IBM PC	N	Z-150 Laptop, Microsoft Works in ROM	1985	1986	$699.00	$699.00
ZSS-184-1	Computer	IBM PC	N	SupersPort Model 2 Laptop with two 3.5" floppy drives	1988	1988	$2,399.00	$2,399.00

Model	Category	Series	Kit	Description	First Year	Last Year	Lowest Price	Highest Price
ZSW-184-2	Computer	IBM PC	N	SupersPort Model 20 Laptop one 3.5" floppy drive and 20MB hard disk	1988	1988	$3,599.00	$3,599.00
ZTC-3034-EB	Computer	IBM PC	N	TurbosPort 386 Model 40 Computer with 2MB RAM, one 3.5" floppy, 40MB hard drive, MS-DOS	1995	1995	$7,999.00	$7,999.00
ZTC-3034-MO	Computer	IBM PC	N	TurbosPort 386 Model 40 Computer with 2MB RAM, one 3.5" floppy, 40MB hard drive, modem, MS-DOS	1995	1995	$8,499.00	$8,499.00
ZW-151-22	Computer	HS-151	N	Assembled Low-Profile Personal Computer, 128K RAM, 10.68 MB 5.25" rigid disk, one 5.25" disk drive with 360 KB total storage	1984	1984	$4,799.00	$4,799.00
ZW-158-42	Computer	H-158	N	Assembled Expandable Personal Computer with 10.6MB Winchester hard disk and one 5.25" disk drive	1985	1985	$3,699.00	$3,699.00
ZWL-183-92	Computer	IBM PC	N	Z-183 Laptop, 640K RAM, 3.5" floppy, 10MB hard drive	1987	1987	$3,499.00	$3,499.00
ZWL-200-2	Computer	IBM PC	N	Laptop, 286 CPU, 1MB RAM, one 3.5" floppy drive, 20MB hard drive	1988	1988	$4,999.00	$4,999.00

Chapter 8: Robots

At the 1939 World's Fair in New York City, audiences were amazed by a human form robot named Elektro. He could walk, move his arms and fingers, answer questions from the audience, and even smoke! In actual fact he was controlled offstage by a human being. His "brain", built from 48 electrical relays, was clearly limited in its capabilities. This was perhaps the first public demonstration of a robot and was to influence the public's perception for decades.

Forty years later, in 1979, Heathkit began the development of a robot kit. HERO (for **H**eathkit **E**ducational **RO**bot) was the marketing name for what became a series of educational robots offered by Heathkit in kit and assembled form. The series started with the HERO 1 which came on the market in 1982, and was followed by the lower-cost HERO Jr, and the more powerful HERO 2000. A revived version of Heathkit in 2007 made an attempt to offer a robot kit built for them by a third party.

In this chapter we'll take a look at the Heathkit robots and related accessories, which are now considered very collectible, and many units still exist and continue to operate.

HERO 1 (ET-18)

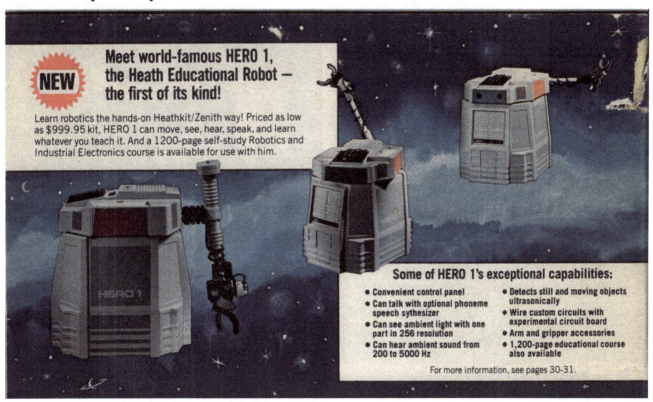

The first in the HERO line was the HERO 1, a self-contained robot capable of moving and turning, sensing light, sounds and motion, and with an optional robotic arm and speech synthesizer. It was offered both as a kit and factory-assembled. Offered from 1982 to 1995, is sold for about $1500 as a kit and $2500 assembled. It is estimated that about 14,000 were sold. Powered by four 6-volt gel cell batteries, the unit weighed 39 pounds (18 kg).

The processor was a Motorola 6808 CPU with 2KB of ROM and 4 KB of RAM. It could be programmed using "learn mode", using a high-level language (Tiny BASIC), or in machine language. Programs could be saved to and loaded from cassette tape or linked to a computer over an optional serial interface.

A top-mounted keyboard allowed the user to enter, verify, and modify programs, and select operating modes. An attachable teaching pendant could control all motor and arm movements or store them for later duplication. The user interface featured a display with six 7-segment LEDs and a hex keypad with 17 keys. There was also an optional remote control unit.

An optional arm could rotate, pivot at the wrist, and open and close a gripper. It was only capable of carrying a weight of up to one pound (0.5 kg).

An optional speech synthesizer used the Votrax SC-01 chip to produce human speech.

The following options were available for the HERO 1:

- ET-18-1 Robot Arm 5 Axis (16 ounces max)
- ET-18-2 Speech (SC-01 Based)
- ET-18-35 Remote control (75.43 MHz) with RS-232
- ET-18-36 Remote control (75.67 MHz) with RS-232
- ET-18-4 DEMO ROM Sings songs, shows off
- ET-18-5 Monitor ROM Listing
- ET-18-6 Memory Expansion board
- ET-18-7 Auto Mode ROM Lets HERO 1 navigate a room
- ET-18-9 BASIC ROM Requires Memory Expansion
- ETW-18-10 RS-232 serial interface (Plugs in Experimenter board on head)
- ET-18-11 DEMO cassette (More Demos)
- ET-18 Basic robot kit
- ET-18-1 arm and gripper mechanism
- ET-18-2 Phoneme speech synthesizer
- ETS-18 A bundle of all above
- ETW-18 Factory assembled with arm and voice
- ET-18-4 Demo ROM
- ET-18-5 Monitor ROM source code listing
- ET-18-7 automatic mode ROM

By 1984 some prices were cut, e.g. $799.95 for the ET-18 and $1199.95 for the ETS-18.

The next few pages show some relevant Heathkit catalog pages for the HERO 1.

NEW Introducing the world's first sophisticated teaching robot, HERO 1 — one of the most

Your new robot will move. See. Hear. Speak. And learn whatever you teach it — while it teaches you robotics with help from the companion Heathkit/Zenith educational course. It's also remarkably inexpensive, with the HERO 1 Robot Kit available for only $999.95 — and the assembled Robot, complete with arm and voice, priced at $2499.95.

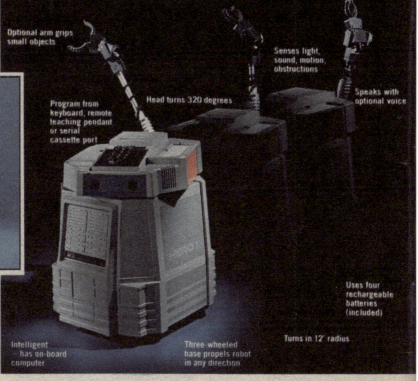

Optional arm grips small objects

Program from keyboard, remote teaching pendant or serial cassette port

Head turns 320 degrees

Senses light, sound, motion, obstructions

Speaks with optional voice

Uses four rechargeable batteries (included)

Intelligent — has on-board computer

Three-wheeled base propels robot in any direction

Turns in 12" radius

HERO 1 is a full-featured robot:

- Controlled by on-board computer
- Exceptional maneuverability — goes in any direction, turns in 12" radius
- Senses light, sound, motion and obstructions in its path
- Can pick up small objects, speak with optional Arm and Voice
- Includes rechargeable batteries, external battery charger and experimental circuit board

One of the most important microprocessor-controlled devices since the introduction of the microcomputer: HERO 1 is a completely self-contained, electro-mechanical robot capable of interacting with its environment.

Functions free of any external control: Controlled by a programmable on-board computer, the robot has electronic sensors to detect light, sound, motion and obstructions in its path. It can travel over pre-determined courses and repeat specific functions on a pre-determined schedule.

It can also be programmed to pick up small objects with the optional ET-18-1 Arm and Gripper Mechanism (below, right), and speak with the optional ET-18-2 Phoneme Voice Synthesizer (also below, right).

Highly maneuverable: Using a three-wheeled base with both drive and steering on one wheel, the robot travels any direction and turns in a 12" radius.

A computer on wheels: Program HERO 1's on-board 6808 microprocessor to guide the robot through various complex maneuvers, activate the robot's sensors and modify the robot's behavior in response to inputs from its on-board sensors and real-time clock. The straightforward programming process allows step-by-step debugging and other corrections, as needed.

HERO 1 can be programmed in three different ways: Through the keyboard mounted on the robot's head, with its hand-held remote-control teaching pendant, or through its serial cassette port (using programming previously stored on a conventional audio cassette tape recorder). The computer can store programs with over 1,000 individual steps.

Program HERO 1 to guard your home, plant: It could automatically detect intruders in its range and warn them away verbally. And HERO 1 can remain on guard for extended periods of time, using its power-conserving "sleep" mode.

Grabs and speaks with optional accessories: Capable of seven axes of motion, the optional ET-18-1 Arm and Gripper Mechanism lets you program HERO 1

to pick up small objects. The arm extends, retracts and turns — performing mechanical tasks with precision. The robot can also be programmed to speak complete sentences with the optional ET-18-2 Speech Synthesizer.

Experimental circuit board included: Expand HERO 1's capabilities to the very limits of the user's skills and imagination. This board allows the user to design circuits for interfacing with the robot's computer.

Includes on-board rechargeable batteries and charger: When HERO 1 tells you that its batteries need charging, use the robot's external battery charger. HERO 1 can be operated while its batteries are charging.

An even more significant "first": Remarkable though the robot is, its companion Robotics Education Course (see opposite page) provides an even more thorough grounding for you or those working with you in robot technology.

HERO 1 and the Robotics Course bring the learning process to life: You quickly get a hands-on grasp of industrial electronics, mechanics, computer theory and programming as applied to robots by putting them into action.

You teach it — it teaches you: HERO 1's only limitations are your imagination and ingenuity in programming, as you challenge its capabilities.

The list of capabilities goes on almost indefinitely: With the appearance of HERO 1, in production now and ready for you, the learning age of robotics has arrived. Now you can work with your own robot to develop your electronics, mechanics and programming skills — at a highly affordable price.

Kit ET-18, Basic HERO 1 Robot (less arm, voice), 69 lbs. **999.95**
ET-18-1, HERO 1's Arm (Arm and Gripper Mechanism), 6 lbs. **399.95**
ET-18-2, HERO 1's Voice (Phoneme Speech Synthesizer), 1 lb. **149.95**
SAVE $50.00! Kit ETS-18, Complete HERO 1 Robot (with arm and voice), Shpg. wt. 91 lbs. . . . . **$1549.85 separately, NOW ONLY 1499.85**
ETW-18, Complete Assembled Robot (with arm, voice), 70 lbs. **2499.95**

 Use your Visa or MasterCard credit cards to purchase your kit!

important microprocessor-controlled devices ever conceived

Exceptional capabilities!

Convenient Control Panel: Control HERO 1 from the keyboard on his head. You can also use the remote teaching pendant, or a program written on cassette tape.

Experimental Circuit Board included: HERO 1's breadboarding area provides direct access to an I/O port, user-defined interrupt, CPU control lines and power.

HERO 1 can see: The robot's light sensor beam can detect ambient light over the entire visible spectrum, with excellent resolution – down to one part in 256.

HERO 1 can hear: The robot's omnidirectional sound sensor can hear ambient sound from 200 to 5000 Hz, with the same one-part-in 256 resolution.

Detects still and moving objects: HERO 1's ultrasonic sensors can "see" movement up to 15 feet away, and can determine the range of an object up to eight feet away.

HERO 1 can talk (with optional accessory): With the optional ET-18-2 Phoneme Speech Synthesizer, the robot can simulate human speech – with four levels of inflection.

HERO 1's Hand, part of its optional Arm, grips small objects: The gripper can hold up to a pound when fully retracted and horizontal – pivots up to 350 degrees.

Optional ET-18-1 Arm available: Rotates up to 250 degrees, pivots wrist up to 180 degrees, extends or retracts gripper over a five-inch track.

"Learn" mode lets you teach HERO 1: Just switch to "Learn" mode and take the robot through your task. It remembers – and repeats the steps at your command.

"Sleep" mode conserves power: This makes HERO 1 ideal for home and plant security duty – when it sees intruders, it "wakes up," and warns them away verbally.

Self-contained rechargeable batteries: Two separate power systems – one for the logic circuits and a second for the drive system. External recharger included.

World-famous Heathkit manual: Easy-to-follow instructions from the world's largest builder of electronic kits guide you through each kitbuilding step.

Highly maneuverable: HERO 1's three-wheel drive system, with one wheel both driving and steering, allows the robot to move any where – and to turn in a 12-inch radius.

Course provides a complete, comprehensive education in robot technology

NEW

$99⁹⁵

- The 1200-page self-instruction text – Heathkit/Zenith's most extensive to date – has 11 chapters covering robot fundamentals
- Progress at your own pace – self-test exams in each unit help you check your progress
- Optional experiments give you hands-on experience with our HERO 1 Teaching Robot
- Earn 8 CEUs and a Certificate of Achievement

The most extensive course ever developed by Heathkit/Zenith Educational Systems: The 1,200-page text, which fills two three-ring binders, consists of 11 separate units covering the basics of robotics – each unit fully illustrated with charts and diagrams.

These subject areas are covered in the Heathkit/Zenith Robotics Course:

1. Robot Fundamentals
2. AC and Fluidic Power
3. DC Power and Positioning
4. Microprocessor Fundamentals
5. Robot Programming
6. Heathkit/Zenith Robot Microprocessor
7. Data Acquisition (Sensors)
8. Data Handling and Conversion
9. Voice Synthesis
10. Interfacing
11. Industrial Robots at Work

Progress at your own pace: The programmed self-study materials guide the student, step-by-step, until important concepts are mastered. Self-test reviews at the end of each unit make sure you understand what you've studied, before moving on to the next unit.

Use the ideal learning aid for robotics: Use the HERO 1 Robot on the opposite page to bring the learning process to life. By letting you apply what you've just learned, you get the type of reinforcement that makes 'learning-by-doing' one

of the most effective education methods ever devised. The course is also fully functional without the robot.

Prerequisites: You should complete EE-3101 DC Electronics (p. 32), EE-3102 AC Electronics (p. 33), EE-3201 Digital Techniques (p. 35) and EE-3401 Basic Microprocessors (pgs. 36-37) – or have a basic knowledge of those subjects – before starting the Robotics Course.

Earn 8 Continuing Education Units (CEUs) and a Certificate of Achievement from Heathkit/Zenith Educational Systems: Pass the optional final examination with a 70 percent or better score.

EE-1800, Robotics Course, Shpg. wt. 12 lbs. **99.95**

ROBOTICS/31

 Discover the fun of kitbuilding at your Heathkit Electronic Center.

HERO Jr. (RT-1)

In 1984 Heathkit introduced a smaller and lower-cost robot dubbed the HERO Jr. Intended to be more affordable for the home consumer market, it sold for about $600. It featured the same 6808 processor as the HERO 1 but came with only 2 KB of RAM and 32 KB of ROM. The RAM could be expanded to 32KB. It included proximity, light, and sound sensors and a Votrax SC-01 speech synthesizer.

The user interface was a hex keypad with 17 keys and a nine LED display. It was powered by two 6 Volt batteries (you could optionally buy two more to extend the operating time). It was 19 inches high and weighed 21.5 pounds.

Options included an infrared sensor, wireless remote controls, and an add-on for using the HERO Jr. with the Heathkit GDA-2800 Home Security System. The robot could detect an intruder, give a spoken warning, and activate the security system if the user did not correctly respond with a password.

Unlike the HERO 1, there was no option for an arm, but it had a storage compartment to carry objects (Heathkit suggested "your favorite beverage"). It also had a real-time clock.

The HERO Jr. was sold from 1984 to 1987 and it is estimated that about 4,000 were produced.

The following options were available for the HERO Jr:
- RTA-1-1 Infra-red motion detector on head. Range about 35' long x 20' wide
- RTA-1-2 Remote control accessory offers manual, wireless control of HERO Jr's movements up to 100 feet away. Operates at 75 MHz.
- RTA-1-3 RS232 interface allows the use of the BASIC cartridge
- RTA-1-4 Two extra batteries (doubles the capacity)
- RTA-1-5 Cartridge Adapter, permits the use of plug-in cartridges, with 8K RAM

Software was available in the form of plug-in cartridges. The following cartridges were offered:
- RTC-1-1 Trivia Quotes (Trivia game)
- RTC-1-2 Songs, phrases and Rhymes #1 (Adds to personality)
- RTC-1-3 Animals, Blackjack, and Tic Tac Toe
- RTC-1-4 Special Occasions (Jungle Bells, Auld Lang Syne)
- RTC-1-5 Math Master a timed math game
- RTC-1-6 Riddle Robot/Tongue Twister
- RTC-1-7 Philosopher
- RTC-1-8 HERO JR. BASIC (program the HERO JR. with simple BASIC commands)
- RTC-1-9 HEROBICS (10 Exercises, 4 levels of difficulty)
- RTC-1-10 HERO JR. Program Language (Program HERO JR. with the keypad)
- RTC-1-11 Musical Chairs with Acey-Ducey and Robot mind reader

A Master Cartridge was also offered that contained all twelve of the above cartridges in a single cartridge.

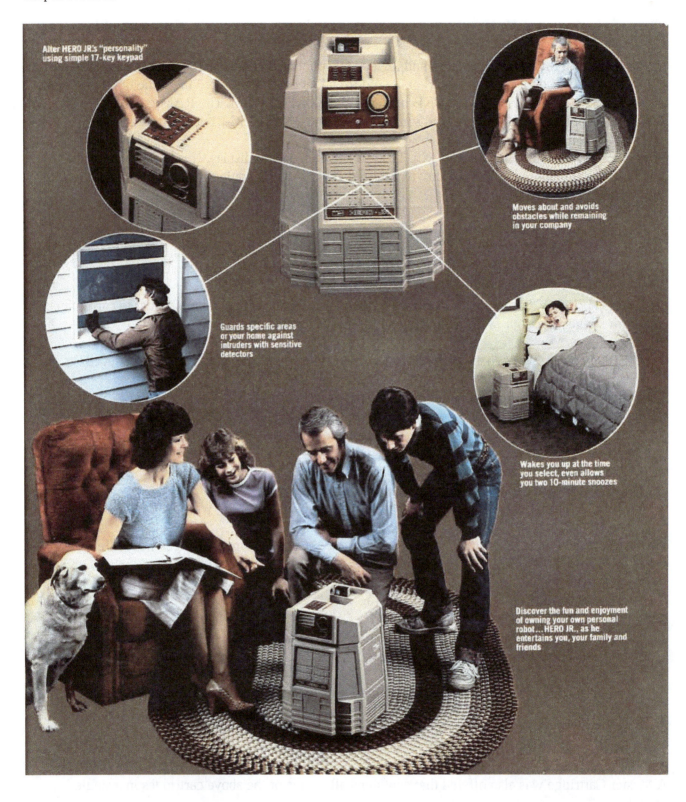

Alter HERO JR.'s "personality" using simple 17-key keypad

Moves about and avoids obstacles while remaining in your company

Guards specific areas or your home against intruders with sensitive detectors

Wakes you up at the time you select, even allows you two 10-minute snoozes

Discover the fun and enjoyment of owning your own personal robot... HERO JR., as he entertains you, your family and friends

Meet HERO JR. – the home and personal robot with an entertaining personality

HERO JR. is fully preprogrammed with speech output, light and sound sensors, an ultrasonic sonar, drive and steering motors and an on-board computer control system.

Low kit price of

$599⁹⁵

with voice

- Has a dynamic personality consisting of six traits
- Sings songs, tells nursery rhymes, plays games
- Performs tasks at specific times in the future
- Guards your home and challenges intruders
- Wakes you up on time and announces special dates
- Lets you modify his personality as desired
- Add capabilities with additional plug-in cartridges

Meet the first affordable, personal robot with a dynamic personality... HERO JR. A very friendly robot, HERO JR. will fit right in with your family and into your home. He sings songs, plays games, tells nursery rhymes, recites poems, guards your home and he can even wake you in the morning. Without supervision or help, HERO JR. will explore his surroundings and will seek to remain near his human companions. HERO JR.'s personality is preprogrammed and doesn't require any computer programming skills to operate.

HERO JR.'s personality consists of six individual traits. Each trait is assigned a level of priority depending on how frequently or how seldom you want each task performed. You can change the Robot's personality by simply changing the priority level of any given trait. Press the SET-UP key and select a level of activity from zero to nine for each trait. This gives you the unique capability of modifying HERO JR.'s behavior to fit any situation.

The traits comprising HERO JR.'s dynamic personality include: singing songs like "Daisy" and "America"; speaking preprogrammed English phrases; exploring and moving about, using his sensors to avoid most obstacles and seeking out humans; playing games such as "Cowboys and Robots," "Let's Count" and "Tickle Robot"; telling a nursery rhyme; and gabbing in "Roblish" (a robot gibberish that sounds like English). All routines are stored in *32K of built-in ROM*. Additional functions can be easily added to HERO JR. through optional plug-in cartridges.

In addition to these six traits, HERO JR. has an internal clock with a 100-year calendar that even compensates for Daylight Savings Time (if observed in your area). With this time-keeping ability, HERO JR. can act as an alarm clock and awaken you at a specified time. After your wake-up call, the Robot listens to be sure you are awake or permits two ten-minute snoozes if you desire. You can also make HERO JR. announce the day of the week, date and time at predetermined intervals or just at one important time and date. With his on-board 2K of RAM, HERO JR. can store and then remind you of birthdays and anniversaries, or other calendar events — up to sixteen dates per year.

To see, hear and speak, and to move about; HERO JR. uses a light sensor, ultrasonic sonar and motion detector, sound detector, speech synthesizer and an internal clock which are controlled by an on-board computer using a Motorola 6808 microprocessor. The light sensor has an adjustable 256-part resolution range and a 30-degree reception angle. A Polaroid ultrasonic sonar transceiver is used for the Robot's sonar and motion detector which is accurate from four inches to 26 feet. The sound sensor has a 256-part adjustable resolution range and a 200-5000 Hz bandwidth. An optional infrared sensor easily installs to add superior heat/motion detection capability.

Show off HERO JR.'s many talents to your friends using the single-button DEMO feature. In this mode, a built-in "Robot Variety Show" demonstrates the Robot's ability to see, hear, speak, tell time and move. You can even participate in the show as HERO JR. tells you what to do and when.

HERO JR. can perform other very useful tasks, including security guard. In this mode, HERO JR. will guard your home against intruders with a coded security system. You can even leave HERO JR. in the Guard mode while you are at home. If you are detected by one of the Robot's sensors, you simply respond with the proper password when requested by the Robot. Should an intruder be detected, the Robot gives a verbal warning and requests the password. If you own the Heath GD-2800 Security System (page 20), HERO JR. can activate a GDA-2800-3 RF Security Transmitter (page 20) when it challenges someone and an incorrect password or no response is given. HERO JR. can guard a specific area or patrol randomly around the house.

HERO JR. also has another human-like characteristic, it can go to sleep. This occurs randomly as part of his personality and allows the Robot to conserve battery power by keeping only critical circuits energized. You can make HERO JR. go to sleep with the SLEEP switch or by activating the Wake-Up Alarm feature.

HERO JR. can duplicate all English sounds using its built-in Votrax SC-01 phoneme synthesizer. This permits the Robot to say just about anything. Volume and pitch

adjustments tailor the Robot's voice to whatever sounds best to you. All of HERO JR.'s vocabulary is preprogrammed for you.

Although HERO JR. normally speaks, sings and performs tasks between moving about at random, an optional wireless remote unit allows the Robot to be manually driven from place to place. HERO JR. will also speak while moving about on the remote control. Four buttons on the handheld RF remote transmitter control the Robot's forward and backward movement, stop, and left and right steering. The remote operates at 75 MHz and provides control from up to 150 feet away.

A number of easy-to-install accessories are available for HERO JR. Install the Infrared Motion Detector Accessory to improve HERO JR.'s ability to seek out humans and to detect intruders. An RS-232 Accessory allows you to program the Robot using a special BASIC language through the console of a video terminal or computer. Add two extra batteries to double HERO JR.'s operating time. And, extend HERO JR.'s capabilities even further by adding on the Cartridge Adapter Accessory. It enables you to plug in a variety of preprogrammed cartridges that expands HERO JR.'s list of routines, songs, games and phrases. Even a BASIC cartridge that will allow you to program the Robot through a home computer.

Once you understand all the facets of the Robot's personality, you can advance your skill level to that of "Robot Wizard" which permits HERO JR. to identify you by name. Other wizardry enables you to change the Robot's name, adjust the sensitivity of the light and sound sensors, and make HERO JR. measure distances and more. Learn secret passwords and become a Robot Wizard.

HERO JR. is powered by two six-volt rechargeable batteries that allow the Robot to operate from 4 to 6 hours, with an average amount of exploring. The batteries recharge overnight from a plug-in wall charger that's included with the kit. HERO JR. is 19 inches tall, weighs 21½ lbs. and can carry your favorite beverage (up to 10 pounds) on a 94 cubic inch compartment built into the top of his head. Three wheels, including a single rear drive and steering wheel, enable him to move about. HERO JR. is easily assembled in approximately twenty hours.

HERO JR. is also equipped with a 17-key keypad which permits the owner to modify the Robot's personality or initiate a special task. The alphanumeric keypad features clearly marked function keys including Sing, Play, Poet, Gab, Alarm, Guard, Help, Plan, Set Up and Enter. Eight data LEDs flash in time with his speech.

Kit RT-1, HERO JR., Shpg. wt. 32 lbs. **599.95**
SAVER! Kit RTR-1-1, HERO JR. with RS-232 and Cartridge Adapter Accessories. Shpg. wt. 35 lbs. **649.95**
SAVER! Kit RTR-1-2, HERO JR. with Infrared Motion Detector, Remote Control, RS-232, and Cartridge Adapter Accessories, Shpg. wt. 38 lbs. **849.95**

Accessory kits for HERO JR.:

RTA-1-1, Infrared Motion Detector Accessory detects rapid changes in temperature within a zoned range of approximately 35' long x 20' wide. Includes two window stickers that read "Warning, This Area Protected By A Security Robot." Shpg. wt. 1 lb. **119.95**
RTA-1-2, Remote Control Accessory offers manual, wireless control of HERO JR.'s movements up to 150 feet away, operates at 75 MHz, Shpg. wt. 2 lbs. . . **179.95**
RTA-1-3, RS-232 Accessory allows you to program HERO JR. in BASIC (RTC-1-8) from a terminal or computer (requires HCA-10 or HCA-11 RS-232 cable on page 95 and terminal emulation software such as CPS), Shpg. wt. 1 lb. **49.95**
RTA-1-4, Two extra batteries, Shpg. wt. 5 lbs. **59.95**
RTA-1-5, Cartridge Adapter, permits use of optional plug-in cartridges that increase HERO JR.'s capabilities. Includes additional 8K RAM, 1 lb. **49.95**

Plug-in, preprogrammed cartridges for HERO JR. (all require the installation of the RTA-1-5 Cartridge Adapter Accessory):

RTC-1-2, Songs, Phrases and Rhymes #1 Cartridge increases HERO JR.'s vocal routines and automatically adds to the Robot's personality, 1 lb. **19.95**
RTC-1-3, Animals, Blackjack and TicTacToe Cartridge enables you to play these additional games with HERO JR., Shpg. wt. 1 lb. **39.95**
RTC-1-4, Special Occasions Cartridge adds songs for special occasions, includes two versions of Happy Birthday (one using master's name), Jingle Bells and Auld Lang Syne, Shpg. wt. 1 lb. **19.95**
RTC-1-5, Math Master Cartridge, a timed math game, Shpg. wt. 1 lb. **24.95**
RTC-1-6, Riddle Robot/Tongue Twister Cartridge, Shpg. wt. 1 lb. **24.95**
RTC-1-8, HERO JR. BASIC Cartridge contains special enhancements for speech, movement, sensors and integer math; and allows the owner to write programs using a video terminal or home computer running a terminal emulation program (such as CPS), requires RTA-1-3 RS-232 port, Shpg. wt. 1 lb. **49.95**

 Use your Visa or MasterCard credit cards to purchase your kit!

HERO 2000 (ET-19)

Introduced in 1986, the HERO 2000 was a more powerful robot that reflected advancements and cost reductions in computing.

The main processor was essentially an IBM-compatible PC: a 16-bit Intel 8088 CPU running MS-DOS. With BASIC in 64K or ROM, it came with 24 KB of RAM expandable to 576 KB using up to three 192K memory cards. A backplane supported up to 11 expansion cards.

The main CPU was augmented by six Z80 8-bit slave processors (11 when using the optional arm) which performed hardware control functions. It offered speech synthesis with text-to-speech conversion, 360-degree ultrasonic ranging, and temperature, sound and light level sensors. There were two RS-232 serial ports and a cassette tape interface.

The user interface was a top-mounted hex keypad with an optional wireless remote control with an ASCII keyboard and 80-character LCD display. Output indicators were sixteen head-mounted status LEDs.

The unit could operate for up to six days on a 24 amp-hour battery. An optional auto docking accessory allowed the HERO 2000 to automatically dock with its charger when the battery was low.

Options included a 5-1/4 inch floppy disk drive, an experimenter board for prototyping circuits, and a demonstration ROM with over a dozen programs.

An optional multi-jointed robot arm had a gripper with a sense of touch and could lift up to one pound/0.5 kg.

The unit was 32 inches/81 cm in height and weighed 78 pounds/35 kg.

The HERO 20000 sold for about $3,000 as a kit, $4,500 assembled and it is estimated that about 3,000 were sold.

The following options were available:
- ET-19-3 Robot carrying cart
- ET-19-35 Two-way Remote control 75.43 MHz, full keyboard, teaching pendant, 80-character LCD display, and RS-232 port
- ET-19-36 Same as above except 75.67 MHz
- ET-19-5 Auto-Dock (Enables robot to find charger on low battery)
- ET-19-51 Demo ROM
- ET-19-14 Experimenter card dual breadboard and buffered I/O
- ETW-19-15 Static memory card 192k max on each
- ETW-19-6 360K Floppy disk drive and controller

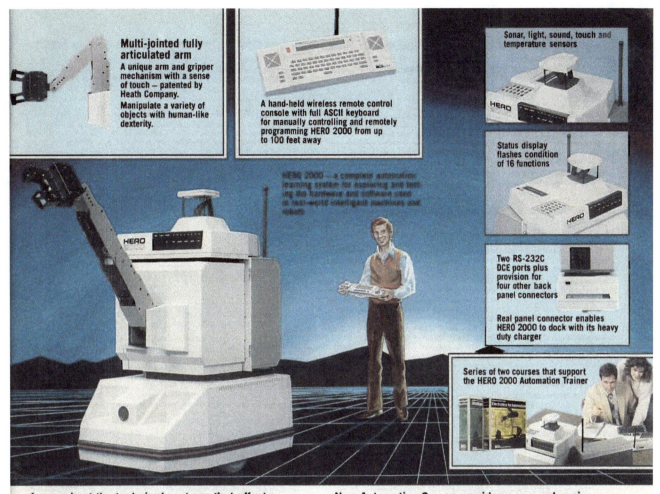

Multi-jointed fully articulated arm
A unique arm and gripper mechanism with a sense of touch — patented by Heath Company. Manipulate a variety of objects with human-like dexterity.

A hand-held wireless remote control console with full ASCII keyboard for manually controlling and remotely programming HERO 2000 from up to 100 feet away

Sonar, light, sound, touch and temperature sensors

Status display flashes condition of 16 functions

Two RS-232C DCE ports plus provision for four other back panel connectors

Real panel connector enables HERO 2000 to dock with its heavy duty charger

Series of two courses that support the HERO 2000 Automation Trainer

Learn about the technical systems that affect all of us in the New Intelligent Machines Course

$99⁹⁵

- Ties together computers, robotics and sensor systems
- Written so that even a novice can understand the technical aspects of intelligent machines

This course is an introduction to intelligent machines. The basic parts of these machines are detailed as well as how they make decisions. Input and output devices are covered including keyboards, mice, digitizers and others. Transducers and sensors are introduced with such complex devices as vision and tactile sensor systems. Concluding the course is a discussion of robotics including characteristics, classifications and programming.

Other subjects covered include basic signal conditioning, analog-to-digital and digital-to-analog conversion, and the hardware and software involved in machine communication. Also touched on are computer aided manufacturing, computer-aided design and flexible manufacturing systems.

To better understand the text material of this course, we recommend the completion of the DC and AC electronics courses on page 65 or equivalent knowledge of the contents of these courses. A knowledge of BASIC is also helpful.

Earn 3.0 Continuing Education Units by passing the optional final exam with a 70% or higher score. Also receive a Certificate of Achievement.

Fifteen interesting experiments transform textbook material into exciting, practical hands-on experience. All the experiments are designed to operate on the HERO 2000 Automation Trainer equipped with its versatile Arm Accessory. No other test equipment is required.

EE-1900, Shpg. wt. 8 lbs. **99.95**

New Automation Course provides a comprehensive look at the electronics used at the component level

$99⁹⁵

- A component by component look at the electronics used in automated industrial robotic systems
- Used with the HERO 2000 Automation Trainer to transform textbook theory into exciting, hands-on experience

A second course in the Heathkit/Zenith series on industrial automation. It presents a sweeping and all-inclusive examination of the electronics used at the component level in automated systems. Covered are industrial controllers and active and passive sensory devices and circuits.

Also covered are signal conditioning circuits including analog sampling and analog-to-digital conversion circuits. Industrial control devices and circuits, motors and digital-to-analog conversion circuits are explained. In addition, actual industrial applications for automated systems are explored including visual and tactile sensing systems.

Thirteen practical and exciting experiments help develop a thorough understanding of the material contained in the text. All experiments are conducted on the unbeatable HERO 2000 Automation Trainer.

Earn 6.0 Continuing Education Units by passing the optional final exam with a 70% or higher score and also receive a Certificate of Achievement.

Completion of the Intelligent Machines Course and the Fundamental Electronic Series which includes the DC Electronics, AC Electronics, Digital Techniques, and Semiconductor courses (pages 65-67) are recommended. A working knowledge of the BASIC Programming Language is also helpful.

EE-1901, Shpg. wt. 11 lbs. (Available in May) **99.95**

HERO® 2000

NEW

HERO 2000 is a high-technology tool that enables you to explore and learn about controlling real-world automated systems which are intelligent machines. HERO 2000 is also an educational trainer for use in simulating industrial robotic applications. And HERO 2000 is an imagination machine with enormous capability that can stimulate, challenge and inspire the user.

Unmatched technology at

$1999⁹⁵

- A master microprocessor plus eleven other processors that control motors, sensors and interfacing
- A multi-jointed, fully articulated arm
- A synthesized voice with an unlimited vocabulary
- Five different senses; remote wireless control

The most advanced automated systems and robotics trainer in the world

HERO 2000 is a highly versatile and powerful automation trainer. Specially designed as an educational tool, HERO 2000 will help you learn about, explore and test the interrelated technologies of robot automation programming, electronics for automation, intelligent machines and robotics. HERO 2000 is also a comprehensive test environment for developing a thorough understanding of basic robotic processes including electricity and electronics, microprocessors and microcomputers, instrumentation and mechanics.

No other educational robot can match the on-board computing power of HERO 2000. The Robot features a 16-bit 8088 master microprocessor that is dedicated to running user programs plus controlling eleven 8-bit peripheral microprocessors. These eleven slave microprocessors perform separate input/output tasks simultaneously thus relieving the main microprocessor from performing the time-consuming task of interfacing to the outside world.

More computing power is contained in 64K of on-board ROM. Stored in ROM is powerful HERO 2000 BASIC that enables easier user programming. More than 20 special robot commands have been added so you can control any additional functions not usually included in standard BASIC. One of these is a direct text-to-speech conversion that allows you to type in what you want the Robot to say in plain text. Also stored in ROM are six robot demonstration routines plus diagnostic, service and sensor adjustment routines.

More computer features include 24K of RAM that can be expanded up to 576K with the addition of three optional memory boards. The Robot also comes equipped with two RS-232 DCE ports configured for a terminal and printer, plus a cassette port for storing your programs on an inexpensive standard tape recorder.

No other educational robot can be expanded or its hardware accessed as easily as HERO 2000. A rear panel card cage swings open for easy access to a tremendous amount of expansion capability; 12 circuit card slots. Five of these slots have openings for back panel connectors. Separate CPU, input/output and motor controller cards use three slots in a minimum Robot configuration. Optional RAM boards can be added to expand memory up to 576K and an Experimenter Board can be installed for conducting experiments or testing your own circuits.

No other educational robot can match HERO 2000's potential for intelligent behavior. Many sophisticated on-board sensors enable HERO 2000 to gather information about its surrounding environment. Then, under your program control, the Robot can alter its behavior in response to changing surrounding conditions to exhibit truly intelligent behavior.

HERO 2000 features an impressive array of senses. A unique scanning sonar system enables the Robot to see objects up to 10 feet away in a complete 360° circle. An auxiliary sonar detector watches for low-lying objects directly in front of the Robot. A light detector uses the same scanning system as the sonar to detect 255 separate levels of light intensity all around HERO 2000. HERO can also hear and measure 255 direct levels of sound 360° around the Robot. This high-tech Robot can also sense the temperatures ranging from 60 to 90 degrees F.

HERO 2000 communicates using an electronically synthesized voice. This system generates 64 sounds that make up human speech to give HERO 2000 an unlimited vocabulary in virtually any language. The voice synthesizer system can also be software controlled through 4096 inflection levels, 16 rate and volume levels, and four full octaves of musical sound. With this capability HERO 2000 can produce a wide range of voices from husky bass to high soprano, including regional accents plus a variety of musical effects and various sound effects.

No other educational trainer can match the robot simulation ability of HERO 2000. The optional arm accessory (standard on an assembled HERO 2000) is a multi-jointed, fully articulated arm with a gripper that has a sense of touch. The Heath Company patented gripper enables the Robot not only to determine the size of a grasped object, but also to adjust the gripping pressure over a nine-level range. The arm has five axis of motion and can manipulate objects up to a pound in weight. DC servo motors are used to provide the arm with speed, power and a high

degree of accuracy. A closed loop system is used so HERO always knows the position of the motors and its arm.

No other education robot can match the programmability of HERO 2000. From the top-mounted hexadecimal keypad, you can execute programs from memory or cassette tape and perform diagnostic procedures and tests. You can also maneuver HERO around and select several ROM-stored functions among other commands. Sixteen head-mounted LED status indicators (eight are user definable) show what function HERO 2000 is performing. Next to the keypad is a seven-digit data display that shows addresses and their current data contents.

A hand-held wireless remote control console puts you in complete charge of HERO 2000 from up to 100 feet away. With the optional Remote Console (included with an assembled HERO 2000) you can control in real time or teach HERO complex tasks involving its arm and base using special speed and position keys. The full ASCII typewriter-style keyboard on the console enables you to create, execute or edit a program. Programs are written in HERO BASIC which is permanently stored in ROM. An RS-232C connector on the remote also allows you to connect the remote to the Robot like a terminal. The Remote Accessory features a 2 line by 40 character LCD display and is powered by included rechargeable nickel-cadmium batteries. A 120 VAC charging cube is also included.

No other educational robot has a sophisticated power management system like HERO 2000. A single 24 amp-hour battery provides HERO with up to four full hours of operating power under normal use. Operating time is extended up to six hours when only the electronics are used. This operating time can be further extended by taking advantage of HERO's sleep mode. Using this mode you can power down all HERO's systems except memory and its real-time clock to extend battery life up to six days. An internal warning system alerts the user when the battery reaches a low-charge level. A 120 VAC charger is included.

HERO 2000 is a complete automation learning system that stands 32.4 inches high on a four wheel suspension system. Two side-mounted wheels are servomotor driven providing a maximum pulling force of 26 pounds. The Robot has eight speeds in both forward and reverse, and it can turn in its own diameter giving the Robot extreme maneuverability. HERO has girth dimensions of 16.5 inches wide by 22.5 inches long. The Robot's torso rotates on its base which gives a sixth axis of motion to an installed arm. HERO 2000 weighs 78 pounds with arm.

And HERO 2000 is fun to build with the experience and promise of "We won't let you fail" from the world leader in robotics education and training. Let HERO 2000 aid you in understanding the nuts, bolts, bits and design concepts of this new microprocessor hardware and software, and industrial electronics technology.

Kit ET-19, HERO 2000, Shpg. wt. 108 lbs. **1999.95**

Kit ETS-19-1, HERO 2000 Arm with Controller Card, Shpg. wt. 14 lbs. . . **699.95**

ET-19-14, Experimenter Board includes two solderless breadboards and bidirectional, buffered interface lines to entire operating system plus regulated power supply outputs, Shpg. wt 2 lbs. **99.95**

ET-19-51, Demonstration ROM containing eleven entertaining programs illustrating the versatility of HERO 2000's voice synthesizer plus a demonstration of a number of the Robot's sensors. ROM installs in either a socket on the CPU board or a socket on an accessory RAM board. Shpg. wt. 1 lb. **29.95**

Kit ETS-19-35, Remote Keyboard Control operates at 75.43 MHz for 2-way wireless communication with HERO 2000 from up to 100 feet away. Includes rechargeable nickel-cadmium batteries and two frequency modules. Shpg. wt. 5 lbs. **499.95**

Kit ETS-19-36, Remote Keyboard Control operates at 75.67 MHz for 2-way wireless communication with HERO 2000 from up to 100 feet away. Includes rechargeable nickel-cadmium batteries and two frequency modules. Shpg. wt. 5 lbs. **499.95**

ETW-19-15, 192K Static RAM Expansion Board includes 64K RAM that can be expanded up to 192K with the addition of ETA-19-15 RAM Chip Sets. Shpg. wt. 2 lbs. **99.95**

ETA-19-15, 64K RAM Chip Set includes eight 8K x 8 RAM chips for use in expanding the RAM capability of the ETW-19-15 Static RAM Board. Shpg. wt. 1 lb. **49.95**

Kit ETS-19, HERO 2000 Robot with Arm, Shpg. wt. 123 lbs. **2499.95**

EWS-19-35, Assembled HERO 2000 Robot, Arm and Remote control with two 75.43 MHz frequency modules, Shpg. wt. 121 lbs. **4499.95**

EWS-19-36, Assembled HERO 2000 Robot, Arm and Remote Control with two 75.67 MHz frequency modules, Shpg. wt. 121 lbs. **4499.95**

© Heath Company. "Heath" and "Heathkit" are registered trademarks of Heath Company. "Zenith" is a registered trademark of Zenith Electronics Corporation.

 Credit Card Orders Call TOLL-FREE: 800-253-0570. Alaska and Michigan Residents Call: 616-982-3411.

HE-RObot

In 2007, Heathkit (no longer in the kit business but still existing as the Educational Systems Division) announced the HE-RObot. It was the result of a partnership with the company White Box Robotics. The HE-RObot was a rebadged version of the White Box Robotics 914 PC-Bot. It was powered by an Intel CPU running Windows XP, with 1 GB of RAM and an 80 GB hard disk drive.

Sold fully assembled at a cost of about $8,000, it is estimated that only about 50 units were sold before Heathkit went out of business in 2012.

In 2014 the PC-Bot line was discontinued when White Box Robotics was acquired by Cohort Systems Inc.

Figure 21: The HE-RObot

The Robot Arm Trainer

The ETS-19-32/ETW-19-32 Robot Arm Trainer was a standalone robot arm sold by Heath Educational Systems to teach the use and programming of industrial robots. Essentially it was the arm from the HERO 2000 sold as a standalone unit mounted on a base. It featured five axes of motion, a gripper with touch sensing, and could lift up to one pound/0.5 kg. It could be controlled using menu-driven software or programmed with steps.

It featured an on-board main CPU and six slave CPUs that allowed it to be operated without an external computer. The main CPU was a 4 MHz Z80A microprocessor with 32KB ROM and 48 KB RAM. It used six slave Z80 processors, one for each servo motor. A teaching pendant provided a 7-key keypad and a 16-character LCD display. An RS-232 serial port could be connected to an external terminal or computer.

Options included a cassette tape interface for program storage and an 8-bit parallel i/o board.

Training Material

With the release of the HERO 1, Heathkit offered the EE-1800 course in robotics. At a cost of about $100, it had 1200 pages of material in 11 chapters with optional hands-on experiments.

An advanced EE-1812 Robot Applications course covered vision systems, tactile sensing, CAM, etc.

Product Listing

The table below lists Heathkit products related to robots, options, and accessories.

Figure 22: List of Robot Products

Model	Category	Series	Kit	Description	First Year	Last Year	Lowest Price	Highest Price
EE-1800	Robot	HERO 1	N	Robotics Course	1984	1984	$99.95	$99.95
EE-1812	Robot	HERO 1	N	Robot Applications Course	1984	1984	$99.95	$99.95
ET-18	Robot	HERO 1	Y	Basic HERO 1 Robot (less arm, voice)	1983	1984	$799.95	$999.95
ET-18-1	Robot	HERO 1	N	HERO 1's Arm (Arm and Gripper Mechanism)	1983	1984	$349.95	$399.95
ET-18-2	Robot	HERO 1	N	HERO 1's Voice (Phoneme Speech Synthesizer)	1983	1984	$99.95	$149.95
ET-18-4	Robot	HERO 1	N	Demo ROM	1984	1984	$49.95	$49.95
ET-18-5	Robot	HERO 1	N	Monitor ROM Listing	1984	1984	$39.95	$39.95
ET-18-7	Robot	HERO 1	N	Automatic Mode ROM	1984	1984	$29.95	$29.95
ET-19	Robot	HERO 2000	Y	HERO 2000	1986	1986	$1,999.95	$1,099.95
ET-19-14	Accessory	HERO 2000	Y	Experimenter Board	1986	1986	$89.95	$89.95
ET-19-51	Accessory	HERO 2000	Y	Demonstration ROM	1986	1986	$29.95	$29.95
ETA-19-15	Accessory	HERO 2000	Y	64K RAM Chip Set	1986	1986	$49.95	$49.95
ETS-18	Robot	HERO 1	Y	Complete HERO 1 Robot (with arm and voice)	1983	1984	$1,199.85	$1,499.95
ETS-19	Robot	HERO 2000	Y	HERO 2000 Robot with Arm	1986	1986	$2,499.95	$2,499.95
ETS-19-1	Accessory	HERO 2000	Y	HERO 2000 Arm with Controller Card	1986	1986	$699.95	$699.95
ETS-19-32	Robot	n/a	Y	Robot Arm Trainer				
ETS-19-35	Accessory	HERO 2000	Y	Remote Keyboard Control 75.43 MHz	1986	1986	$499.95	$499.95
ETS-19-36	Accessory	HERO 2000	Y	Remote Keyboard Control 75.67 MHz	1986	1986	$499.95	$499.95
ETW-18	Robot	HERO 1	N	Assembled Robot (with arm, voice)	1983	1984	$2,199.95	$2,499.95
ETW-19-15	Accessory	HERO 2000	Y	192K Static RAM Expansion Board	1986	1986	$99.95	$99.95
ETW-19-32	Robot	n/a	N	Robot Arm Trainer				
EWS-19-35	Robot	HERO 2000	N	Assembled HERO 2000 Robot, Arm, and Remote Control with two 75.43 MHz frequency modules	1986	1986	$4,499.95	$4,499.95
EWS-19-36	Robot	HERO 2000	N	Assembled HERO 2000 Robot, Arm, and Remote Control with two 75.67 MHz frequency modules	1986	1986	$4,499.95	$4,499.95
HE-Robot	Robot	n/a	N	HE-RObot (became PC-BOT)	2012	2012	$8,000.00	$8,000.00
RT-1	Robot	HERO JR.	Y	HERO JR.	1984	1984	$599.95	$599.95
RTA-1-1	Accessory	HERO JR.	N	Infrared Motion Detector	1984	1984	$119.95	$119.95
RTA-1-2	Accessory	HERO JR.	N	Remote Control Accessory	1984	1984	$179.95	$179.95
RTA-1-3	Accessory	HERO JR.	N	RS-232 Accessory	1984	1984	$49.95	$49.95
RTA-1-4	Accessory	HERO JR.	N	Two extra batteries	1984	1984	$59.95	$59.95
RTA-1-5	Accessory	HERO JR.	N	Cartridge Adapter	1984	1984	$49.95	$49.95
RTC-1-2	Accessory	HERO JR.	N	Preprogrammed Cartridge: Songs, Phrases and Rhymes #1	1984	1984	$19.95	$19.95

Model	Category	Series	Kit	Description	First Year	Last Year	Lowest Price	Highest Price
RTC-1-3	Accessory	HERO JR.	N	Preprogrammed Cartridge: Animals, Blackjack and TicTacToe	1984	1984	$39.95	$39.95
RTC-1-4	Accessory	HERO JR.	N	Preprogrammed Cartridge: Special Occasions	1984	1984	$19.95	$19.95
RTC-1-5	Accessory	HERO JR.	N	Preprogrammed Cartridge: Math Master	1984	1984	$24.95	$24.95
RTC-1-6	Accessory	HERO JR.	N	Preprogrammed Cartridge: Riddle Robot/Tongue Twister	1984	1984	$24.95	$24.95
RTC-1-8	Accessory	HERO JR.	N	Preprogrammed Cartridge: BASIC	1984	1984	$49.95	$49.95
RTR-1-1	Robot	HERO JR.	Y	HERO HR. with RS-232 and Cartridge Adapter Accessories	1984	1984	$649.95	$649.95
RTR-1-2	Robot	HERO JR.	Y	HERO HR. with Infrared Motion Detector, Remote Control, RS-232, and Cartridge Adapter Accessories	1984	1984	$849.95	$849.95

(this page intentionally left blank)

Chapter 9: Terminals

Before the introduction of graphical user interfaces (the so-called WIMP interface for **W**indows-**I**cons-**M**enus-**P**ointer), most interactions with computers were entirely text-based. The early operating systems like CP/M and MS-DOS only directly supported a command line interface. This was an advancement over the earlier front panel interfaces with switches and lights.

Interaction was often through an external standalone terminal[3] connected to the computer over a serial interface. These typically provided from 24 to 40 lines of text and up to 132 columns per line (but more commonly 80), with a monochrome (white, green, or amber) display.

Sometimes called a "glass typewriter", the video terminal was descended from the printing terminal (like the Teletype model ASR 33) which had a keyboard and could print on paper. Hardcopy printing terminals specifically designed for computers like the DEC Writer (which Heathkit offered) also continued to be used into the 1980s and had the advantage of producing a permanent paper copy of work that was done.

On a typewriter or printing terminals, when the printing head approached the end of a line, a bell would ring. With video terminals, the feature of making an audible sound continued to be called a "bell".

As well as characters and common control codes like Carriage Return and Line Feed, terminals typically supported "escape codes" for other control and display functions to do things like move the cursor, select bold, underline, flashing text, etc. These were initially proprietary and manufacturer-specific, but some popular common terminals became de facto standards that many terminals supported, most notably the DEC VT52 and VT100 codes. Later, an ANSI standard was written to standardize this.

The asynchronous serial interface for communications used industry standard protocols: either RS-232 or 20 mA current loop. Characters could be encoded in ASCII (now called ANSI) or less commonly older systems like BAUDOT, Murray, or EBCDIC.

A modern computer can emulate a video terminal by running a terminal emulator application communicating over a serial interface.

H-9

The Heathkit H-9 (also referred to as the H9) was Heathkit's first video terminal. Introduced in 1977 at a price of $530 it was designed for use with the H-8 or H-11 computers but could be used with other computers.

Key features included:
- A 12" CRT.
- 12 lines of 80 characters. Also 48 20-character lines in 4 12-line columns.

---

3 I have a special place in my heart for serial terminals. My first job in the early 1980s used DEC VT52 and VT100 terminals and I spent many hours in front of one.

- 67-key keyboard with function keys.
- Fully wired and tested controller board.
- Wiring harness to simplify assembly.
- Upper case only display using a 5x7 character dot matrix.
- Speaker produces a 4800 Hz "bell".
- Automatic line feed on end of line.
- On-screen cursor. Can move cursor up, down, left, right, home.
- Baud rates from 110 to 9600.
- Erase page or end of line.
- Page transmit function.
- Plot mode for graphs.
- RS-232C, 20 mA current loop, and TTL -level interfaces. Also 8-bit TTL parallel interface with 4 handshaking lines.
- Weight 32 pounds.

The H-9 was quite limited: it could only display uppercase characters as twelve 80-character lines or 48 20-character lines in four columns. It was not compatible with ANSI, DEC or other terminal escape codes: it only recognized CR, LF, BS, BEL, and ESC. It didn't make use of a microprocessor in its design. While inexpensive, it was somewhat ugly in appearance and used low-quality switches for its keyboard.

H-19

In 1980 Heathkit introduced the H-19 terminal which offered a higher-quality display with 23 80-character lines with upper and lower case, graphics characters, and DEC VT52 escape code compatibility. The keyboard featured 80 keys including 12 function keys and a numeric keypad. It was controlled by a Z80 microprocessor.

Key features included:
- A 12" CRT with white phosphor.
- 95 ASCII characters and 33 graphic characters.
- 24 80-character lines with a 25th status line.
- 5x7 dot matrix display with upper low case and descenders.
- 84 key keyboard: 60 alphanumeric plus 12 function keys and 12 key numeric keypad.
- Cursor, cursor positioning, bell, and normal and reverse video.
- RS-232C serial interface from 110 to 9600 bps (could also do 19200 but was not recommended as it could not guarantee to keep up).

It supported DEC VT52 compatible escape codes as well as a native Heathkit mode. It was designed for the H-8 and H-11A computers but would work with any compatible device as a serial terminal.

The WH-19 was a factory-assembled version of the H-19.

The H-19 was essentially half of an H-88 All-In-One computer. Heathkit offered the H-19-2 kit that would upgrade an H-19 to an H-88 computer (at about the same price as the H-19).

Other accessories for the H-19 included non-glare filters and a plastic dust cover.

H-19A

The H-19A, introduced in 1981, was a minor update to the H-19 terminal. There were no changes in features or appearance from the H-19, just some electrical design differences. Note that the kit to convert the H-19A to an H-88 All-in-One computer was slightly different from the kit to convert an H-19.

As well as being offered with standard white phosphor, at a slightly higher cost you could have an anti-glare white or anti-glare green CRT.

Heathkit also sold source code listings for the ROM of the H-19 which, unlike the H-9, used a microprocessor.

The Z-19 was a factory-assembled version of the H-19A which was identical except for Zenith branding on the front panel.

H-29

The Heathkit H-29 terminal was introduced in April, 1983. It featured an 80 character by 25 line display on a 12-inch green phosphor screen. It could emulate DEC VT100, Hazeltine 1500, and Lear Siegler ADM-3A terminal codes. It used an Intel 8051 CPU. The terminal was available in assembled form as the Zenith Z-29.

H-36

The H-36 was an assembled LA36 DEC Writer II printing terminal. It was intended for use for the H-8 and H-11 computers but was compatible with many others. It sold for $1,495 in 1979.

Output was a 7x7 dot matrix on fanfold tractor feed paper up to 14-7/8" wide. It provided a full typewriter-style keyboard and had an integral stand. The data rate was 10, 15, and 30 cps (100, 150, and 300 bits per second) and used a 20 mA current loop interface. Support for RS-232 required the optional H36-2 kit which was $65.

Z-39

The Z-39 was a Zenith branded fully-assembled terminal. It features a 12-inch screen with green phosphor with 25 rows of 80 characters.

It supported ANSI, Lear Siegler ADM3A, Hazeltine 1500, or Zenith terminal escape codes and sold for $749 in 1985.

Z-49

This was a Zenith branded fully-assembled terminal featuring a 14" display with amber CRT. It could display 25 rows of 80 or 132 characters. The terminal supported H/Z-20, H/Z-19, DEC VT52, and VT100 terminal codes. It sold for $1,099 in 1984.

HT-10/ZT-10/ZTX-10

This was a low cost terminal for data entry compatible with the DEC VT52. It was a keyboard unit only and required an external video monitor. It had support for an external modem and parallel port for use with a printer.

The HT-10 was a kit that came bundled with a monitor and sold for $399 in 1984. The HTX-10 was a kit without a monitor and sold for $279.

Model ZT-10 was a Zenith-branded assembled version that came with a monitor and sold for $499. The ZTX-10 was similar with omitted the monitor and sold for $399.

A suitable modem was the HTX-10-1 auto-dial and auto-answer 300 baud modem which sold for $69.95.

HT-1011/ZT-11/ZTX-11

This was a terminal designed for accessing time-sharing services over a phone line using a modem. It had an internal modem but required an external monitor. You could program it with phone numbers, login, and passwords for single key access to up to 26 information sources.

The following models were offered:
- HT-1011: Kit version with monitor and serial port.
- ZT-11: Assembled version with monitor and serial port.
- ZTX-11 Assembled version without monitor, with a serial port.
- ZT-1-U: assembled version with monitor and without a serial port.
- ZTX-1-U: Assembled version without monitor and serial port.

THE HEATHKIT H9 VIDEO TERMINAL

One of the lowest-cost ASCII terminals available anywhere — features a bright 12" CRT display with twelve 80-character lines, 67-key keyboard, all standard serial interfaces, plus a fully wired and tested control board and a wiring harness for simplified assembly.

$899 95 Kit

The H9 video terminal is a general-purpose peripheral designed for use with the Heathkit H8 or H11 computers. It provides keyboard input and a CRT for the convenient entry and display of computer programs and data. It can be used with any computer in dedicated stand-alone applications or in time-sharing systems.

Character format is standard upper case 5x7 dot matrix. The long form display is twelve 80-character lines. The short form display is forty-eight 20-character lines in four 12-line columns. An automatic line carry over feature executes line feed and return when line exceeds character count on both long and short-form displays. A built-in oscillator/speaker generates a 4800 Hz tone and serves as audible end-of-line warning.

Auto-Scrolling is featured in both long and short-form. In the long form, as the line enters at bottom, the top line scrolls off screen; in the short form, as the column enters from the right, the left column scrolls off screen. Auto-scrolling can be defeated with a front panel switch. The cursor mark indicates the next character to be typed for accurate positioning. Cursor controls include up, down, left, right and home. Serial data baud rates are selectable from 110-9600. Baud rate clock output and reader control are available on the rear panel connector.

The erase mode permits automatic full page erase or erase to end of line starting at cursor position. A transmit page function allows a full page to be formatted, edited and modified, then transmitted as a block of continuous data.

The plot mode permits graphs, curves and simple figures to be displayed. Plotting can be accomplished via the front panel keyboard or from external inputs.

The H9 serial interface provides EIA RS-232C levels, a 20 mA current loop and standard TTL levels. Parallel interfacing includes standard TTL levels, 8 bits input and 8 bits output and 4 handshaking lines for connection to H10.

Ultra-compact size, only 12½" H x 15⅝" W x 20¾" D, makes the H9 ideal for desktop or console applications. For 110 VAC, 60 Hz or 230 VAC, 50 Hz.

Kit H9, Shpg. wt. 50 lbs. **899.95**

Long-form Display — Twelve 80-character lines

Short-Form Display — forty-eight 20-character lines in four columns

Plot Mode — Curves, graphs and simple figures

Full ASCII 67-Key Keyboard

Function keys are positioned away from keyboard to prevent miskeying.

Typewriter keyboard for easy, more accurate input.

Wide, easy-to-use space bar aids accurate typing.

THE HEATHKIT H10
PAPER TAPE READER/PUNCH
$499 95 Kit

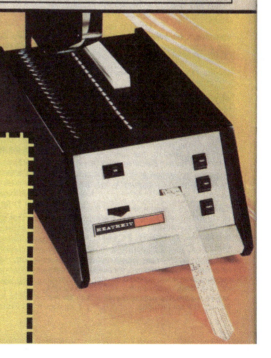

A general-purpose mass storage peripheral designed for use with the H8 and H11 computers plus any other computer. Features a heavy-duty built-in power supply, totally independent punch and reader and a copy node for fast, easy tape duplication.

- *Solid-state reader with stepper motor*
- *Precise ratchet/solenoid drive for high accuracy and consistent punching*
- *Totally independent punch and reader*
- *Copy mode for easy tape duplication*
- *Heavy-Duty Built-in power supply*
- *For Heathkit H8 and H11 computers, others too*
- *Styling matches H8 and H11 computers for total system design*
- *Includes 24-pin interface connector and mating cable*

The H10 paper-tape reader/punch is a general-purpose mass storage peripheral using reliable low-cost paper tape. It's fully compatible and styled to match the H8 and H11 computers, and it works reliably with any other computer through a parallel interface. The H10 uses standard 1″ wide roll or fanfold 8-level paper tape. Standard punched paper tape gives you the reliability, durability and trouble-free handling you need for effective mass storage of programs and data.

The reader reads tape up to a maximum rate of 50 characters per second. A full sensitivity adjustment on each channel permits any color, thickness, quality (oiled or unoiled) paper tape to be used. Sensitive Darlington photo transistors and an incandescent lamp reader head provide reliable reading. The powerful stepper motor drive insures accurate tape positioning and movement.

The punch operates up to maximum speed of 10 characters per second. Ratchet/solenoid drive and solenoid control of punches provide high-accuracy and consistent punching.

Controls include power on-off, read and punch start. A feed control feeds blank tape through the punch for leader tape, a copy control provides fast, easy tape duplication.

Interfacing is provided by separate 8-bit parallel input and output buses with standard TTL logic levels and handshaking lines for both reader and punch. A rear panel 24-pin interface connector and mating cable are supplied.

Accessories include holder for roll paper tape, chad collector tray and collector box for fan-fold tape, 8″ roll 900 ft. blank paper tape. Cabinet with metal top and rugged steel chassis, 12⅝″ H x 9¾″ W x 19⅝″ D. For 110-130 VAC, 60 Hz or 220-240 VAC, 50 Hz.

Kit H10, Shpg. wt. 29 lbs. **499.95**

Three Rolls Blank paper tape, each 8″ diameter, 900-ft. min.
H10-2, Shpg. wt. 5 lbs. **15.95**

Three Boxes Fan-Fold Tape. Approx. 1000 ft. each.
H10-3, Shpg. wt. 5 lbs. **15.95**

77

The Heath H-19A Professional Video Terminal features two new optional anti-glare CRTs

- Z-80 microprocessor-based for fast, efficient data handling
- Heavy-duty typewriter-format keyboard with separate 12-key numeric keypad
- Eight user-definable function keys
- DEC VT-52 software-compatible
- Expandable to an All-In-One Computer

As low as
$695.00 Kit
with standard white CRT

CHOOSE FROM ANTI-GLARE WHITE, ANTI-GLARE GREEN OR STANDARD WHITE CRTS

The Heath H-19A Professional Video Terminal features exceptional capabilities in its price range. It's designed for the H-8 or H-11A Computers – or with any device using an RS-232C Serial Interface.

The H-19A's professional keyboard, laid out in typewriter format, lets you begin entering data right away. The terminal's 32 functions can be controlled from the keyboard, or a computer. A separate 12-key numeric keypad, in calculator format, makes the entry of mathematical programs faster and easier.

Baud rates ranging from 110 to 9600 are keyboard-selectable for easier changes. Eight separate user-function keys give extra flexibility.

The H-19A displays the entire ASCII character set, including upper and lower case letters. The terminal can also display thirty-three graphics characters, which can be arranged for a variety of graphic displays and effects.

The video display screen can show up to twenty-four 80-character lines (with a software-controlled 25th line). Using the H-19A's direct or relative cursor addressing capabilities, you can make corrections or edit text – anywhere on the video display screen.

The 12" (30.48 cm) diagonal cathode-ray tube (CRT) features an extremely wide bandwidth for outstanding resolution and bright, clear, easy-to-read video displays. A reverse video capability allows you to emphasize any portion of the video screen by reversing white on black.

Now you have a choice of two anti-glare screens (green or white) to make the H-19A easier on your eyes – as well as the standard white CRT.

You'll be able to change your H-19A into an H-88A All-In-One Computer, with the H-19-3 Conversion Kit (available 4th quarter 1981). And the H-19's ROM listing is available (also below) to help you understand how this powerful, versatile terminal operates – or to allow you to alter its personality and cursor control protocols to match those of other terminals. For 120/240 VAC, 50/60 Hz power. Draws just 45 Watts. Overall Dimensions of the H-19 Video Terminal are 13" H x 17" W x 20" D (33.02 x 43.18 x 50.80 cm).

H-19A Professional Video Terminal Kit with Anti-Glare White CRT.
Kit HS-19-1, Shpg. wt. 52 lbs. 725.00

H-19A Professional Video Terminal Kit with Anti-Glare Green CRT.
Kit HS-19-2, Shpg. wt. 52 lbs. 725.00

H-19A Professional Video Terminal Kit with Standard White CRT.
Kit HS-19-3, Shpg. wt. 52 lbs. 695.00

An assembled commercial product of this type is also available. Please see the Z-19 Professional Video Terminal on page 78.

H-19-1, Source Listings for ROM of H-19 Video Terminal, 1 lb. 25.00

Black Fabric Anti-Glare CRT Filter for the H-19 or H-19A Video Terminals. Sun-Flex nylon cover makes video displays stand out, cuts eye strain.
HCA-4, Shpg. wt. 1 lb. 19.95

Clear Plastic Anti-Glare CRT Filter for the H-19 or H-19A Video Terminals. Pannelgraphix cover makes video displays easier to see.
HCA-3, Shpg. wt. 1 lb. 12.95

Dust Cover for the Heath H-19 or H-19A Professional Video Terminals.
HCA-5-89, Shpg. wt. 1 lb. 14.00

Convert the Heath H-19 Professional Video Terminal (not H-19A) into an H-88 All-In-One Computer! Featuring easy kit assembly, this conversion kit includes a detailed, step-by-step assembly manual and all necessary parts. When finished, you'll have an H-88 All-In-One Computer with 16K bytes of Random Access Memory (RAM) – without giving up any of the features of your powerful video terminal. Add an H-88-4 5.25" Floppy Disk Drive with Controller (sold on page 71), and you can expand to a full-fledged H-89! Not for H-19A Video Terminal; a version of this kit, designed for use with the H-19A, will be available in the fourth quarter of 1981.

Kit H-19-2, Shpg. wt. 19 lbs. 695.00

H-19A SPECIFICATIONS: CRT: 12" (30.48 cm) diagonal. **Display Format:** 25 lines x 80 characters (25th line software-controlled). **Display Size:** 6.5" H x 8.5" W (16.51 x 21.59 cm). **Character Size:** Approximately 0.2" H x 0.1" W (0.508 x 0.254 cm). **Character Set:** 128 (95 ASCII, 33 graphic). **Character Type:** 5 x 7 dot matrix (upper and lower case) and 5 x 9 dot matrix (lower case with descenders). **Keyboard:** 84 keys (60 alphanumeric, 12 function), 12-key numeric pad. **Cursor:** Blinking nondestructive underline or block. **Cursor Controls:** Up, down, left, right, home, CR, LF, back space and tab. **Cursor Addressing:** Relative and direct. **Tab:** Standard 8-column tab. **Refresh Rate:** 60 Hz at 60 Hz line frequency and 50 Hz at 50 Hz line frequency. **Edit Functions:** Insert and delete character or line. **Erase:** Erase page, erase to end of line, erase to end of page, erase to beginning of line, erase to beginning of page and erase line. **Scroll:** Automatic scrolling, line/page freeze. **Bell:** On receipt of control G. **Video:** Normal and reverse (using escape sequence), by character. **Communications: Interfacing:** Standard EIA RS-232 Serial Interfacing. **Baud Rates:** 110 to 9600. **Mode:** Full or half-duplex. **Parity:** Even, odd, stick and none. **Handshaking:** Software, control S – control Q; all RS-232 Serial lines tied high internally. Buffered terminal is capable of keeping up with most operations and normal scrolling text output, at 9600 baud or less. **Operating Temperature Range:** 32-104 degrees F (0-40 degrees C). **Power Requirement:** 120/240 VAC, 50/60 Hz, 45 Watts. **Overall Dimensions:** 13" H x 17" W x 20" D (33.02 x 43.18 x 50.80 cm). **Net Weight:** 45 lbs. (20.4 kg).

74/COMPUTERS

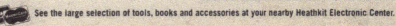

See the large selection of tools, books and accessories at your nearby Heathkit Electronic Center.

Versatile and compatible terminals that are priced to meet the most demanding budgets

Z-49 uses the latest in solid-state technology for expanded flexibility

$1099⁰⁰

- All advanced features are set through the keyboard and stored in nonvolatile memory
- A large 14-inch nonglare screen provides 25 rows of a selectable 80 or 132 characters

State-of-the-art terminal: The very friendly Z-49 Video Display Terminal is designed to satisfy all your business and personal needs while providing the greatest degree of user convenience. As soon as you turn it on, this smart terminal goes to work and performs a series of internal self-check tests to verify proper operation. All functions, even screen brightness, are easily set up by programming selections through the keyboard as they are displayed on-screen in plain-talk menus. These selections can be stored in nonvolatile memory until changed by the user.

Advanced keyboard features: The 92-key, detached keyboard uses a standard typewriter key layout. Included are five user-programmable special function keys, eight LED indicators, and an 18-key keypad with 14 numeric and four user-programmable function keys. The tilt-adjusted, low-profile keyboard connects to the display by a six-foot coiled cord.

Professional display: A smoothly scrolling display can be seen on the non-glare 14-inch diagonal Chromogold II™ (amber) screen. This special screen provides a larger and more easily readable viewing area for 25 lines of either a user-selectable 80 or 132 characters. These include 95 printing ASCII characters of upper and lower case, numerics and punctuation plus 33 graphic characters. Alternate characters include 32 graphic representations of non-printing ASCII, seven foreign language sets, 32 special Greek symbols and 32 VT-100 graphic characters. The Z-49 is compatible with the H/Z-19, H/Z-29, DEC VT52 and DEC VT100.

Interfacing: The Z-49 Terminal includes a DTE and DCE connector.

Zenith data systems	Z-49, Assembled and tested, Shpg. wt. 37 lbs.	1099.00
Zenith data systems	Z-49-G, Z-49 with green CRT, Shpg. wt. 37 lbs.	1099.00

Z-49 SPECIFICATIONS: DISPLAY: CRT: 14" diagonal, enhanced contrast, video screen. **Display Format:** 25 rows of 80 characters or 25 rows of 132 characters. **Display Size:** 6.75" H x 9.25" W. **Character Type:** 80-column display, 10 x 12 character cell. 132-column display, 8 x 12 character cell. **Character Size (approx.):** 80-column display, 0.255" H x 0.12" W. 132-column display, 0.255" H x 0.07" W. **Video Attributes:** Normal or reverse character, normal or underlined character, half intensity character and background, normal or blinking display. **Refresh Rate:** 50 or 60 Hz. **CURSOR: Type:** Underline or reverse (solid) video block. **Attributes:** On, off, blinking. **Controls:** Up, Down, Left, Right, Backspace, Tab, Back Tab, Home, Carriage Return, Line Feed and Brightness. **Addressing:** Direct or relative. **COMMUNICATIONS: Type:** EIA RS-232C. **Baud Rates:** 50 – 19,200 baud. **Mode:** Half or full duplex. **Code:** ASCII. **Format:** Serial asynchronous. **Word length:** 7 data bits, one parity bit. **Stop Bits:** 1 or 2. **Sync:** Auto XON and XOFF. **Parity:** Even, odd, mark, space, or none. **Power:** 105 – 127/210 – 254 VAC, 50/60 Hz, 73 watts.

H-29 provides more functions and versatility in a smart, user-friendly video display terminal

$599⁰⁰

- Built-in flexibility provides you with the room to grow as your requirements increase
- Complete communications compatibility with many ANSI protocol terminals and host computers

User-oriented operation: One of the most user-friendly terminals available, the H-29 allows a user to configure parameters from on-screen selections. Even a user-settable 24-hour clock is accessible for keeping track of standard or elapsed time. A keyboard HELP key is also provided for prompts or help messages used with some software. A special screen saver automatically shuts off the display after 15 minutes of nonuse for those forgetful moments.

Popular compatibility: The H-29 is compatible with the popular H/Z-19, Lear Siegler ADM-3A, Hazeltine 1500A display terminals. And, it is also compatible with the DEC VT52 and has many attributes of the DEC VT100 terminal.

Screen and keyboard capabilities: Information is clearly displayed in 25 lines of 80 characters on a 12-inch non-glare CRT in normal or reverse video. The detached keyboard has 91 keys and includes a separate numeric keypad. It generates the entire 128-character ASCII set and codes for an alternate character set of 33 special symbols in an 8 x 10 dot matrix.

Accessible editing features: Available are character and line insert and delete as well as erase a page, line, to the beginning or end of a line or a page.

Interfacing: Two RS-232C standard connectors are available, a DTE connector for computers or a modem and DCE connector for an auxiliary device.

Heathkit	Kit H-29, Terminal, Shpg. wt. 41 lbs.	599.00
Zenith data systems	Z-29, Assembled and tested Terminal, 38 lbs.	849.00
	Z-29-1, Palm Rest Accessory, Shpg. wt. 1 lb.	15.00
	Z-29-2, ROM Source Listing, Shpg. wt. 4 lbs.	25.00

H/Z-29 SPECIFICATIONS: DISPLAY: CRT: 12" P31, green, non-glare video screen. **Display Format:** 25 rows of 80 characters. **Display Size:** 6" H x 8½" W. **Character Type:** 8 x 10 character cell. **Character Size:** 0.2" H x 0.1" W (approx.). **Video Attributes:** Normal or reverse character, normal or underline character, normal or half-intensity character, normal or blinking. Can be in any or all combinations. **Refresh Rate:** 60 Hz. or 50 Hz. **CURSOR: Type:** Underline or reverse (solid) video block. **Attributes:** On, off, blinking. **Controls:** Up, Down, Left, Right, Backspace, Tab, Back Tab, Back, Home, Carriage Return and Line Feed. **Addressing:** Direct and relative. **COMMUNICATIONS: Type:** EIA RS-232C. **Baud Rates:** 75 – 19,200 baud. **Mode:** Half or full duplex. **Code:** ASCII. **Format:** Serial asynchronous. **Word Length:** 7-data bits, one parity bit. **Stop Bits:** 2 at 75 and 110 baud rates, 1 at all other baud rates. **Sync:** Auto XON and XOFF. **Parity:** Even, odd, mark or space. **Operating Temperature:** 32° to 105° F (0° to 40° C). **Operating Humidity:** 10-90% (relative) noncondensing. **Power Requirements:** 105 – 127 VAC at 60 Hz and 45 watts.

Personal Information Terminal provides quality and economy in data entry and access systems

A low-cost entry point data terminal for use in communicating with a computer and a printer

- Instant and user-friendly access to mainframe computers, minicomputers and microcomputers
- Professional data display and keyboard capabilities with DEC VT-52 terminal compatibility

Information processing terminal: The HT-10 features an integral RS-232 standard port that can function at speeds from 110 to 9600 baud for communicating with personal, business and other computers. In addition, this versatile terminal is compatible with a DEC VT-52.

Plain talk: Built-in prompts and cues in simple English make it easy to communicate with and use this friendly terminal.

Easy-to-use keyboard: The keyboard features a standard 63-key layout including the full ASCII set with CTRL, ESC, BREAK, TAB and RETURN. Four cursor control keys and a special HELP key add further convenience.

Electronic typewriter: Connect a parallel-type printer to the rear Centronics interface and take advantage of the terminal's printing features.

Heathkit	**Kit HT-10,** Terminal includes ZVM-121 video monitor without modem, Shpg. wt. 36 lbs.	**399.00**
Heathkit	**Kit HTX-10,** Terminal less video display monitor and without modem, Shpg. wt. 10 lbs.	**279.00**
Zenith data systems	**ZT-10,** Assembled and tested Terminal, includes video display monitor and without modem, Shpg. wt. 32 lbs.	**499.00**
Zenith data systems	**ZTX-10,** Assembled and tested Terminal less video monitor and without modem, Shpg. wt. 6 lbs.	**399.00**

Accessories for the Personal Information Terminal

ZT-1-2, Terminal Carrying Case, Shpg. wt. 2 lbs.	**24.99**
ZTA-1-1, Parallel Cable, Shpg. wt. 1 lb.	**25.00**
ZVM-121, Optional Monochrome Video Display, for use with HTX and ZTX Terminals. Features high resolution 12" green CRT that can display 25 lines of 80 characters each, Shpg. wt. 18 lbs.	**139.95**
HTX-10-1, Auto-dial and auto-answer 300 baud modem for use only with HTX and ZTX model terminals, Shpg. wt. 1 lb.	**69.95**
ZT-1-3, Universal ROM set for upgrading older ZT-1s into programmable one-key access models, Shpg. wt. 1 lb.	**49.95**

A rapid access terminal for use with remote computers, information services, data banks...

- Single button accessing of up to 26 pre-selected information sources with universal log-on capability
- System setup allows automatic answering of incoming calls and permits unattended operation capability

Telecomputing system: With its internal modem, the HT-10 can be connected anywhere there is a modular phone jack to gain complete access to computer data services. After preprogramming in a menu of up to 26 pre-selected information sources, a user simply presses one button to automatically select a desired information source or place a normal voice call.

Memory capability: Besides dialing a desired source, the terminal can transmit all required codes. A special universal log-on feature allows the user to program in log-on procedures including account numbers, escape codes and passwords into a battery-protected memory system. When left unattended, the terminal can be set up to receive incoming calls with automatic answering.

High-resolution display: Included with some models is the ZVM-121 monochrome monitor which features a green 12-inch CRT with excellent character definition.

Heathkit	**Kit HT-1011,** Includes ZVM-121 video display monitor, RS-232C port and 300 baud modem, Shpg. wt. 44 lbs.	**449.00**
Zenith data systems	**ZT-11,** Assembled and tested HT-1011 with video display, RS-232C port and modem, Shpg. wt. 32 lbs.	**579.00**
Zenith data systems	**ZTX-11,** Assembled and tested HT-1011 with modem RS-232C port less video display monitor, Shpg. wt. 6 lbs.	**479.00**
Zenith data systems	**ZT-1-U,** Assembled and tested Terminal with monitor and modem less RS-232C serial port, Shpg. wt. 30 lbs.	**549.00**
Zenith data systems	**ZTX-1-U,** Assembled and tested Terminal with modem less monitor, RS-232C serial port, 6 lbs.	**449.00**

HT-10 SPECIFICATIONS: KEYBOARD/TERMINAL: Character Set: 95 ASCII, 33 graphics. **Keyboard:** 63 keys (26 alphabet, 10 numeric, 4 cursor/special function, 12 control, 11 punctuation). **Storage:** Up to 26 names (to 12 characters) and telephone numbers (to 16 digits). **Cursor:** Blinking or steady block, or off. **Cursor Controls:** Up, down, left, right. **Cursor Addressing:** Direct (VT-52 compatible). **Tab:** Standard 8-column tab stops. **Refresh Rate:** 60 Hz. **Edit Functions:** Insert line, delete line. **Erase Functions:** Page, line, beginning of line to cursor, cursor to end of line, beginning of page to cursor, cursor to end of page. **Bell:** Audible alarm on receipt of ASCII BEL. **Video:** Normal, reverse, half-intensity, blink. **INTERFACES: Telephone Connections (modem models only):** Standard RJ-11, RJ-12, or RJ-13 telephone jack. **Data Rate (modem models only):** 110, 150, 300 baud Bell 103 compatible. **Dial Method (modem models only):** Pulse. **Video:** RS170 compatible. **Serial Equipment I/O:** RS-232 levels at 110, 150, 300, 600, 1200, 2400, 4800 and 9600 baud. **Printer:** Parallel (Centronics-type).

 Discover the fun of kitbuilding at your Heathkit Electronic Center.

COMPUTERS/39

Product Listing

The table below lists the Heathkit models that fall under the category of terminals.

Figure 23: List of Terminal Products

Model	Category	Series	Kit	Description	First Year	Last Year	Lowest Price	Highest Price
GDC-21	Terminal	n/a	N	LEX-21 Portable Terminal	1982	1982	$1,795.00	$1,795.00
H-19	Terminal	H-19	Y	Professional Video Terminal	1980	1980	$675.00	$675.00
H-19-1	Accessory	H-19	N	Source Listings for ROM of H-19 and H-19A Terminals	1981	1983	$25.00	$30.00
H-29	Terminal	n/a	Y	Video Display Terminal	1983	1985	$449.00	$599.00
H-36	Terminal	H-8/H-11	N	LA36 DEC Writer II keyboard Printer Terminal	1978	1978	$2,195.00	$2,195.00
H-9	Terminal	H-8/H-11	Y	Serial Terminal	1977	1977	$299.95	$530.00
HCA-5-89	Accessory	H-19	N	Dust Cover for H-19 and H-19A	1981	1984	$14.00	$14.00
HS-19-1	Terminal	H-19	Y	Professional Video Terminal with anti-glare white CRT	1981	1982	$725.00	$1,035.00
HS-19-2	Terminal	H-19	Y	Professional Video Terminal with anti-glare green CRT	1981	1983	$549.00	$899.95
HS-19-3	Terminal	H-19	Y	Professional Video Terminal with standard white CRT	1981	1983	$549.00	$899.95
HT-10	Terminal	n/a	Y	Video Display Terminal, includes ZVM-121 video monitor without modem	1983	1985	$399.00	$399.00
HT-1011	Terminal	n/a	Y	Video Display Terminal, includes ZVM-121 video display monitor, RS-232C port and 300 baud modem	1983	1985	$449.00	$449.00
HTX-10	Terminal	n/a	Y	Video Display Terminal, less video display monitor and without modem	1983	1985	$279.00	$279.00
WH-19	Terminal	H-19	N	Factory Assembled and Tested H-19 Video Terminal	1980	1980	$995.00	$995.00
WH-9-1	Terminal	H-9	N	Interface Adapter Cable	1980	1980	$15.00	$15.00
Z-19	Terminal	H-19	N	Assembled version of H-19	1981	1983	$995.00	$1,395.00
Z-22	Terminal	n/a	N	Economical user user-friendly terminal	1985	1985	$649.00	$649.00
Z-29	Terminal	n/a	N	Video Display Terminal	1983	1984	$849.00	$849.00
Z-39	Terminal	n/a	N	Terminal	1985	1985	$749.00	$749.00
Z-49	Terminal	n/a	N	Video Display Terminal	1984	1985	$1,099.00	$1,099.00
Z-49-G	Terminal	n/a	N	Video Display Terminal with green CRT	1984	1984	$1,099.00	$1,099.00
ZT-1	Terminal	ZT-1	N	Low-Cost Personal Terminal, with one-button access to CompuServe, with monitor	1983	1983	$569.00	$1,089.00
ZT-1-3	Terminal	n/a	N	Universal ROM set for upgrading older ZT-1s into programmable one-key access models	1984	1985	$49.95	$49.95
ZT-1-U	Terminal	n/a	N	Assembled and tested Terminal with monitor and modem less RS-232C serial port	1983	1984	$549.00	$549.00

Model	Category	Series	Kit	Description	First Year	Last Year	Lowest Price	Highest Price
ZT-1-UZ	Terminal	n/a	N	Assembled and tested Terminal with monitor and modem less RS-232C serial port	1985	1985	$549.00	$549.00
ZT-10	Terminal	n/a	N	Assembled and tested Terminal, includes video display monitor without modem	1983	1985	$499.00	$499.00
ZT-11	Terminal	n/a	N	Assembled and tested HT-1011 with video display, RS-232C port and modem	1983	1984	$579.00	$579.00
ZT-11-Z	Terminal	n/a	N	Assembled and tested HT-1011 with video display, RS-232C port, 300 baud modem	1985	1985	$579.00	$579.00
ZT-1A	Terminal	n/a	N	Low-Cost Personal Terminal, with one-button access to The Source, with monitor	1983	1983	$569.00	$1,089.00
ZT-1A	Terminal	n/a	N	Low-Cost Personal Terminal, with one-button access to The Source, with monitor	1983	1983	$569.00	$569.00
ZTX-1	Terminal	n/a	N	Low-Cost Personal Terminal, with one-button access to CompuServe, needs video monitor	1983	1983	$449.00	$449.00
ZTX-1-U	Terminal	n/a	N	Assembled and tested Terminal with modem less monitor, RS-232C serial port	1983	1984	$449.00	$449.00
ZTX-1-UZ	Terminal	n/a	N	Assembled and tested Terminal with model less monitor and RS-232C serial port	1985	1985	$449.00	$449.00
ZTX-10	Terminal	n/a	N	Assembled and tested Terminal less video monitor and without modem	1983	1985	$399.00	$399.00
ZTX-11	Terminal	n/a	N	Assembled and tested HT-1011 with modem RS-232C port less video display monitor	1983	1984	$479.00	$479.00
ZTX-11-Z	Terminal	n/a	N	Assembled and tested HT-1011 with RS-232C port, 300 baud modem, less video display monitor	1985	1985	$479.00	$479.00
ZTX-1A	Terminal	n/a	N	Low-Cost Personal Terminal, with one-button access to The Source, needs video monitor	1983	1983	$449.00	$449.00

Chapter 10: Peripherals and Accessories

Heathkit sold many peripherals and accessories for their computer products. Some of these were kits unique to Heathkit, some were kit versions of other manufacturer's products, and many were standard OEM products that they resold for convenience to buyers of their computers. Most of these should be familiar to computer users today, although a few, such as modems and paper tape readers, are now obsolete.

In the early 1980s, a typical Heathkit catalog had as many as 25 pages of computer-related products. The following is a list of the more common categories:

Printers: Using dot matrix and daisy wheel technologies (inkjet and laser printers were not yet commonly available). Most used either a serial or Centronics parallel interface. Low-cost printers usually used traction feed with continuous fan-fold paper although some supported friction feed which accepted standard sheets of paper. In most cases, these were preassembled although a few were offered in kit form.

Modems: For data communications over a phone line. Initially ran at 300 bps and later 1200 bps and higher. Early models used an acoustic coupler to a telephone handset, later they supported direct connection to a modular phone wall jack.

Paper tape punches and readers: Perforated/punched paper tape, originally used by Teletype machines, was a common data storage format used by early computers for loading and saving programs if the user did not have a floppy drive or other storage. Heathkit offered the H-10 Paper Tape Reader/Punch.

Cassette tape recorders: Used for low-cost data storage up to the early 1980s. Heathkit offered suitable units like the ECP-3801 Cassette Recorder which was a standard General Electric model.

Video monitors: Uses for computers without an integral display. Early units usually used composite video (based on the NTSC television standard), while later models accommodated industry standards for PCs. These were almost always offered as factory assembled and many were manufactured by Zenith.

Floppy and hard drives: Used for mass storage. There were various formats for 8", 5.25", and 3.5" floppy discs. Eventually, hard drives (often referred to as Winchester drives before the IBM PC era) became affordable and small enough to be integrated inside the computer.

Some representative catalog pages are included here to give you an idea of the types of products offered at the time.

51

Get good performance and extra-value features, at a price you can afford, with the MX-80

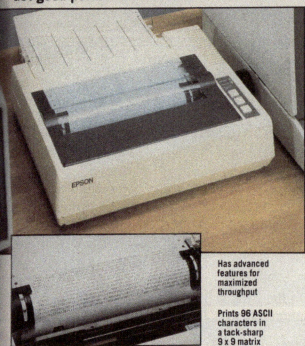

Has advanced features for maximized throughput

Prints 96 ASCII characters in a tack-sharp 9 x 9 matrix

$899⁰⁰

- Bi-directional printing and advanced logic seeking circuitry maximize throughput rate
- Can interface with many different computers

Many printers, costing a lot more, can't touch the MX-80's performance. Using bi-directional printing and logically seeking the shortest lines, its throughput is a fast 46 lines per minute (using 80-character lines) – printing at speeds up to 80 characters per second.

Printing the full 96-character ASCII set and 64 block graphics characters, the MX-80 gives you a choice of 40-, 66-, 80- or 132-character lines – in as many as four distinct printing density modes. This provides a total of 12 different printing combinations, which can accommodate nearly any printing requirement. More than half of these printing combinations use multi-strike or multi-pass techniques to generate correspondence-quality printing.

An internal bell warns the user of paper out conditions or errors, with a periodic three-second tone that continues for 30 seconds. A self-testing mode prints all characters in ROM.

This printer communicates with Heath/Zenith computers with the optional MX-80-2 RS-232C Serial Interface (below). A Centronics-style 8-bit parallel interface is included with the MX-80 as standard equipment.

Includes paper tray and one ribbon. For 120 VAC, 60 Hz power. The MX-80 Printer measures 4.2" H x 14.7" W x 12" D.

MX-80, Assembled, Shpg. wt. 8 Kg 899.00
RS-232C Serial Interface for MX-80 Printer.
MX-80-2, Shpg. wt. 1 Kg 110.00
HCA-5-80, Dust Cover for MX-80, Shpg. wt. 1 Kg 19.95

MX-80 SPECIFICATIONS: Printhead: 9-pin, replaceable. **Printing Method:** Serial impact dot matrix. **Print Rate:** 80 cps. **Print Direction:** Bidirectional. **Line Spacing:** ⅙", ⅛", ⁷⁄₇₂" – plus programmable. **Character Set:** Full 96-character ASCII set with descenders. **Graphics Characters:** 64 block characters. **Printing Modes:** Standard, double (advance paper ¹⁄₂₀₀th page and repeat line), emphasized (shift right and double strike), double emphasized (combination of above). **Tabs:** Horizontal, 112 positions; Vertical, 64 positions. **Paper Feed:** Adjustable tractor-type pin feed. **Paper Width:** 4-10". **Forms:** 1-3. **Communications: Interfacing:** Buffer Size: 1 line. **Operating Temperature:** 41-95 deg. F. (5-35 deg. C). **Operating Humidity:** 10-80%, non-condensing. **Net Weight:** 12 lbs.

H-14 Line Printer features big $ savings, in kit and assembled forms! Act Now as Quantities are Limited

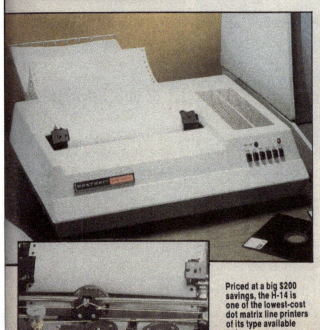

Priced at a big $200 savings, the H-14 is one of the lowest-cost dot matrix line printers of its type available today

NOW ONLY

$595⁰⁰ Kit

- Has extra features you won't find on comparably priced dot matrix line printers
- Use with most computers — communicates via RS-232C or 20 mA current loop interfacing

Here's an outstanding value in a microprocessor-based dot matrix line printer! Priced at a $200 savings, the H-14 provides hard copy — for added convenience in reading, editing, debugging and modifying your programs. It can also print address lists or other data you need for almost any applications.

The H-14 prints the standard 96-character ASCII set (upper and lower case letters), using a 5 x 7 dot matrix print head. Maximum throughput rate is 75 characters per second, with selectable 80, 96 or 132 character line length. Vertical line spacing is 6 lines per inch, with a software-selectable option of 8 lines per inch.

Baud rates are user-selectable, from 110 to 4800. Adjustable width sprocket feed handles edge-punched, 2.5-9.5" wide fan-fold paper, up to 0.006" thick.

The H-14 connects to most computers with an RS-232C Serial Interface or 20 mA current loop. Includes 25-pin male EIA connector for fast, convenient hookup – and a matching paper catch which keeps printer output handy and organized. 120/240 VAC. 4.80" H x 18.33" W x 14.33" D. Requires HDOS or CP/M for H/Z-89; H-88-18 for H-88; any Heath-offered operating system for H-8.

SAVE $200! Kit H-14 Shpg. wt. 14 Kg .... Was $795.00, **NOW ONLY 595.00**
SAVE $500! WH-14, Assembled 13 Kg .... Was $1295.00, **NOW ONLY 795.00**
HCA-5-14, Dust Cover for H/WH-14, Shpg. wt. 1 Kg 19.95

H/WH-14 SPECIFICATIONS: Printing Speed: Initial time per full line is approx. 1.75 seconds on 60 Hz power line, 2.1 seconds on 50 Hz power line. Avg. throughput approx. 40 cps with 96 character lines. Print head temperature controlled by varying print speed. **Format:** 80, 96 or 132 cpi (96 cpi software selectable only). **Forms Handling:** Sprocket feed with adjustable (2.5-9.5") widths. **Ribbon System:** Standard typewriter ribbon with automatic reversing mechanism.

Use one of these high-quality modems to communicate with other computers

Hayes Smartmodems

Choose 300 baud or 1200 baud models: Automatically places and receives calls to/from other computer systems. Program-controlled by ASCII strings. Accepts commands from terminal or under program control. Full- or half-duplex operation. Bell 103 (300 baud) and 212 (1200 baud) compatible. Includes phone-modem cable. Requires HCA-11 Cable below and single-line telephone for use with terminals; for computers, serial I/O and CPS (p. 77) also required. 120 VAC adapter included. 2″ H x 5½″ W x 9½″ L.

WH-43, Assembled 300 Baud Smartmodem, Shpg. wt. 3 lbs. **279.00**
WH-53, Assembled 1200 Baud Smartmodem, Shpg. wt. 4 lbs. **695.00**
HCA-11, RS-232C Computer-Modem Cable, Shpg. wt. 1 lb. **20.00**

Versatile Acoustic Modem is ideal for any phone

Many practical and useful applications: The economical, fully assembled Lexicon Lex-11 Acoustic Modem lets your computer talk to other computers over standard telephone lines. This stand-alone FSK (frequency shift keying) modem has selectable originate and answer modes. Operates in half-duplex or full-duplex modes. Compatible with Bell 103 modems. Two self-testing modes verify the Lex-11's capabilities. RS-232C Serial Interface included. Powered from 120 VAC, 60 Hz line by UL- and CSA-listed AC Adapter (included). Measures 2.4″ H x 10″ W x 5.5″ W (6.90 x 25.4 x 13.95 cm).

SAVE $20! WH-23, Assembled and tested, Shpg. wt. 3 lbs. **NOW ONLY 139.00**

Lowest-priced Direct-Connect Modem **NEW**

Sets a new standard for quality, reliability and value: The Muraphone MM-100 is an inexpensive, self-contained FSK (frequency shift keying) telephone interface that lets your computer communicate with other computers over standard phone lines. Direct, non-acoustic connection helps ensure fewer data errors. Sends, receives at 0-300 baud for compatibility with most time-share systems. Selectable originate/answer modes for remote or host operation. Full duplex communication. Powered by phone line; phone-modem cable included. Requires HCA-11 Cable above for terminals and computers; serial I/O also needed for computers.

WH-63, Assembled and tested, Shpg. wt. 3 lbs. **99.00**

Hayes Chronograph for time-keeping

Perfect for time-sharing, electronic mail and home security applications: Keep any RS-232C-compatible computer system up-to-date. Provides for timed-access, dated messages and recording elapsed on-line access time. Use with Hayes Stack Smartmodem above to send electronic mail at night, when phone rates are lowest. Quartz crystal control for precise timekeeping. 120 VAC, 60 Hz. Three 1.5 VDC "AA" cells (not included) provide battery backup during power failures. 2.6″ H x 5.5″ W x 9.6″ D. NOTE: Not recommended for novice users; software interfacing not currently available from Heath/Zenith.

SAVE $50! WH-42, Assembled and tested, Shpg. wt. 4 lbs. **NOW ONLY 199.00**

Add video, color or sound to your system with these high-quality accessories

High-resolution ZVM-121 Monochrome Video Display

Use with Z-100, most popular computers: Accepts direct EIA monochrome video, gives performance comparable with higher-priced units. Green 25 x 80 CRT display is easy on the eyes, has excellent character definition. Select 40- or 80-character lines. 120 VAC. 11.75″ H x 16.25″ W x 12″ D.

ZVM-121, Assembled in Orchard Tan, Shpg. wt. 18 lbs. **139.95**
ZVM-121-Z, Assembled in Z-100 earthtone colors, 18 lbs. **139.95**

Type-'N-Talk Text-to-Speech Synthesizer

Has many computers talking: Unlimited vocabulary. Built-in microprocessor has 750-character memory. Has 1-Watt, 8 ohm amplifier; speaker not included. Uses one RS-232 port at 75-9600 baud. 120 VAC. 3.1″ H x 7.7″ W x 5.2″ D. NOTE: Not recommended for novices at this time; requires HCA-13 Cable and a modified print driver routine.

WH-12, Assembled and tested, Shpg. wt. 5 lbs. **299.00**
HCA-13, Custom RS-232 Cable to connect WH-12 to H-8 and H/Z-89, 1 lb. **20.00**

High-resolution Color Video Display

Outstanding 640(H) x 225(V) pixel resolution: Ideal for most systems needing high-resolution capability, including H/Z-100s. Takes direct RGB video inputs; displays twenty-four 80-character lines. 20 MHz bandwidth, 20 nS rise time for better definition. Use in home or office — has UL, CSA, FCC Class B approvals. 120 VAC, 60 Hz. Measures 13½″ H x 20″ W x 15″ D.

ZVM-134, Assembled and tested, Shpg. wt. 38 lbs. **699.00**
ZVM-134-1, Cable to connect ZVM-134 to Z-100 Computer, 2 lbs. .. **20.00**
ZVM-134-21, ZVM-134 to IBM PC 16-Color Cable, 2 lbs. **20.00**

Color Video Display for computers, VCRs, cameras

Accepts direct NTSC composite video: Modulation interference is eliminated by special Heath/Zenith circuitry. This 13″ diagonal display uses fully automatic color processing for a stable picture. An audio amplifier and speaker are built-in. Has 75-ohm RCA-type phone jack for video input, miniature phone jack for Hi-Z audio input. UL and CSA listed; meets requirements of 21 CFR, Subchapter J for X-radiation. For 120 VAC, 60 Hz power. Measures 14″ H x 20.25″ W x 14.75″ D (35.56 x 51.44 x 37.47 cm).

GDZ-1320, Assembled and tested, Shpg. wt. 42 lbs. **399.95**

High performance video monitors for high-resolution monochrome and brilliant color displays

High-resolution monochrome displays offer unmatched quality at an economical price

- Excellent character definition and intensity
- Easy-on-the-eyes 40 or 80 column display
- Compatible with most popular computer systems

High quality: Both the ZVM-122A Amber and the ZVM-123A Green displays offer crisp character definition because of a wide 15 MHz bandwidth and a fast 30 nanosecond rise time. Special DC-coupling circuitry permits the video to retain its brightness even when their screens are full of information. A special deflection system helps to provide a display that is easy to read and also very easy on the user's eyes. Front panel controls allow easy adjustment.

Versatile and compatible: Both monitors, with their 12-inch diagonal screens, offer a large 25 line by 80 character capacity with a switchable 40 or 80 character column display. Use with H/Z-100, Atari, IBM-PC and PC Jr. and others.

ZVM-122A, Assembled and tested monitor with amber CRT, 18 lbs. **139.95**

ZVM-123A, Assembled and tested monitor with green CRT, 18 lbs. **139.95**

ZVM-124, Assembled monitor for use with IBM-PC and PC compatible computer systems, amber CRT needs monochrome printer adapter card. 18 lbs. ... **199.00**

ZVM-123-2, Tilt Base for HVM/ZVM-122/123, Shpg. wt. 2 lbs. **15.00**

ZVM-121-1, Cable to connect HVM/ZVM-121/122/123, to IBM, 1 lb. **5.00**

ZVM-121-2, Cable to connect HVM/ZVM-121/122/123, to Atari 1200, Shpg. wt. 1 lb. **15.00**

NEW ### Build your own monochrome video display

Kit **HVM-122A:** Get all these features: non-glare amber CRT, excellent character definition and intensity, a 40/80 column display, versatile front exterior controls contemporary styling, portability and compatibility with most popular computer systems. The HVM-122 uses the same cables as the ZVM-122/123 monitors which are listed above.

HVM-122A, Kit video display, 22 lbs. .... **Was $109.95 NOW ONLY 89.95**

13-inch color monitors for home computers, VCRs, modular TV tuners, and video games

- Full-featured ZVM-131 and ZVM-135 Color Monitors with sound
- ZVM-133 economical high-resolution monitor for RGB inputs only
- ZVM-136 long-persistence monitor with features of ZVM-133

ZVM-131 and ZVM-135: Both feature composite video and analog RGB inputs and are capable of displaying a full range of colors and intensities. A unique feature of each is a switch that cancels all colors except green so that monochrome text material can be displayed for easier reading. Both adjust screen brightness automatically. The one difference between the two is that the ZVM-131 has a 25 line by 40 character display for use with home computers and the ZVM-135 has a 25 line by 80 character display which makes it ideal for use with the H/Z-100 Computer. The ZVM-135 displays 80 characters using the RGB input or 40 characters using the composite input. Easy-to-reach front-panel display and sound controls are other assets of these monitors. With the purchase of a ZVM-135 monitor, you receive a free computer cable of your choice from those listed below.

ZVM-133 and ZVM-136: Both of these Displays are special versions of the monitors above for use with RGB inputs only. User adjustments include a green-only switch and contrast control, and a front panel brightness control. The ZVM-136 uses a long persistence CRT to reduce flicker when the interlace mode is used. Both monitors support 16 colors including the IBM-PC's brown.

ZVM-131, Assembled medium-resolution monitor, Shpg. wt. 38 lbs. ... **379.00**

ZVM-135, Assembled high-resolution monitor, Shpg. wt. 39 lbs. **599.00**

ZVM-133, Assembled high-resolution RGB-only monitor, 39 lbs. **559.00**

ZVM-136, Assembled long-persistence RGB-only monitor, 39 lbs. **799.00**

Cables for use with the ZVM-131/133/135/136 Color Video Displays:

ZVM-135-1, to the H/Z-100 Computer (ZVM-135/133/136 only), 1 lb. ... **25.00**

ZVM-135-2, to the IBM Personal Computer, Shpg. wt. 1 lb. **25.00**

ZVM-135,3, to the Apple III Computer, Shpg. wt. 1 lb. **25.00**

ZVM-135-4, to the Texas Instruments and Atari Computers, 1 lb. **25.00**

Discover the fun of kitbuilding at your Heathkit Electronic Center.

HVM-122A shown with optional tilt base

Available in non-glare amber and green CRT displays

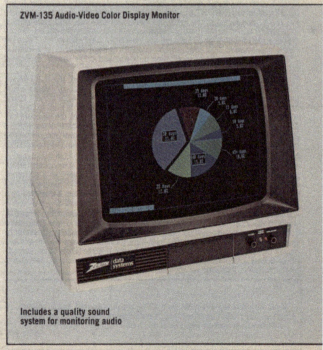

ZVM-135 Audio-Video Color Display Monitor

Includes a quality sound system for monitoring audio

COMPUTERS/35

NEW LOW PRICES on increased disk storage for your H/Z-89 or Z-90 Computer

Add up to 1.28 megabytes of on-line disk storage: Designed especially for use with the H/Z-89 and Z-90 Computers, these external floppy disk systems give you even more flexibility in configuring the amount of disk storage you need for your computer system applications.

Your choice of data storage capacity: The H-37 provides up to 1.28 megabytes of additional data storage capacity — while the H-77 provides up to 320K bytes.

Use up to three drives in your system: When you use one of these systems with your H/Z-89 or Z-90, you have room for up to three 5.25-inch disk drives on a single controller board. With multiple drives, you can mount operating system and program disks at the same time. And because these peripherals work with the H/Z-89 and Z-90, your system will work harmoniously.

Space-saving design: Each 5.25" floppy disk drive installs vertically into the durable metal cabinet, so the H-37 and H-77 systems take up less space than units with horizontally-mounted disk drives.

The H-37 features high-capacity disk drives: Its double-sided 96 tpi disk drives provide up to 6.4 times the storage capacity of our single-sided 5.25-inch drive: Store up to 640K bytes per drive — for a total capacity of up to 1.28 megabytes! For easier kitbuilding, the disk drives are assembled and tested.

Enhanced software capabilities: With the double-sided H-37's ability to store a much greater amount of data on each disk (double the capacity of single-sided 5.25-inch disk drives), you can more fully utilize most of our software programs. And many of those software packages are available on soft-sectored 5.25-inch floppy disks, compatible with the H-37. See pages 10-13 for more details on Heath/Zenith soft-sectored software.

Field-proven H-77 available: Using single-sided 5.25" disk drives, this reliable data storage system is available with one or two drives — to provide up to 200K bytes of data storage (up to 320K bytes of data storage when the Z-89-37 Soft-Sectored Disk Controller Board is used).

Compatible disk controller boards: The H-77 Floppy Disk System can be run from either the H-88-1 Single-Density Controller Board (standard with H-Z-89 Computers) or the Z-89-37 Double-Density Controller Board (standard with Z-90 Computers; with H/Z-89s, see below). The H-37 Floppy Disk System requires the Z-89-37 Double-Density Disk Controller Board.

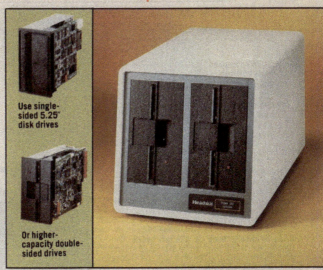

Use single-sided 5.25" disk drives

Or higher-capacity double-sided drives

Designed to complement the H/Z-89, Z-90 Computers

Easy ordering method: Use the configuration and ordering charts (below, right) to order the H-37 or H-77 Floppy Disk System that's right for your H/Z-89 or Z-90 Computer System. For 120/240 VAC, 50/60 Hz power. The H-37 and H-77 Floppy Disk Systems measure 8⅝" H x 8⅞" W x 15" D (21.92 x 22.56 x 38.1 cm).

Disk storage accessories

Soft-Sectored Disk Controller Board for H/Z-89 Computers: Increases data storage capacity of disk drives below
Z-89-37, Assem., 2 Kg **495.00**

Hard-Sectored Disk Controller Board for H/Z-89 Computers, Use only with H-17-1 Single-Sided Floppy Disk Drives below.
H-88-1, Assem., 1.5 Kg **229.95**

Double-Sided Floppy Disk Drive for H/Z-37 Disk Systems: Stores up to 640K bytes on a compatible disk. Requires Z-89-37 above.
H-17-4, Assem., 2.5 Kg Was 795 NOW **695.00**

Single-Sided Floppy Disk Drive for H-77/Z-87 Disk Systems: Stores up to 160K bytes per disk when used with Z-89-37, 100K when used with H-88-1 Controller Board. Also for H-88, H/Z-89 and Z-90 Computers.
H-17-1, Assem., 2.5 Kg Was 425.00 NOW **395.00**

Dust Cover: Protects H/Z-37 and H-77/Z-87 Disk Systems from airborne contaminants.
HCA-5-77, Shpg. wt. 1 Kg **19.95**

ZENITH DATA SYSTEMS DISK DRIVES
These Zenith Data Systems Disk Drives are factory assembled and tested for use with the H/Z-89 or Z-90 Computers and include two drives.

Z-37 Dual-Sided Floppy Disk System: Provides 1.28 Megabytes of data storage. Requires Z-37-89 Dual Density Controller Board listed above.
Z-37, Assembled, with two drives,
Shpg. wt. 13 Kg **2495.00**

Z-87 Single-Sided Floppy Disk System: Provides 320,000 bytes of storage when used with Z-89-37 Controller (above), or 200,000 bytes if used with H-88-1 Controller (above).
Z-87, Assembled, with two drives,
Shpg. wt. 13 Kg **1695.00**

H/Z-89 Computer/5.25" Disk System Configuration Chart

System Components	Hard-Sectored Disk Storage	Soft-Sectored Disk Storage	Total Disk Storage Capacity
H/Z-89 (Note 1)	One 100 KB internal drive	—	100 KB
H/Z-89 (Note 1) H-77 (Note 2)	One 100 KB internal drive, one or two 100 KB external drives		200 or 300 KB
H/Z-89 (Note 1) Z-89-37	—	One 160 KB, single-density internal drive	160 KB
H/Z-89 (Note 1) Z-89-37 H-77 (Notes 2, 3)	One 100 KB internal drive	One (or two) 160 KB, single-density external drive	260 or 420 KB
H/Z-89 (Note 1) Z-89-37 H-37 (Notes 2, 3)	One 100 KB internal drive	One (or two) 640 KB, double-density external drives	740 KB or 1.38 MB

NOTES: (1) When ordering an HS-89, use -2 or -3 for desired CRT. (2) When ordering an HS-77 or HS-37, use -1 or -2 for desired number of drives. (3) H-37s require Z-89-37 Disk Controller.

How to order external 5.25" disk storage for H/Z-89s, Z-90s

All disk systems below require either H-88-1 Hard-Sectored Disk Controller (included with H/Z-89) or Z-89-37 Soft-Sectored Disk Controller (included with Z-90), as listed (order from right).

Drives	Storage Capacity		Order Model	Shpg. wt.	Price
	With H-88-1	With Z-89-37			
One H-17-1 (Single-Sided)	100K bytes	160K bytes	Kit HS-77-1	16 Kg	Was 825.00 NOW 699.95
Two H-17-1 (Single-Sided)	200K bytes	320K bytes	Kit HS-77-2	22 Kg	Was 1125.00 NOW 999.95
One H-17-4 (Double-Sided)	—	640K bytes	Kit HS-37-1	16 Kg	Was 1195.00 NOW 898.95
Two H-17-4 (Double-Sided)		1.28 megabytes	Kit HS-37-2	22 Kg	Was 1895.00 NOW 1599.95

COMPUTERS/5

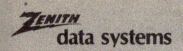

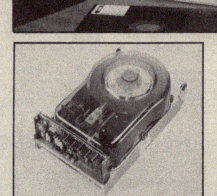

Product Listing

Listed here are some Heathkit products for peripherals and other accessories.

Figure 24: List of Peripheral and Accessory Products

Model	Category	Series	Kit	Description	First Year	Last Year	Lowest Price	Highest Price
GDC-11	Modem	n/a	N	Acoustic Modem	1982	1983	$199.95	$260.00
GDC-21-1	Accessory	GDC-21	N	Acoustic Cup for coupling LEX-21 to telephone	1982	1982	$69.95	$69.95
GDZ-1320	Monitor	n/a	N	Color Video Display for computers, VCRs, cameras	1980	1983	$399.95	$659.95
H-125	Printer	n/a	Y	Dot Matrix Printer	1983	1984	$899.00	$899.00
H-14	Printer	n/a	Y	Dot Matrix Printer	1980	1982	$495.00	$595.00
H-17-2	Accessory	WH17	N	5 5.25" Diskettes	1978	1978	$34.95	$34.95
H-25	Printer	n/a	Y	Dot Matrix Printer	1982	1983	$1,695.00	$1,850.00
H-27-2	Accessory	H-27	N	Package of 5 Blank 8-inch Floppy Disks	1980	1980	$25.00	$25.00
H-36-1	Accessory	H-36	N	Fan-fold Paper for H-36	1978	1978	$44.95	$44.95
H-36-2	Accessory	H-36	N	EIA RS-232C interface	1978	1978	$149.95	$149.95
H-36-3	Accessory	H-36	N	Acoustic Coupler	1978	1978	$339.95	$339.95
HBT-40-1	Accessory	IBM PC	N	40MB DC2000 tape cartridge	1992	1992	$14.95	$14.95
HBT-40-AT	Accessory	IBM PC	Y	40MB streaming tape drive	1992	1992	$99.95	$99.95
HCA-1	Accessory	n/a	N	Bi-Directional Tractor Feed Accessory for WH-44K/Diablo 1640 KSR and WH-54 Printers	1980	1982	$259.00	$479.95
HCA-10	Accessory	MX-80A	N	Male-to-Male RS-232C Cable	1983	1983	$20.00	$20.00
HCA-11	Accessory	WH-53	N	RS-232 Computer-Modem Cable	1983	1983	$20.00	$29.95
HCA-13	Accessory	WH-12	N	Custom RS-232 Cable to connect WH-12 to H-8 and H/Z-89	1982	1983	$20.00	$29.95
HCA-14	Accessory	MX-80A	N	Parallel Cable	1983	1983	$25.00	$25.00
HCA-2	Accessory	WH-55	N	Printer Stand for WH-55 Printer	1980	1984	$99.00	$99.00
HCA-4	Accessory	H-19	N	Black Fabric Anti-Glare CRT Filter for H-19/H-19A	1980	1983	$19.95	$19.95
HCA-5-14	Accessory	H-14	N	Dust Cover for H/WH-14	1981	1982	$14.00	$19.95
HCA-5-17	Accessory	H-17	N	Dust Cover for H-17 Floppy Disk System	1981	1982	$14.00	$19.95
HCA-5-77	Accessory	Z/Z-90,Z-90	N	Dust Cover for H-37,H-77,Z-87	1981	1984	$14.00	$19.95
HCA-5-80	Accessory	MX-80A	N	Protective Dust Cover for MX-80/MX-80A	1982	1983	$14.00	$14.00
HCA-9	Accessory	H/Z-125	N	Printer Stand for Z/Z-125 Printer	1981	1984	$99.00	$99.00
HDC-125	Accessory	H/Z-125	N	Dust Cover for H/Z-125 Printer	1983	1984	$16.00	$16.00
HFM-9600	Modem	n/a	N	Internal fax/modem, 9600/2400 bps, for Heathkit laptops and ZDS equivalents.	1992	1992	$149.00	$149.00

Model	Category	Series	Kit	Description	First Year	Last Year	Lowest Price	Highest Price
HTX-10-1	Modem	n/a	N	Auto-dial and auto-answer 300 baud modem for use only with HTX and ZTX model terminals	1983	1985	$69.95	$69.95
HVM-1220A	Monitor	n/a	Y	Economical 12" Monochrome Monitor	1986	1987	$59.95	$89.95
HVM-122A	Monitor	n/a	N	Video display	1984	1984	$89.95	$109.95
ICA-2009-1	Accessory	IC-2009	N	Carrying Case for IC-2009 Calculator	1974	1974	$3.95	$3.95
MPI-150	Printer	n/a	N	Impact Matrix Printer	1984	1984	$995.00	$995.00
MPI-99	Printer	n/a	N	Impact Matrix Printer	1984	1984	$599.00	$599.00
MX-100	Printer	n/a	N	Epson MX-100 printer	1983	1983	$1,199.00	$1,199.00
MX-80	Printer	n/a	N	Epson MX-80 printer	1982	1982	$899.00	$899.00
MX-80-2	Accessory	MX-80	N	Serial interface for MX-80 Printer	1982	1982	$110.00	$110.00
MX-80-3	Accessory	MX-80A	N	Buffered RS-232C Serial Interface	1983	1983	$135.00	$199.95
MX-80-4	Accessory	MX-80A	N	ROM Set to add extended graphics set to MX-80s	1983	1983	$60.00	$99.95
MX-80A	Printer	n/a	N	Epson MX-80A Dot Matrix Printer	1983	1983	$499.00	$899.95
SK-203	Accessory	n/a	Y	Printer Buffer, serial and parallel interfaces	1987	1987	$199.95	$199.95
WH-12	Accessory	n/a	N	Votrax Type 'N' Talk Speech Synthesizer	1982	1984	$299.00	$599.95
WH-14	Printer	n/a	N	Assembled H-14 line printer	1980	1982	$595.00	$795.00
WH-23	Modem	n/a	N	Modem, LEX-11 acoustic, 300 bps	1981	1984	$139.00	$159.00
WH-24-1	Printer	n/a	N	TI-810 Doc Matrix Printer	1980	1981	$1,695.00	$1,695.00
WH-33	Modem	n/a	N	Direct-Connect Modem	1981	1982	$195.00	$295.00
WH-34	Printer	n/a	N	DECwriter Teleprinter	1980	1981	$1,095.00	$1,095.00
WH-42	Accessory	n/a	N	Hayes Chronograph	1983	1984	$199.00	$199.00
WH-43	Modem	n/a	N	Modem, Hayes Smartmodem 300	1982	1984	$279.00	$499.95
WH-44K	Printer	n/a	N	Assembled and Tested Diablo 1640 RO Printer	1980	1980	$2,995.00	$2,995.00
WH-44K	Printer	n/a	N	Letter Quality Printer/Terminal for Word Processing	1980	1981	$2,995.00	$3,295.00
WH-53	Modem	n/a	N	Modem, Hayes Smartmodem 1200	1983	1984	$695.00	$1,199.95
WH-54	Printer	n/a	N	Diablo Daisy-wheel printer	1981	1983	$2,295.00	$3,995.00
WH-54B	Printer	n/a	N	Diablo Daisy-wheel printer	1984	1984	$1,999.00	$1,999.00
WH-55	Printer	n/a	N	Diablo Daisy-wheel printer	1984	1984	$1,199.00	$1,199.00
WH-63	Modem	n/a	N	Modem, Muraphone MM-100 300 bps direct connect	1983	1984	$99.00	$99.00
WH-9121	Printer	n/a	N	Daisy Wheel Printer/Electronic Typewriter	1982	1983	$1,995.00	$2,695.00
WHA-34-2	Accessory	n/a	N	Tractor Feed for WH-34	1980	1981	$179.00	$179.00
Z-125	Printer	n/a	N	Dot Matrix Printer	1983	1984	$1,499.00	$2,495.00
Z-207-7	Accessory	Z-200	N	5.25" 360K Floppy Disk Drive	1985	1985	$250.00	$250.00
Z-25	Printer	n/a	N	Dot Matrix Printer	1981	1982	$1,595.00	$2,495.00
Z-29-1	Accessory	Z-29	N	Palm Rest Accessory	1983	1985	$15.00	$15.00
Z-29-2	Accessory	Z-29	N	ROM Source Listing	1984	1985	$25.00	$25.00

Model	Category	Series	Kit	Description	First Year	Last Year	Lowest Price	Highest Price
Z-329	Accessory	Z-200	N	High-Resolution Monochrome Video Card	1985	1985	$200.00	$200.00
Z-37	Disk	Z-89	N	Dual-Sided Floppy Disk System	1982	1983	$2,495.00	$2,495.00
Z-405	Accessory	Z-200	N	1.5MB Memory Board, 128K installed	1985	1985	$399.00	$399.00
Z-409	Accessory	Z-200	N	Standard Video Card with monochrome and RGB outputs, 320x200 pixel resolution	1985	1985	$239.00	$239.00
Z-416	Accessory	Z-200	N	80287 Numeric Co-Processor	1985	1985	Call	Call
Z-47-BA	Disk	Z-89	N	Dual 8" Floppy Drive	1981	1981	$3,500.00	$3,500.00
Z-67	Disk	Z-89	N	10.782 Megabyte Commercial Winchester Disk System	1981	1982	$5,800.00	$8,995.00
Z-87	Disk	Z-89	N	Single-Sided Floppy Disk System	1981	1983	$1,195.00	$1,695.00
ZCM-1390	Monitor	n/a	N	13" Diagonal Color Monitor	1987	1987	$699.00	$699.00
ZCM-1490	Monitor	n/a	N	14" Diagonal Flat Technology Monitor	1987	1987	$999.00	$999.00
ZCM-1492	Monitor	n/a	N	14" Diagonal Flat Technology Monitor	1990	1990	Call	Call
ZD-12	Disk	Z-200	N	5.25" 1.2MB Floppy Disk Drive	1985	1985	$599.00	$599.00
ZD-200	Disk	Z-200	N	20MB Winchester Disk Drive	1985	1985	$1,499.00	$1,499.00
ZD-400	Disk	Z-200	N	40MB Winchester Disk Drive	1985	1985	$2,499.00	$2,499.00
ZMM-1470-G	Monitor	n/a	N	14" Diagonal Monochrome Monitor	1986	1987	$299.00	$299.00
ZMM-149-A	Monitor	n/a	N	14-inch Diagonal Monochrome Monitor, amber	1987	1987	$299.00	$299.00
ZMM-149-P	Monitor	n/a	N	14-inch Diagonal Monochrome Monitor, white	1987	1990	$299.00	$299.00
ZT-1-2	Accessory	ZT-1	N	Terminal Carrying Case	1983	1985	$24.99	$24.99
ZTA-1-1	Accessory	n/a	N	Parallel Cable	1983	1985	$25.00	$25.00
ZVM-121	Monitor	n/a	N	Monochrome Video Display	1982	1984	$139.95	$199.95
ZVM-121-1	Accessory	n/a	N	Cable to connect HVM/ZVM-121/12/123, to IBM	1984	1984	$5.00	$5.00
ZVM-121-1	Monitor	Z-100	N	Monochrome Video Display, Orchard Tan	1983	1983	$139.95	$139.95
ZVM-121-1	Monitor	n/a	N	Optional Monochrome Video Display, for use with HTX and ZTX terminals	1984	1984	$139.95	$139.95
ZVM-121-2	Accessory	n/a	N	Cable to connect HVM/ZVM-121/12/123, to Atari 1200	1984	1984	$15.00	$15.00
ZVM-121-Z	Monitor	Z-100	N	Monochrome Video Display, Earthtone color	1983	1985	$139.95	$199.95
ZVM-1220-A	Monitor	n/a	N	12" Diagonal Monochrome Monitor, amber	1986	1987	$119.95	$119.95
ZVM-122A	Monitor	n/a	N	Assembled and tested monitor with amber CRT	1983	1984	$139.95	$169.95
ZVM-123	Monitor	n/a	N	Assembled and tested monitor with green CRT	1983	1983	$139.95	$139.95
ZVM-123-2	Accessory	n/a	N	Tilt Base for HVM/ZVM-122/123	1984	1984	$15.00	$15.00
ZVM-1230-A	Monitor	n/a	N	12" Diagonal Monochrome Monitor, green	1986	1987	$119.95	$119.95
ZVM-123A	Monitor	n/a	N	Assembled and tested monitor with green CRT	1984	1984	$139.95	$139.95

Model	Category	Series	Kit	Description	First Year	Last Year	Lowest Price	Highest Price
ZVM-124	Monitor	n/a	N	Assembled monitor for use with IBM-PC and PC compatible computer systems, amber CRT needs monochrome printer adapter card	1984	1984	$199.00	$199.00
ZVM-1240	Monitor	n/a	N	12" Diagonal Monochrome Monitor, amber, TTL compatible	1986	1987	$169.95	$169.95
ZVM-131	Monitor	n/a	N	Assembled medium-resolution monitor	1983	1984	$379.00	$379.00
ZVM-133	Monitor	n/a	N	Assembled high-resolution RGB-only monitor	1984	1984	$559.00	$559.00
ZVM-1330	Monitor	n/a	N	13" Diagonal Color Monitor	1987	1987	$649.00	$649.00
ZVM-1330	Monitor	n/a	N	13" Diagonal Color Monitor	1986	1986	$649.00	$649.00
ZVM-134	Monitor	n/a	N	Assembled High-resolution color video display	1983	1983	$699.00	$1,099.00
ZVM-134-1	Accessory	ZVM-134	N	Cable to connect ZVM-134 to Z-100 Computer	1983	1983	$20.00	$34.95
ZVM-134-2	Accessory	ZVM-134	N	Cable to connect ZVM-134 to IBM Personal Computer	1983	1983	$34.95	$34.95
ZVM-134-21	Accessory	ZVM-134	N	ZVM-134 to IBM PC 16-Color Cable	1983	1983	$20.00	$20.00
ZVM-135	Monitor	n/a	N	Assembled high-resolution monitor	1983	1986	$599.00	$599.00
ZVM-136	Monitor	n/a	N	Assembled long-persistence RGB-only monitor	1984	1984	$799.00	$799.00
ZVM-1360	Monitor	n/a	N	13" Diagonal Color Monitor, long persistence	1986	1986	$799.00	$799.00
ZVM-1380	Monitor	n/a	N	13" Diagonal Color Monitor	1986	1986	Call	Call
ZVM-1380-C	Monitor	n/a	N	13" Diagonal Color Monitor	1987	1987	$799.00	$799.00

Chapter 11: Trainers, Educational Courses, and Miscellaneous

As Heathkit got into the technical training market, primarily with courses in electronics, they offered several products to assist students in performing the lab experiments in the courses.

Often called design experimenters or trainers, they were essentially solderless breadboards with additional features such as power supplies, switches, clocks, and indicators. Specific models were aimed at either analog or digital electronics. Examples include the ET-3100 Electronic Design Experimenter and ET-3200 Digital Design Experimenter products.

Heathkit also offered trainers for learning microprocessor hardware design and software programming. These could be purchased and used on their own, or in conjunction with Heathkit training courses.

Manufacturers typically offered development systems for their microprocessor products, but these tended to be expensive and beyond what a student or hobbyist could afford. The Heathkit trainers were less expensive (in part, because they were kits assembled by the end user) and more geared to the needs of training than development systems. The hardware provided a microprocessor with facilities for entering and running programs.

ET-3400/ET-3400A

In 1977 Heath introduced the ET-3400 Microprocessor Trainer at a price of around $200. It was built around the popular Motorola 6800 microprocessor and included an LED display and keyboard for entering and running programs. A breadboard area allowed the user to perform hardware experiments and gain access to the signals of the microprocessor. An extensive training course, EE-3401, was offered that taught microprocessor hardware and software using the board. It came as a set of binders, cassette tapes or records, and with all of the electronic components needed for the labs.

The basic features of the ET-3400 were the following:
- 6800 microprocessor running at 0.5 MHz.
- Monitor program contained in a 1K ROM.
- 256 bytes of RAM expandable to 512 bytes.
- 6 seven-segment LEDs for display.
- 17-key keypad.
- A breadboard area for prototyping circuits.
- 8 LEDs that can indicate logic high/low levels.
- 8 DIP switches that can produce logic high/low levels.
- Access to all address, data, and control signals on the breadboard.
- Access to ground, +5V, +12V, and -12V power supplies.
- 1 Hz and 60 Hz clock signals.
- An optional expansion connector for use with the ETA-3400 memory i/o expander.
- A power on/standby switch with power LED.
- A self-contained AC power supply.

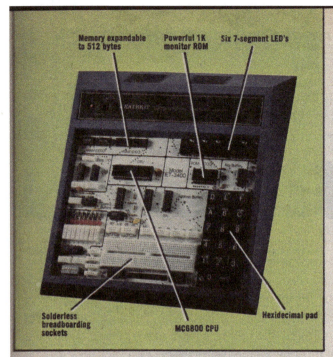

Memory expandable to 512 bytes — Powerful 1K monitor ROM — Six 7-segment LED's

Shielded 110V section — Standard RS232 connector for terminal — Kansas City standard audio cassette I/O

Heath/Pittman Tiny BASIC ROM

Terminal monitor ROM

Add up to 4K user RAM

Connector cable for ET-3400

Solderless breadboarding sockets — MC6800 CPU — Hexidecimal pad

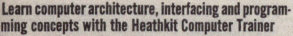

The ETA-3400 Microprocessor Trainer Accessory converts the ET-3400 Microprocessor Trainer to a full personal computer system.

Learn computer architecture, interfacing and programming concepts with the Heathkit Computer Trainer

The ET-3400 Computer Trainer is designed for use with the EE-3401 Microprocessor Self-Instruction Program on page 74. Once you complete the EE-3401 experiments, add the ETA-3400 Trainer Accessory and a terminal such as the H-9 or H-19 for a complete system.

Functioning as a miniature digital computer, the ET-3400 Microprocessor Trainer is used with the experiments in the EE-3401 Self-Instruction Program. The ET-3400 features a built-in 1K ROM monitor program for controlling unit operation. It also has a 6-digit hexadecimal 7-segment LED display for address and data readout. The 17-key hexadecimal keyboard permits you to access memory location to examine contents, then step forward or backward from that memory location to examine more memory locations, to change a memory location, to examine and/or alter any of the MC6800 CPU's internal registers, to set break points for program debugging, or to reset the CPU. The flexible instruction set of the MC6800 permits relative addressing, and makes use of two accumulators.

The ET-3400 has 256 bytes of random access memory (RAM) built-in and is expandable to 512 bytes with the RAM's supplied in the EE-3401 Self-Instruction Program. It also features 8 buffered binary LED's for display of breadboard logic states, 8 SPST DIP switches for binary input to breadboarding circuits, and a breadboarding socket for prototyping, interfacing and memory circuits. All microprocessor address, control and data busses are buffered and terminated on the front panel for ease of connection to prototyped circuits. There's also provision for a 40-pin external connector to expand memory and I/O capacity. The Heathkit ET-3400 Microprocessor Trainer features built-in +5, +12 and −12 volt power supplies. Power requirement: 120/240 volts, 60/50 Hz, 30 watts maximum. The unit measures 3½" H x 12⅛" W x 11¾" D.

All of the programming and hardware interface experiments supplied with the EE-3401 Microprocessor Self-Instruction Program are implemented on the ET-3400 Trainer. While designed primarily for use with the EE-3401 Program, the Trainer is a flexible, general purpose training unit and microprocessor breadboard. It can be used in many other applications that require a low-cost microprocessor-based software development system or as a design aid for developing special interfaces. Team it up with the ETA-3400 Trainer Accessory (description at right) for real computing power.

Kit ET-3400, Shpg. wt. 7 lbs. 199.95
ETW-3400, Factory assembled and tested, Wt. 6 lbs. 279.00

The ET-3400 Accessory turns Microprocessor Trainer into a complete system

When you add the ETA-3400 Trainer Accessory, you turn your ET-3400 Microprocessor Trainer into a complete computer system. The Accessory provides you with more computing power — an additional 1K bytes of memory — so you are able to run longer and more sophisticated programs through your ET-3400 Trainer. The Accessory's memory can even be expanded to 4K bytes by adding the optional 3K Chip Set (ET-3400-1). Order the Chip Set from the listing below.

A serial I/O with EIA or 20 mA loop format in the Accessory allows you to hook up a terminal such as the H-9 or H-19 (described on page 42), or a 20 mA ASCII teletype machine. It also provides an audio cassette interface enabling you to store programs on convenient audio cassettes. The ROM monitor/debugger program lets you implement the standard Trainer monitor functions through the external terminal. Memory locations can be examined or changed, break points can be initiated, and program debugging can be accomplished with a single instruction step feature.

A Tiny BASIC interpreter is provided in ROM allowing you to program using BASIC (see the EC-1100 BASIC Self-Instruction Program on page 50). Tiny BASIC features 26 variables (A-Z), integer math, 15 BASIC statements and two functions: random and user. User function allows you to run machine code routines from BASIC — the same machine code routines you learn to write in the EE-3401 Self-Instruction Program.

The ETA-3400 Accessory connects to the Trainer by means of a 40-pin ribbon cable supplied. Parts required to modify the Trainer are included. Since this modification changes the clock frequency of the Trainer, the experiments in the Microprocessor Self-Instruction Program using timing loops will be changed. It is recommended that all of the EE-3401 experiments be completed before adding this modification kit. The cabinet of the Accessory measures 3" H x 11" W x 12" D. Power requirement: 120/240 VAC, 60/50 Hz, 11 watts.

As with all Heathkit electronic kits, our step-by-step instruction manual even includes directions on soldering for the first-time builder.

Kit ETA-3400, Shpg. wt. 8 lbs. 150.00
EWA-3400, Factory assembled and tested, Wt. 8 lbs. 250.00
ETA-3400-1, Optional 3K Chip Set, Wt. 1 lb. 47.00

NOTE: A terminal such as the H-9 or H-19 (see page 42) is required to use the BASIC and monitor software with the Trainer Accessory.

EDUCATION/75

Everything was contained in a rugged and compact plastic case and the unit weighed about four pounds. All ICs and the LED displays were installed in sockets and the chip functions and signal names were listed on the board silkscreen. Like most of their products, the ET-3400 was sold as a kit that the user would assemble. A factory-assembled version, the ETW-3400, was also available at a higher cost.

Note that if you happen to obtain an ET-3400 which is missing the custom masked ROM (as I did) it is possible to rewire it to accept a standard 2716 EPROM. Instructions can be found in the internet.

The trainer was expandable by purchasing the ETA-3400 Memory and Input/Output Accessory which added additional RAM and ROM, a serial port for communication with a serial terminal, and an interface to allow loading and saving programs to cassette tape. This made the unit more convenient for programming and also offered the Tiny BASIC programming language in ROM.

A hobbyist named Scott Baker has designed a version of the ETA-3400 expansion board that uses slightly more modern components and provides more memory. I've built one and have used it with my ET-3400.

I've also designed and built my own single-board computer based on the ET-3400 and ETA-3400 expander using more modern and available parts and made the schematic and PCB layout available as an open-source hardware design.

The ET-3400 was slightly updated as the ET-3400A model around 1981 or 1982. The ET-3400A used the 6808 version of the 6800 that included an on-chip clock oscillator that had required an additional MC6874 chip on the ET-3400. It also ran at a 1 MHz clock speed rather than the 0.5 MHz of the ET-3400 (the ET-3400 could be modified to run at 1 MHz using a crystal and needed to be when using the ETA-3400). The ROM was changed from a 1K MCM6830A to a 2K 2316 which was compatible with commonly available 2716 EPROMs. It also switched from 2112 (256x4) static RAM to 2114 (1Kx4) RAM chips, offering 1K of RAM as standard.

Heathkit offered a course, EE-3404, for the Motorola 6809 microprocessor, a more powerful successor to the 6800. Heathkit never offered a 6809-based trainer, but the EE-3404 course included an adapter board that replaced the processor chip in the ET-3400/ET-3400A and included a 6809 CPU and ROM with new firmware. On the ET-3400A the adapter simply replaced the 6808 chip. On the ET-3400 there were some additional hardware changes required to use it. The 6809 adapters are rarely seen, but it is possible to build one yourself using the Heathkit published design, and several people have done so.

One Heathkit catalog I came across claimed the ET-3400A was the world's top-selling microprocessor trainer. Tens of thousands are believed to have been sold. I have a very late Heathkit catalog from 1992 as they were leaving the kit business and it was one of the few kits still being offered. I believe the factory assembled model was still offered when Heathkit continued as Heathkit Educational Systems.

ET-6800

Introduced around 1979, the ET-6800 was a cost-reduced version of the ET-3400 that only had a display and keypad. It used a 6808 processor with 1K of RAM and 265 bytes of ROM. Offered in conjunction with the EC-6800 course, it was suited to learning 6800 programming but didn't support any of the lab experiments for hardware interfacing. It was housed in a cardboard case and used the same ROM as the ET-3400.

ET-100/ETA-100

The ET-100, introduced around 1984, was a trainer based on the Intel 8088 processor used in the IBM PC and some Heathkit desktop computers. It featured 16K of RAM expandable to 64K, a 32K ROM with assembler, editor, and debugger, a full 95-key keyboard, solderless breadboard, switches and LEDs, serial port, access to processor address, data, and control lines, and a video interface to a TV or monitor.

It was offered in conjunction with the EE-8088 programming course. The ETW-100 was the factory assembled version.

The ETA-100 accessory kit expanded it into a desktop computer with 128K of RAM expandable to 192K, two serial ports, a parallel printer port, timer, floppy disk controller and floppy disk drive, and support for video graphics. A boot ROM allowed it to run MS-DOS/Z-DOS and other software for the Heathkit H-100/Z-100 computers.

The EWA-100A was a factory assembled version of the accessory. ETS-100 was a bundle of the ET-100 and ETA-100, and EWS-100-A was an assembled version of ETS-100 bundle. Also offered was an additional breadboard and RF modulator for use with a TV.

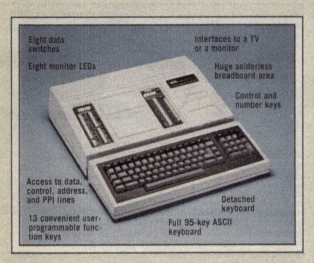
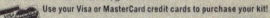

ETW-3800

Not technically a Heathkit, since it was sold when Heathkit only existed as Heathkit Educational Systems, this was the last trainer offered, introduced around 1993. Although I have seen references to an ET-3800 kit version in manuals, as far as I can tell it was only ever offered as the ETW-3800 factory wired model.

The trainer offered a breadboard area, 20 character by 2 line text LCD display, 21 key keypad, switches and LEDs, serial port, and access to all processor bus signals.

The processor was determined by a plug-in module. The ETC-8085 CPU module provided an Intel 8085 CPU and the ETC-6811 CPU module provided a Motorola 6811 CPU (a successor to the 6800 series). The optional ETC-128 memory module provided up to 128K of program storage.

The unit had an expansion connector for the ETW-3567 accessory backback. This added power supplies for lab experiments, a 3-1/2 digit digital multimeter, and connectors for accepting experiment circuit boards from Heathkit/Zenith Educational Systems courses.

Several courses were offered for the trainer. Following is a representative page from the course *8-Bit Microprocessor Interfacing and Applications*, which used the 6811 version of the trainer.

EXPERIMENT 14

A MICROPROCESSOR-CONTROLLED THERMOMETER

PURPOSE

1. *To demonstrate the operation of a semiconductor temperature-sensing IC.*

2. *To show how to condition the output of a temperature-sensing IC to be compatible with the input of an analog-to-digital converter.*

3. *To show how to interface a temperature-sensing circuit to the Microprocessor Trainer to produce a microprocessor-controlled thermometer.*

4. *To show how to write the software required to control the analog conversion process and display temperature in °F.*

Materials Required

1 ETW-3800 Microprocessor Trainer

1 LM35 temperature-sensing integrated circuit (#442-783)

1 ADC0809 analog-to-digital converter (#443-1122)

1 6821 PIA integrated circuit (#443-1014)

1 741C op amp integrated circuit (#442-22)

1 1,000 Ω, 1/4-watt, 5% resistor

1 10 kΩ, 1/4 watt, 5% resistor

1 Ice cube. (User supplied.)

1 Household thermometer. (User supplied.)

Miscellaneous

Several Heathkit products used microprocessors in their design, even if the end user was not able to program them.

The MK3870 was a single-chip 8-bit microprocessor based on the Fairchild F8 architecture that had on-board RAM, ROM, I/O ports, and a programmable timer. It was used in several Heathkit products, including the Heathkit PT-1500 Darkroom Timer, SA-5010 MicroMatic Memory Keyer, HD-8999 UltraPro CW Keyboard, OC-1401 Aircraft Navigation Computer, GC-1000 Most Accurate Clock, ID-4001 Digital Weather Computer, ET-19 HERO 2000 Robot, and GR-3000 Television.

Note that the IC has an internal masked programmed ROM which is programmed at the factory, so the chips are unique to each Heathkit product.

The Heathkit SS-9000 amateur radio transceiver used a similar Mostek 3850 processor, an earlier version than the 3870 that also required a 3851 Program Storage Unit (PSU) and some other support chips.

Product Listing

The following table lists the Heathkit trainers and related products that I have been able to identify.

Figure 25: List of Trainers and Related Products

Model	Category	Series	Kit	Description	First Year	Last Year	Lowest Price	Highest Price
EE-3404	Accessory	n/a	N	6809 Programming Course, includes 6809 adapter for ET-3400 or ET-3400A.	1984	1984	$99.95	$99.95
ET-100	Trainer	n/a	Y	Basic Learning Computer	1956	1984	$799.95	$799.95
ET-1000	Trainer	n/a	Y	Analog/Digital Circuit Design Trainer	1984	1992	$199.95	$229.95
ET-1000-1	Accessory	ET-1000	N	Extra Removable Breadboard Accessory	1984	1984	$29.95	$29.95
ET-3100	Trainer	n/a	Y	Trainer, Electronic Design Experimenter	1976	1980	$59.95	$92.95
ET-3100A	Trainer	n/a	Y	Trainer, Electronic Design Experimenter	1981	1982	$79.95	$149.95
ET-3100AS	Trainer	n/a	Y	Trainer, Electronic Design Experimenter, with Spanish manual	1981	1981	$79.95	$79.95
ET-3100B	Trainer	n/a	Y	Trainer, Electronic Design Experimenter	1983	1984	$89.95	$89.95
ET-3100S	Trainer	n/a	Y	Trainer, Electronic Design Experimenter, with Spanish manual	1980	1980	$79.95	$79.95
ET-3200	Trainer	n/a	Y	Trainer, Digital Techniques	1976	1980	$69.95	$89.95
ET-3200A	Trainer	n/a	Y	Trainer, Digital Techniques	1981	1983	$89.95	$99.95
ET-3200B	Trainer	n/a	Y	Trainer, Digital Techniques	1984	1984	$99.95	$99.95
ET-3300	Trainer	n/a	Y	Laboratory Breadboard	1976	1981	$79.95	$94.95
ET-3300A	Trainer	n/a	Y	Laboratory Breadboard	1982	1983	$199.95	$199.95
ET-3300B	Trainer	n/a	Y	Laboratory Breadboard	1983	1984	$99.95	$99.95
ET-3400	Trainer	n/a	Y	Trainer, Microprocessor, 6808 CPU, 256 bytes RAM, 1K ROM	1978	1981	$199.95	$224.95

Model	Category	Series	Kit	Description	First Year	Last Year	Lowest Price	Highest Price
ET-3400-AE	Trainer	n/a	Y	Trainer, Microprocessor, 6808 CPU, 512 bytes RAM, 1K ROM, 240VAC 50 Hz	1983	1984	$249.95	$249.95
ET-3400A	Trainer	n/a	Y	Trainer, Microprocessor, 6808 CPU, 512 bytes RAM, 1K ROM	1982	1992	$229.95	$229.95
ET-3600	Trainer	n/a	Y	Analog trainer	1992	1992	$139.95	$139.95
ET-3700	Trainer	n/a	Y	Digital trainer	1992	1992	$139.95	$139.95
ET-6800	Accessory	n/a	N	Trainer, 6800 CPU, 1K ROM	1980	1983	$99.95	$129.95
ETA-100	Accessory	ET-100	Y	Expansion Accessory	1984	1984	$1,299.95	$1,299.95
ETA-100-1	Accessory	ET-100	N	Extra Removable Breadboard	1984	1984	$29.95	$29.95
ETA-100-2	Accessory	ET-100	N	Channel 4 Modulator, use with TVs	1984	1984	$39.95	$39.95
ETA-100-3	Accessory	ET-100	N	Channel 3 Modulator, use with TVs	1984	1984	$39.95	$39.95
ETA-3400	Accessory	ET-3400A	Y	Microprocessor Trainer Accessory	1980	1984	$150.00	$175.00
ETA-3400-1	Accessory	ET-3400A	N	Optional 3K Chip Set	1981	1984	$47.00	$49.95
ETA-3600-1	Accessory	ET-3600	N	Extra breadboard block for ET-3600/ETW-3600	1992	1992	$19.95	$19.95
ETS-100	Trainer	ET-100	Y	ET-100 and ETA-100	1984	1984	$1,999.00	$1,999.00
ETW-100	Trainer	n/a	N	Basic Learning Computer	1984	1984	$1,095.00	$1,095.00
ETW-1000	Trainer	n/a	N	Analog/Digital Circuit Design Trainer	1984	1984	$349.95	$349.95
ETW-3100	Trainer	n/a	N	Trainer, Electronic Design Experimenter	1980	1980	$134.95	$134.95
ETW-3100A	Trainer	n/a	N	Trainer, Electronic Design Experimenter	1981	1982	$139.95	$269.95
ETW-3100B	Trainer	n/a	N	Trainer, Electronic Design Experimenter	1983	1984	$159.95	$159.95
ETW-3200	Trainer	n/a	N	Trainer, Digital Techniques	1980	1980	$149.95	$149.95
ETW-3200A	Trainer	n/a	N	Trainer, Digital Techniques	1981	1983	$159.95	$169.95
ETW-3200B	Trainer	n/a	N	Trainer, Digital Techniques	1984	1984	$179.95	$179.95
ETW-3300	Trainer	n/a	N	Laboratory Breadboard	1980	1981	$149.95	$159.95
ETW-3300A	Trainer	n/a	N	Laboratory Breadboard	1982	1983	$199.95	$199.95
ETW-3300B	Trainer	n/a	N	Laboratory Breadboard	1983	1984	$179.95	$179.95
ETW-3400A	Trainer	n/a	N	Trainer, Microprocessor, 6808 CPU, 256 bytes RAM, 1K ROM	1980	1980	$279.00	$279.00
ETW-3400A	Trainer	n/a	N	Trainer, Microprocessor, 6808 CPU, 256 bytes RAM, 1K ROM	1981	1981	$299.95	$299.95
ETW-3400A	Trainer	n/a	N	Trainer, Microprocessor, 6808 CPU, 512 bytes RAM, 1K ROM	1983	1992	$329.95	$329.95
ETW-3600	Trainer	n/a	N	Analog trainer	1992	1992	$229.95	$229.95
ETW-3700	Trainer	n/a	N	Digital trainer	1992	1992	$229.95	$229.95
EWA-100-A	Trainer	ET-100	N	Basic Learning Computer	1984	1984	$1,650.00	$1,650.00
EWA-3400	Trainer	ET-3400A	N	Microprocessor Trainer Accessory	1980	1984	$250.00	$275.00
EWA-3400-1	Accessory	ETA-3400	N	Optional 3K Chip Set	1980	1980	$47.00	$47.00
EWS-100A	Trainer	ET-100	N	ET-100 and ETA-100	1984	1984	$2,750.00	$2,750.00

(this page intentionally left blank)

Chapter 12: Software

In this chapter, I'll give an overview of the software that was available for the various Heathkit computers.

While some computers (like the H-8 and CPU trainers) supported rudimentary entering and running of programs from a front panel, this was slow, tedious, and error-prone for all but the smallest programs.

The next step up was the ability to load programs from cassette tape or a paper tape reader. The H-8, for example, supported this, and Heathkit offered software including Benton Harbor BASIC, an assembler, text editor, and debugger. Similar software was offered for the H-11.

Operating Systems

Loading from paper tape or cassette tape was slow, and as the cost of computer hardware came down, in most cases some type of disk-based operating system was provided. I give here a short description of the different operating systems offered for Heathkit computers.

Most OSes included some utilities such as an assembler, editor, debugger, and file and disk management tools. The operating systems here were all command line/text-based.

HDOS was the Heath-written operating system for the H-8. It was a proprietary operating system (although you could purchase the source code), and was not compatible with anything else. It was written by J. Gordon Letwin, who later went to Microsoft to become the chief architect of their OS/2 operating system for which they partnered with IBM.

CP/M, standing for Control Program for Microcomputers, was a popular operating system created in 1974 for Intel 8080-based microcomputers by Gary Kildall of Digital Research, Inc. It became an industry standard for computers using 8080 and compatible (like Z80) microprocessors. Applications written for CP/M would generally run on any CP/M computer. Later CP/M was extended to run on 16-bit processors (CP/M 85 and CP/M 86) and to support multiple users (MP/M). CP/M was supported on the Heathkit H-8, Z-89/Z-90, H-89A, and H-100/Z-110/Z-120 models.

Z-DOS was the name given to Heathkit's OEM version of Microsoft's MS-DOS. As mentioned earlier, it was not entirely compatible with IBM's version of MS-DOS due to BIOS and hardware differences from the IBM PC.

HT-11 was a modified version of DEC's RT-11 time operating system that was offered for the Heathkit H-11. RT-11 (for Real-time 11) was a small, single-user real-time operating system for Digital Equipment Corporation's line of PDP-11 16-bit minicomputers. RT-11 was first implemented in 1970 and was widely used for real-time computing systems, process control, and data acquisition as well as general-use computing.

The *UCSD P-System* was a portable, highly machine-independent operating system, developed at the University of California, San Diego (UCSD) and first released in 1977. It supported UCSD Pascal, a

Pascal programming language system. It was offered as an alternative operating system for the H-11. It was also supported on the H-8/H-19, H-11A/H-19, an H/Z-89. Note that Borland offered a version of Pascal called Turbo Pascal that ran under CP/M, and later MS-DOS.

Programming Languages

Developing software requires programming tools and language compilers. Listed here are some of the more popular languages that were supported on Heathkit computers. Heath also offered training courses for many of these languages.

Assembly Language or Assembler is a low-level programming language that has a direct correspondence to the binary machine language instructions executed by the hardware, but uses mnemonic names for instructions and offers features like comments, constants, and labels to make programming easier for humans. It is unique to each processor (e.g. 6800, Z80, 8088). Assemblers were included with the software for the H-8, as part of CP/M and HDOS, and available for MS-DOS.

BASIC (for **B**eginners' **A**ll-purpose **S**ymbolic **I**nstruction **C**ode) is a general-purpose, high-level programming language designed for ease of use and learning. The original version was created by John Kemeny and Thomas Kurtz at Dartmouth College in 1963. Versions available for Heathkit computers ranged from Pittman Tiny BASIC offered on the HERO 1 robot and ET-3400 trainer, to Benton Harbor BASIC, which ran standalone on the H-8, to interpreted and compiled versions of Microsoft BASIC for CP/M and MS-DOS.

FOCAL (for **F**ormulating **O**n-line **C**alculations in **A**lgebraic **L**anguage or **FO**rmula **CAL**culator) was an interactive interpreted programming language used on Digital Equipment Corporation PDP series minicomputers. Little known today, it was offered for the Heathkit H-11.

FORTRAN[4] (for **FOR**mula **TRAN**slator) is a general-purpose, compiled programming language especially suited to numeric computation and scientific computing. It was originally developed by IBM in the 1950s and is still used today. Heathkit offered FORTRAN compilers for its CP/M and MS-DOS computers.

COBOL (for **CO**mmon **B**usiness-**O**riented **L**anguage) is a compiled English-like computer programming language designed for business use. It is still in use today, mostly for legacy systems for government and financial institutions. Heathkit offered COBOL compilers for its CP/M and MS-DOS computers.

Software Applications

Heathkit sold their own and third-party applications for their computer products.

They offered software that had been tested and offered on floppy disk under the SOFTSTUFF brand, mostly for HDOS and CP/M.

---

4   Since about 1990 the preferred capitalization is *Fortran*.

The Heath User Group (HUG) was a yearly subscription program that gave access to several hundred software programs in the software library, a monthly subscription to REMark magazine, and access to an online forum (BBS). Many programs were written by HUG members and most ran on HDOS or CP/M.

H-11 users could also join DECUS, the Digital Equipment Corporation User's Group.

Some of the major categories of application programs included:
Databases, including DBase II, Multilog, JTBase, Infostar, and Lotus 1-2-3.
Spreadsheets such as Multiplan and Supercalc.
Word processors like WordStar, Magic Wand, and Magic Spell.
Accounting software, such as Peachtree.
Communications programs, for use with a modem.

On the following pages are some representative pages from Heathkit catalogs listing some of the available software offered directly from Heath.

58

Industry standard CP/M Operating System

- Over 200,000 microcomputer owners use CP/M
- Provides common hardware interface with flexibility

Features: CP/M, Version 2.2.03, frees the user from having to understand the details of underlying hardware. It has fully dynamic named-file allocation, program and peripheral output control and random or sequential data access. Has two-pass assembler, general-purpose editor, advanced 8080 debugger, file dump and copy between devices, system generation/relocation and file size/disk usage displays. CP/M requires an H-8/H-19 or H/Z-89 computer system with a minimum of 48K bytes of RAM and one disk drive (two disk drives are highly recommended). H-8 systems also require HA-8-8 Extended Configuration Option or HA-8-6 Z-80 CPU Card.

Related educational course: EC-1120 CP/M Course on page 65.
HOS-8917-2 (Needs Sublicense, p. 57), hard-sectored 5.25" disk, 2.5 Kg **195.00**
HOS-8937-2 (Needs Sublicense, p. 57), soft-sectored 5.25" disk, 2.5 Kg **195.00**
HOS-8947-2 (Needs Sublicense, p 57), 8" disk for H-47, 2.5 Kg **195.00**
HOS-8967-2 (Needs Sublicense, p. 57), 8" disk for Z-67, 2.5 Kg **195.00**

Modular UCSD P-System with Pascal, Version II

- Easy-to-use system responds quickly to changing needs
- Runs on any microcomputer with a resident interpreter

A complete environment for program development and execution: Includes a Pascal compiler to produce universal P-code, an efficient P-code interpreter, screen-oriented and character-oriented editors for programs and text, a filer for rapid file manipulation, a macro-assembler which produces code to be linked with Pascal programs, and a system library of frequently-used utilities. Modular structure allows division of large tasks into smaller, easier tasks. Support, updates available from Softech Microsystems, San Diego, CA. Requires H-8/H/19, H-11A/H-19 or H/Z-89 (as listed below) with 48K RAM (64K recommended) and two disk drives (HOS-817-3 requires, supports only two hard-sectored 5.25" drives).

HOS-817-3, hard-sectored 5.25" disk for H-8/H-19 and H/Z-89, 4 Kg **380.00**
HOS-1127-3, soft-sectored 8" disk for H-11A/H-19/H-27, 4 Kg **380.00**

Peachtree business software includes CP/M with Microsoft BASIC (where needed), facilities to backup disks and sample data for practicing. They require an H/Z-89 with 64K RAM, an H/Z-37, H/Z-47 or Z-67 Disk System and a basic knowledge of accounting and computers. For a smooth transition, consultation with an accountant or data processing professional may be required.

General Ledger simplifies accounting functions

- Keeps records; writes balance sheet/income statement
- Provides comparative (current vs. year-ago) financial data

Maintains your financial history: Describes what has happened during a given period. Fully linked to other Peachtree business systems.
HRS-837-1 (Requires Sublicense Grants, p. 57), on soft-sectored, double-density, double-sided 5.25" disk, Shpg. wt. 2 Kg **495.00**
HRS-847-1 (Requires Sublicense Grant, p. 57), on soft-sectored 8" disk for H/Z-47 Floppy Disk System, Shpg. wt. 2.5 Kg **495.00**

Automated Accounts Receivable System

- Complete invoicing and monthly statement generating system
- Tracks current and aged accounts receivable

HRS-837-2 (Requires Sublicense Grant, p. 57), on soft-sectored, double-density, double-sided 5.25" disk, Shpg. wt. 1.5 Kg **495.00**
HRS-847-2 (Requires Sublicense Grant, p. 57), on soft-sectored 8" disk for H/Z Floppy Disk System, Shpg. wt. 2 Kg **495.00**

Compatible Accounts Payable System

- Keeps track of both current and aged accounts payable
- Maintains separate records for each vendor

HRS-837-3 (Requires Sublicense Grant, p. 57), on soft-sectored, double-density, double-sided 5.25" disk, Shpg. wt. 2 Kg **495.00**
HRS-847-3 (Requires Sublicence Grant, p 57), on soft-sectored 8" disk for H/Z-47 Floppy Disk System, Shpg. wt. 1 Kg **495.00**

OPERATING SYSTEMS

HDOS has many functions of larger systems

- Sophisticated system controls your H-8 or H/Z-89
- Designed for efficient use of memory and disk space

Provides complete operating environment: The Heath Disk Operating System, Ver. 2.0, allows program writing, editing and storage – with assembly and checkout facilities. Features Extended Benton Harbor BASIC (Ver. 6.0) and ASM 8080 Assembly Language. 17 versatile commands list content, manipulate disks and files; run programs, select device driver options, display status reports and more. Facilities test disk drives and media; initialize disks and generate system images onto disks; allow you to debug programs and edit text. Supports all disk systems except Z-67. HDOS requires an H-8/H-19 or H/Z-89 computer system with a minimum of 48K bytes of RAM and one disk drive. Two drives are highly recommended, and may be required to use some other software with HDOS.

HOS-817-1, on hard-sectored 5.25" disk, Shpg. wt. 5 Kg **195.00**
HOS-847-1, on soft-sectored 8" disk, Shpg. wt. 2.5 Kg **195.00**

Useful H-8/H-88 Cassette Operating Software

- Helps form a solid base for future computer programming
- On audio cassettes, in convenient 1200 baud form

Convenience features make this system easier to use than others: Includes Extended Benton Harbor BASIC Language (Version 6.0), HASL-8 Assembly Language (a two-pass absolute 8080 assembler), TED-8 Text Editor, BUG-8 Console Debugger. Features automatic command completion, dynamic syntax checking and a special user configuration feature.

Min. hardware, software requirements: H-8 or H-88 Computer with 16K bytes of RAM, cassette interface (see below) and ECP-3801A (page 68)
H-8-18, for H-8/H-8-5/ECP-3801A systems, Shpg. wt. 5 Kg **40.00**
H-88-18, for H-88/H-88-5/ECP-3801A systems, Shpg. wt. 2.5 Kg **40.00**

BUSINESS SOFTWARE

Inventory Management for up-to-date information

- Provides better control of merchandise on hand

HRS-837-5 (Requires Sublicense Grant, p. 57), on soft-sectored, double-density, double-sided 5.25" disk to handle approx. 4,000 items, 1.5 Kg **495.00**
HRS-847-5 (Requires Sublicense Grant, p. 57), on soft-sectored 8" disk for use with H/Z-47 Disk System to handle approx. 5,800 items, 2.5 Kg **495.00**

Full-featured Peachtree Sales Invoicing System

- Check credit limits, stock levels before printing invoice

HRS-837-6 (Requires Sublicense Grant, p. 57), on soft-sectored, double-density, double-sided 5.25" disk, Shpg. wt. 1.5 Kg **350.00**
HRS-847-6 (Requires Sublicense Grant, p. 57), on soft-sectored 8" disk for H/Z-47 Floppy Disk System, Shpg. wt. 2 Kg **350.00**

Property Management for multiple properties

- Versatile system helps track properties, leases, renters

HRS-837-7 (Requires Sublicense Grant, p. 57), on soft-sectored, double-density, double-sided 5.25" disk, Shpg. wt. 2 Kg **1195.00**
HRS-847-7 (Requires Sublicence Grant, p 57), on soft-sectored 8" disk for H/Z-47 Floppy Disk System, Shpg. wt. 2 Kg **1195.00**

Multiple General Ledger System for CPAs and others

- Keeps unlimited number of general ledgers (up to 3/disk)

HRS-837-8 (Requires Sublicense Grant, p. 57), on soft-sectored, double-sided, double-density 5.25" disk, Shpg. wt. 5 Kg **1195.00**
HRS-847-8 (Requires Sublicence Grant, p 57), on soft-sectored 8" disk for H/Z-47 Floppy Disk System, Shpg. wt. 2.5 Kg **1195.00**

PROGRAMMING LANGUAGES

Available on both hard- and soft-sectored disks, these languages let you write microcomputer programs with surprising ease. And each program includes famous Heath/Zenith support — at your Heathkit Electronic center, by telephone or by mail.

Popular, powerful Microsoft BASIC Interpreter

- One of the most versatile general-purpose languages for micros

Scores of practical utility and applications programs available: MBASIC features an IF-THEN-ELSE control structure, which provides highly-structured programming capabilities. Also has direct access to CPU ports and memory locations, string and numeric constants, double-precision floating point number and double precision math, the ability to perform algebraic and trigonometric functions, powerful string processing functions and extensive program editing facilities.

All models require an H-8/H-19 or H/Z-89 system with 48K RAM, one disk drive, HDOS or CP/M (as indicated below) and the Sublicense Grant on page 57.
H-8-21, Ver. 4.82 on hard-sectored 5.25" disk for HDOS, 2 Kg **195.00**
HMS-817-1, Ver. 5.21 on hard-sectored 5.25" disk for CP/M, 2.5 Kg **230.00**
HMS-837-1, Ver. 5.21 on soft sectored 5.25" disk for CP/M, 4 Kg **230.00**
HMS-847-2, Ver. 5.21 on soft-sectored 8" disk for CP/M, 2.5 Kg **230.00**

Microsoft FORTRAN for science and engineering

- Comparable to FORTRAN compilers used on large mainframes, minis

Write and execute powerful scientific and engineering programs: This enhanced programming system includes all features of ANSI FORTRAN X3.9-1966, except for the COMPLEX data type. Has routines for 32- and 64-bit floating point math, MACRO-80 Assembler, LINK-80 Editor, CREF Cross-Reference Generator, LIB-80 Library Manager and two libraries (one with single- and double-precision scientific functions, the other with FORTRAN utilities).

All models below require an H-8/H-19 or H/Z-89 system with 48K RAM, two disk drives, HDOS or CP/M (as indicated below) and the Sublicense Grant on page 57.
H-8-20, Ver. 3.35 on hard-sectored 5.25" disk for HDOS, 2 Kg **195.00**
HMS-817-2, Ver. 3.4 on hard-sectored 5.25" disk for CP/M, 2.5 Kg **250.00**
HMS-837-2, Ver. 3.4 on soft-sectored 5.25" disk for CP/M, 2 Kg **250.00**
HMS-847-2, Ver. 3.4 on soft-sectored 8" disk for CP/M, 2.5 Kg **250.00**

MBASIC Compiler speeds general programming

All models below require an H-8/H-19 or H/Z-89 system with 48K RAM, two disk drives, HDOS or CP/M (as indicated below) and the Sublicense Grant on page 57.
HMS-817-41, Ver. 5.23 on hard-sectored 5.25" disk for HDOS, 2.5 Kg **325.00**
HMS-837-41, Ver. 5.23 on soft-sectored 5.25" disk for HDOS, 2.5 Kg **325.00**
HMS-847-41, Ver. 5.23 on soft-sectored 8" disk for HDOS, 2.5 Kg **325.00**
HMS-817-4, Ver. 5.23 on hard-sectored 5.25" disk for CP/M, 2 Kg **325.00**
HMS-837-4, Ver. 5.23 on soft-sectored 5.25" disk for CP/M, 2 Kg **325.00**
HMS-847-4, Ver. 5.23 on soft-sectored 8" disk for CP/M, 2.5 Kg **325.00**

C BASIC gives you more programming flexibility

Min. hardware and software requirements: All models below require an H-8/H-19 or H/Z-89 system with 48K bytes of RAM, one disk drive and CP/M.

HCM-817-1, Ver. 2.0 on hard-sectored 5.25" disk for CP/M, 1 Kg **150.00**
HCM-837-1, Ver. 2.0 on soft-sectored 5.25" disk for CP/M, 1 Kg **150.00**
HCM-847-1, Ver. 2.0 on soft-sectored 8" disk for CP/M, 1 Kg **150.00**

Program faster with MACRO-80 Assembly Language

All models below require an H-8/H-19 or H/Z-89 system with 48K RAM, one disk drive (two drives recommended), HDOS or CP/M and the Sublicense Grant on p. 57.
HMS-817-51, on hard-sectored 5.25" disk for HDOS, 1 Kg **90.00**
HMS-837-51, on soft-sectored 5.25" disk for HDOS, 2 Kg **90.00**
HMS-847-51, on soft-sectored 8" disk for HDOS, 2 Kg **90.00**
HMS-817-52, on hard-sectored 5.25" disk for CP/M, 1 Kg **90.00**
HMS-837-52, on soft-sectored 5.25" disk for CP/M, 1.5 Kg **90.00**
HMS-847-52, on soft-sectored 8" disk for CP/M, 2 Kg **90.00**

Run powerful, business-oriented COBOL-80

All models below require H-8/H-19 or H/Z-89 with 48K RAM, two disk drives, HDOS or CP/M and the Sublicense Grant on page 57. 64K RAM and the H/Z-37 or Z-67 Disk Systems recommended for applications involving large disk files.
HMS-817-31, Ver. 4.0 on hard-sectored 5.25" disk for HDOS, 2 Kg **495.00**
HMS-837-31, Ver. 4.0 on soft-sectored 5.25" disk for HDOS, 2 Kg **495.00**
HMS-847-31, Ver. 4.0 on soft-sectored 8" disk for HDOS, 2 Kg **495.00**
HMS-817-3, Ver. 4.0 on hard-sectored 5.25" disk for CP/M, 2.5 Kg **495.00**
HMS-837-3, Ver. 4.0 on soft-sectored 5.25" disk for CP/M, 2 kg **495.00**
HMS-847-3, Ver. 4.0 on soft-sectored 8" disk for CP/M, 2.5 Kg **495.00**

COMMUNICATIONS PROGRAMS

Using these programs, your Heath/Zenith computer can communicate with the outside world. One program lets your H/Z-89 emulate certain IBM terminals. CPS gives you access to CompuServe's time-sharing MicroNet mainframe. Use the RTTY Communications Processor to communicate with other Hams via computer.

Remote Batch Terminal Emulator Software to communicate with IBM, other mainframes

- Allows your H/Z-89 microcomputer to emulate IBM 3780, 2780, 3741 and 2770 terminals

Use in remote job entry, down-line loading and distributed processing network applications: The Remote Batch Terminal Emulator (RBTE) Program allows the H/Z-89 microcomputer to emulate various IBM terminals (the IBM 3780, IBM 2780, IBM 3741 and IBM 2770) — so that your microcomputer can communicate with most major mainframe computers, using IBM- and industry-standard binary synchronous protocol. Also allows user-written terminal emulation.

Features: RBTE runs unattended — no operator interaction is necessary, once the program has been initialized. Both binary and ASCII data can be transmitted or received. RBTE performs its own on-line diagnosis of communication problems. An off-line diagnostic verifies the operation of the serial port when connected to a modem in loop-back test mode.

Minimum hardware requirements: The Remote Terminal Batch Emulator (RBTE) Software Program requires a Heath H-89 or Zenith Data Systems Z-89 microcomputer system equipped with at least 48K bytes of Random Access Memory, one or more disk drives and the Z-89-11 Multi-Mode I/O Board (see page 52).
HWI-8917-1, on hard-sectored 5.25" disk, Shpg. wt. 2 Kg **1095.00**
HWI-8947-1, on soft-sectored 8" disk, Shpg. wt. 2 Kg **1095.00**

Computerized Phone System (CPS) gives your microcomputer access to much more information

- Allows data transfer between computer and the time-sharing mainframe computers of MicroNet and the Source

Experience time-sharing: After you write a computer program, the Computerized Phone System (CPS) allows you to store that program on either the CompuServe MicroNet or Source time-sharing systems. Run your own programs, access other computers via modem and access programs in the MicroNet or Source libraries. Features automatic log-in, screen elapsed time clock and programmable keys for functions like mail check. Compatible with SF-8512 HDOS-to-CP/M (and vice versa) File Converter — for translation of file onto compatible media.

SF-9503, on hard-sectored 5.25" disk for HDOS and CP/M, 1 Kg **49.95**
SFS-9103, on soft-sectored 5.25" disk for CP/M, 1 Kg **49.95**

RTTY Communications Processor Software adds more fun to your Ham Radio Hobby

- Use your Heath/Zenith computer to communicate with other Hams
- Send, receive data at same time with split-screen feature

High-technology meets Amateur Radio: Use your computer to send and receive messages with amateur radio operators all over the world. Split-screen display allows copying of incoming messages, editing outgoing messages at the same time. Status board shows time, CW identification and your choice of ASCII or Baudot operation. Requires H-8/H-19 or H/Z-89 with 48K RAM, one disk drive and HDOS.

SF-9006, on hard-sectored 5.25" disk for HDOS, 1 Kg **149.95**

Our broad line of utility tools extends the capabilities of your Heath/Zenith computer in many different ways. Each program includes a manual with complete documentation, and a master copy of the program. And you get famous Heath/Zenith support and consultation with each purchase.

PEARL Level 3 generates software programs to solve your applications problems

- You define the application, PEARL generates the solution
- Can generate both simple and complex applications programs

Greatly reduces program-writing time: Interactive, menu-driven system is designed for most computer owners. Use it to generate programs that fit your unique needs. Requires H-8/H-19 or H/Z-89 system with 64K RAM, two high-capacity disk drives (H/Z-37 or H/Z-47), CP/M and C BASIC.

HCP-837-1, on soft-sectored 5.25" floppy disk, Shpg. wt. 2 Kg 795.00
HCP-847-1, on soft-sectored 8" floppy disk, Shpg. wt. 2 Kg 795.00

WordMaster: tool for program development

Don't waste memory space: WordMaster Video Text Editor, Ver. 1.07, is 80% smaller than WordStar (w/o printer interface or formatting) — and much faster functions. Requires H-8/H-9 or H/Z-89 with 48K RAM, one disk drive and CP/M Operating System.

HMP-817-5, on hard-sectored 5.25" floppy disk, Shpg. wt. 2 Kg 150.00
HMP-837-5, on soft-sectored 5.25" floppy disk, Shpg. wt. 2 Kg 150.00
HMP-847-5, on soft-sectored 8" floppy disk, Shpg. wt. 2 Kg 150.00

These selected Heath/Zenith software products add new capabilities to the CP/M Operating System. They include full documentation, so you can take advantage of those capabilities right away. They also include famous Heath/Zenith support — by mail, by phone or at your Heathkit Electronic Center.

Transform your computer into a versatile electronic spreadsheet with SuperCalc

- Helps planners make better use of time and energy
- Easy-to-read, easy-to-use spreadsheet format

Pencils, paper and a calculator have been replaced: Use SuperCalc to help answer those "what if" and "now what" questions. More versatile than many similar packages, you can examine and alter numbers and text within a 63-column by 254-row matrix. Requires H-8/H-19 or H/Z-89 with 48K RAM, one disk drive and CP/M. If printouts are desired, a printer is also required.

HSC-817-1, on hard-sectored 5.25" floppy disk, Shpg. wt. 2 Kg 295.00
HSC-837-1, on soft-sectored 5.25" floppy disk, Shpg. wt. 2 Kg 295.00
HSC-847-1, on soft-sectored 8" floppy disk, Shpg. wt. 2 Kg 295.00

Condor Relational Data Base Management System has capabilities usually found on larger systems

- Develop data bases without a programmer's assistance
- Use for inventory, accounting, personnel, other functions

Now even the "first-time" computer user can create affordable, productive programs — quickly: Features exceptional speed. Has self-contained English-type language; no host language required. Requires H-8/H-8-6/H-19 or H/Z-89 with 64K RAM, two high-capacity disk drives, CP/M and a printer.

HCD-8937-1, on soft-sectored, double-density, double-sided 5.25" floppy disk (requires H/Z-37 Floppy Disk System), Shpg. wt. 2 Kg 1095.00
HCD-8947-1, on soft-sectored 8" disk, Shpg. wt. 2 Kg 1095.00

Source listings for selected Heath/Zenith software

Complete listings for H-8-18 and H-88-18 Cassette Operating Software: Includes these source listings: H-8-52, H-8-53, H-8-54 and H-8-60. This package would cost $120.00 if purchased separately.

HKS-50, Shpg. wt. 4 Kg 85.00

Source listing for Heath Disk Operating System (HDOS), Version 2.0: Has H-8-51 listing for H-17 (below), all other utilities are device drivers. Purchasers eligible for updates when new releases are availble (at nominal charge).

HOS-1-SL, Shpg. wt. 5 Kg 150.00

UTILITY PROGRAMS

Enter, retrieve, update data with DataStar

Power and facilities usually found only on large key-to-disk systems: Form and file generation are simplified; high-volume operations are allowed. Files compatible with Mail/Merge and SuperSort; compatible with any CP/M-supported language; can be used as data entry portion of your applications programs — usually without modifications. Requires H-8/H-19 or H/Z-89 with 48K RAM, one disk drive and CP/M. If printouts are desired, a printer is required.

HMP-817-4, on hard-sectored 5.25" floppy disk, Shpg. wt. 1 Kg 375.00
HMP-837-4, on soft-sectored 5.25" floppy disk, Shpg. wt. 2 Kg 375.00
HMP-847-4, on soft-sectored 8" floppy disk, Shpg. wt. 1 Kg 375.00

Make sorting faster, easier with SuperSort

Makes sorting so simple, it's in a class by itself: SuperSort can sort and merge up to 32 input files in a single file — at the fast rate of 560 records per minute. Accepts nearly any kind of record format. Specify up to 32 different sorting criteria. Three output options. Can work with BASIC, Assembly, Microsoft FORTRAN and Microsoft COBOL programs — as well as with text editors. Requires H-8/H-19 or H/Z-89 with 48K RAM, one disk drive and CP/M.

HMP-817-1, on hard-sectored 5.25" floppy disk, Shpg. wt. 2 Kg 260.00
HMP-837-1, on soft-sectored 5.25" floppy disk, Shpg. wt. 2 Kg 260.00
HMP-847-1, on soft-sectored 8" floppy disk, Shpg. wt. 2 Kg 260.00

UTILITY/APPLICATIONS PROGRAMS

Advanced MAC-Assembler is easy to use

- Has Intel-compatible definitions
- Generates SID-compatible symbol table file for debugging

Designed for sophisticated Assembly Language programmers: Compatible with CP/M's ASM Assembly Language. Has additional conditional operators, other features. Requires H-8/H-19 or H/Z-89 with 48K RAM, one disk drive, CP/M.

HDR-817-1, on hard-sectored 5.25" floppy disk, Shpg. wt. 1 Kg 110.00
HDR-837-1, on soft-sectored 5.25" floppy disk, Shpg. wt. 1 Kg 110.00
HDR-847-1, on soft-sectored 8" disk, Shpg. wt. 1 Kg 110.00

DESPOOL provides simultaneous printer operation

- Allows you to perform two tasks simultaneously

Wait no more: DESPOOL maximizes your computer system's efficiency. Requires H-8/H-19 or H/Z-89 with 48K RAM, one disk drive and CP/M.

HDR-817-3, on hard-sectored 5.25" floppy disk, Shpg. wt. 1 Kg 65.00
HDR-837-3, on soft-sectored 5.25" floppy disk, Shpg. wt. 2 Kg 65.00
HDR-847-3, on soft-sectored 8" floppy disk, Shpg. wt. 1 Kg 65.00

Upgrade the CP/M DDT Debugger with SID/ZSID

- Get both 8080-compatible SID and Z-80-compatible ZSID in one package — save substantially over separate prices

Two programs in one: Many advanced debugging features. Functional in DDT-type mode w/o symbol file. Requires H-8/H-19 or H/Z-89 with 48K RAM, one disk drive, CP/M and MAC, LINK-80 or D.R. Linkage Editor.

HDR-817-2, on hard-sectored 5.25" floppy disk, Shpg. wt. 1 Kg 165.00
HDR-837-2, on soft-sectored 5.25" floppy disk, Shpg. wt. 2 Kg 165.00
HDR-847-2, on soft-sectored 8" floppy disk, Shpg. wt. 1 Kg 165.00

H-8-51, Source listing for ROM of H-17 Disk System, 1 Kg 30.00
H-19-1, Source listing for ROM of H-19 Video Terminal, 1 Kg 30.00
H-8-60, Source listing for Cassette Version of Extended Benton Harbor BASIC Language, Shpg. wt. 1 Kg 30.00
H-8-54, Source listing for Cassette Assembler, 1 Kg 30.00
H-8-53, Source listing for Cassette Text Editor, 1 Kg 30.00
H-8-52, Source listing for Cassette Console Debugger, 1 Kg 30.00

NOTE: All of these source listings are copyrighted. Reproduction of these listings is expressly prohibited. Updates of source listing for HDOS are available for a nominal charge, as described at above left.

WORD PROCESSING

WordStar Word Processing Software features exceptional power, CP/M compatibility

A CP/M-compatible, screen-oriented word processor with integrated printing capabilities: Text entry, alteration and formatting are done on-screen. Has powerful editing commands, flexible find/replace commands. Hyphen-help stops when a hyphen is necessary, and lets you choose the hyphenation point. Automatic page numbering, print enhancements (underlining, boldfacing, subscripts, superscripts, 1/120" horizontal spacing and 1/48" vertical spacing) and several other options are supported on capable printers). Print spooling (requires 64K RAM) allows you to print one file while working on a second file.

WordStar's unique "Help" system, with four levels of user-selectable menus, eliminates the need to refer to a manual. Includes set-up/operating manual and master disk. Requires H-8/H-19 or H/Z-89 system with 48K RAM, two disk drives, a printer and CP/M. We recommend the WH-54 Letter-Quality Printer on page 54.

HMP-817-2, on hard-sectored 5.25" disk, Shpg. wt. 1 Kg **495.00**
HMP-837-2, on soft-sectored 5.25" disk, Shpg. wt. 2 Kg **495.00**
HMP-847-2, on soft-sectored 8" disk, Shpg. wt. 1 Kg **495.00**

Add mailing list, file merging to WordStar

By adding MailMerge to WordStar, you can create personalized form letters – or store and print an entire list of mailing labels: MailMerge features merging of data from one file to another, automatic chained printing of several files, and printing of "nested" files. Requires H-8/H-19 or H/Z-89 with 48K RAM, two disk drives, CP/M, WordStar and a printer (we recommend the WH-54 on p. 54).

HMP-817-3, on hard-sectored 5.25" disk, Shpg. wt. 2 Kg **180.00**
HMP-837-3, on soft-sectored 5.25" disk, Shpg. wt. 2 Kg **180.00**
HMP-847-3, on soft-sectored 8" disk, Shpg. wt. 2 Kg **180.00**

Magic Wand Word Processing Software combines ease of use, versatility and power

More powerful than Zenith Electronic Typing, has sample learning exercises: Magic Wand features EDIT and PRINT modes. EDIT features full scrolling, insertion by character or full insertion, full deletion, search/replace commands, block moves and copying of blocks, and the ability to include all or part of any pure ASCII file on disk into the text you're editing.

PRINT features printing in background (print spooling) to let you print one file while working on another, underscoring, kerning/strikeover, boldfacing, subscripting and superscripting, automatic hyphenation, proportional spacing and mail list merging, 1/120"horizontal spacing and 1/48"vertical spacing (on capable printers). Requires H-8/H-19 or H/Z-89 with 48K RAM, one disk drive, CP/M and a printer (we recommend WH-54, p. 54).

HRS-817-9, on hard-sectored 5.25" disk, 1.5 Kg **380.00**
HRS-837-9, on soft-sectored 5.25" disk, 2 Kg **380.00**
HRS-847-9, on soft-sectored 8" disk, 1.5 Kg **380.00**

Zenith Electronic Typing — our low-cost, easy-to-use word processing software system

Control the cost of paperwork: Zenith Electronic Typing makes word processing practical for both single-secretary offices and departmentalized secretarial staffs. A self-instruction course (included with the system) shows you how.

Features include upper/lower case video display; creation, addition or revision on up to three 5.25" disk drives; scrolling and two search modes; the ability to copy or move blocks of copy; automatic realignment to save hours of retyping; many other print enhancements; and the ability to print a clean copy of the document on a separate printer (not included) at up to 450 words per minute. Requires H-8/H-19 or H/Z-89 with 48K RAM, one disk drive and a printer. Not for Z-90, Z-37, Z-47 or Z-67. Any Heath/Zenith-offered printer will work; we recommended the WH-54 on page 54.

H-8-40, on hard-sectored 5.25" disk, Shpg. wt. 3 Kg **295.00**

NEW! Typing Tutor: Helps you learn fast, efficient touch typing H-8/H-19 or H/Z-89 with 48K RAM, one disk drive.
SF-9018, on hard-sectored 5.25" disk for HDOS, 1 Kg 49.95

NEW! Vocabulary Builder: Library helps students learn English words. Needs H-8/H-19 or H/Z-89 with 48K RAM, one disk drive.
SF-9019, on hard-sectored 5.25" disk for HDOS, 1 Kg 49.95

NEW! U.S. President's Game: Learn about the men who have led the U.S. Ready to run, has HDOS. Needs H-8/H-19 or H/Z-89 with 48K RAM, one disk drive.
SF-9020, on hard-sectored 5.25" disk for HDOS, 1 Kg 49.95

Full Screen Editor: Uses H-19 or H/Z-89 CRT as window into file. Type changes anywhere on screen; use search, block move, scroll functions. Requires H-8/H-19 or H/Z-89 with 48K RAM, one disk drive and either HDOS or CP/M.
SF-9200, on hard-sectored 5.25" disk for HDOS or CP/M, 1 Kg 64.95

Text Formatter: Performs errorless fill and justification (straight right margin) functions on editor-prepared text. Requires H-8/H-19 or H/Z-89 with 48K RAM, one disk drive and HDOS (as listed below).
SF-9001, on hard-sectored 5.25" disk for HDOS, 1 Kg 69.95
SF-9101, on hard-sectored 5.25" disk for CP/M, 1 Kg 69.95

General Ledger II: Keeps your books up-to-date. Features custom chart of accounts, comprehensive printouts, automatic entry checking and more. Requires H-8/H-19 or H/Z-89 with 48K RAM, two disk drives, HDOS or CP/M (as listed below) and Microsoft BASIC Interpreter. (p. 59).
SF-9004, on hard-sectored 5.25" disk for HDOS, 1 Kg 149.95
SF-9104, on hard-sectored 5.25" disk for CP/M, 1 Kg 149.95
SFS-9104, on soft-sectored 5.25" disk for CP/M, 1 Kg 149.95
595-2500, General Ledger Software Manual (Purchase price refunded when complete General Ledge II System is purchased), 1 Kg 18.00

Small Business Inventory Package: Helps facilitate analysis of a business' inventory. Can provide up to 12 items of information on each part. Requires H-8 or H/Z-89 with 48K RAM, one disk drive, HDOS or CP/M (as listed below) and Microsoft BASIC Interpreter (p. 59).
SF-9005, on hard-sectored 5.25" disk for HDOS, 1 Kg 99.95
SF-9105, on hard-sectored 5.25" disk for CP/M, 1 Kg 99.95
SFS-9105, on soft-sectored 5.25" disk for CP/M, 1 Kg 99.95

Mailpro Package: For use as mailing list system—though most any information can be stored and retrieved. Random access files. Sort and retrieve on any field. Has error trapping routines. Requires H-8/H-19 or H/Z-89 with 48K RAM, one disk drive, HDOS or CP/M and Microsoft BASIC Interpreter (p. 59)
SF-9009, on hard-sectored 5.25" disk for HDOS, 1 Kg 49.95
NEW! SF-9109, on hard-sectored 5.25" disk for CP/M, 1 Kg 49.95

Roots-89 Ancestral Genealogy Software: Helps track your roots. Stores thousands of facts about your family. Computes relationships, shows important anniversaries. Includes 100-page course in genealogy. Requires H-8/H-19 or H/Z-89 with 48K RAM, one disk drive and HDOS or CP/M (as listed below).
SF-9008, on hard-sectored 5.25" disk for HDOS, 1 Kg 174.95
NEW! SF-9108, on hard-sectored 5.25" disk for CP/M, 1 Kg 174.95

HDOS-CP/M File Converter: Effectively doubles the information-handling ability of your computer. Transfer HDOS files to CP/M disks—and vice versa. Requires H-8/H-19 or H/Z-89 with 48K RAM, one disk drive, HDOS and CP/M.
SF-8512, on hard-sectored 5.25" disk for HDOS and CP/M, 1 Kg 39.95

Mychess Computer Chess Game: Provides hours of challenging competition. Consistently beats Sargon. Nine skill levels. Switch sides with computer at any time. Full black-and-white graphics. Requires H-8/H-19/HA-8-6 or H/Z-89 with 48K RAM, one disk drive and HDOS or CP/M (as listed below).
SF-9010, on hard-sectored 5.25" disl for HDOS, 1 Kg 49.95
SF-9110, on hard-sectored 5.25" disk for CP/M, 1 Kg 49.95

Air Traffic Controller Game: Tests your confidence and decision-making ability. Control traffic around your own airport. "Radar" screen tracks planes. Safety rules, operator intelligence ensure a safe, thrilling flight. Requires H-8/H-19 or H/Z-89 with 48K RAM, one disk drive and HDOS or CP/M (as listed below).
SF-9014, on hard-sectored 5.25" disk for HDOS, 1 Kg 39.95
SF-9114, on hard-sectored 5.25" disk for CP/M, 1 Kg 39.95

Get top performance from your system with these supplies, accessories

NEW! Paper Tractor: Inexpensively turns your tractor feed printer into a friction feed printing system. Letter or legal size bond, parchment, onionskin, vellum, NCR or manuscript paper — even letterhead — slides into the sleeve (which is pre-punched to run through most any printer's tractor feed mechanism). No installation or modifications required.
HCA-17, Shpg. wt. 1 Kg 19.95

NEW! Plastic 5.25" Floppy Disk Cabinet: This attractive accessory protects your 5.25" floppy disks from airborne contaminants. Features smoked glass cover. Each cabinet holds up to 50 disks. Has five dividers. 6.5" H x 6.75" W x 8.25" D.
HCA-15, Shpg. wt. 1 Kg 34.95

NEW! Plastic 8" Floppy Disk Storage Cabinet: Protects your 8" floppy disks from airborne contaminants. Features smoked glass cover. Each cabinet holds up to 50 disks. 5 dividers. 9" H x 9.56" W x 10.5" D.
HCA-18, Shpg. wt. 2.5 Kg 49.95

Pre-wired, 10'-long RS-232 Cables: Each cable connects pins 1-8 and 20.
HCA-10, Male to Male Cable, Shpg. wt. 1 Kg 29.95
HCA-11, Male to Female Cable, Shpg. wt. 1 Kg 29.95
HCA-12, Female to Female Cable, Shpg. wt. 1 Kg 29.95

NEW! Pre-wired, 10'-long special-applciation Connecting Cables:
HCA-13, Votrax Cable (connects computer to WH-12 Type-N-Talk Speech Synthesizer), Shpg. wt. 1 Kg 29.95
HCA-14 Parallel Cable (for use with Z-89-11 Multi-Mode I/O Board to connect computer/terminal to MX-80 printer), 1 Kg 39.95

Large selection of durable plastic Diablo printwheels:
HCS-20, Courrier 10 (Diablo 38100), Pica with slashed zero, 1 Kg 12.95
HCS-21, Courrier 72 (Diablo 38107), Pica with unslashed zero, 1 Kg 12.95
HCS-22, Elite 12 (Diablo 38102), Elite with unslashed zero. 1 Kg 12.95
HCS-23, General Scientific Font with Greek letters, susperscripts and math symbols (Diablo 38141), 1 Kg 12.95
HCS-24, APL-10 Computer Language Font (Diablo 38150), 1 Kg 12.95
HCS-25, ANSI Standard OCR Type A Font (Diablo 38144), 1 Kg 12.95
HCS-26, Prestige Elite Legal 12A Font with legal symbols (including ©, ® and TM) (Diablo 38105), Shpg. wt 1 Kg 12.95
HCS-27, Courrier Legal 10 (Pica w/legal symbols) Diablo 38104), 1 Kg .. 12.95

High-quality, long-lasting ribbons for printers:
Cloth Ribbons for Diablo Letter-Quality Daisy Wheel Printers.
HCS-50, Shpg. wt. 1 Kg .... Package of three, 29.95
Plug-in, no-mess Film Ribbon Cartridges for Diablo Daisy Wheel Printers.
HCS-51, Shpg. wt. 1 Kg .... Package of three, 29.95

Ribbons for H/WH-14 Dot Matrix Line Printer. Also fits ASR-33 printers.
HCS-52, Shpg. wt. 1 Kg .... Package of three, 12.95
Ribbons for WH-24 (TI 810) and H-36 (LA-36) Dot Matrix Line Printers.
HCS-53, Shpg. wt. 1 Kg .... Package of three, 34.95
Plug-in Ribbon Cartridges for WH-34 DEC Writer Dot Matrix Line Printer.
HCS-54, Shpg. wt. 1 Kg .... Package of three, 46.95
Plug-in, no mess Ribbon Cartridge for MX-80 Dot Matrix Line Printer.
HCS-55, Shpg. wt. 1 Kg 23.95
Plug-in, no mess Ribbon Cartridges for H/Z-25 Dot Matrix Line Printer.
HCS-56, Shpg. wt. 1.5 Kg .... Package of two, 39.95

Top-quality, competitively-priced paper for printers:
Premium 8.5" x 11" One-Part, Fan-Fold Paper. Continuous form, 2700 sheets. Edge-punched to fit tractor feed mechanisms.
HCS-1, Shpg. wt. 13 Kg 59.95
Standard 8.5" x 11" One-Part, Fan-Fold Paper. 3200 sheets. Edge-punched.
HCS-2, Shpg. wt. 14 Kg 59.95
Standard 14.875" x 11" One-Part, Fan-Fold Paper. Continuous form, 3200 sheets. For all Heath/Zenith printers except H/WH-14 and MX-80. Edge-punched.
H-36-1 Shpg. wt. 22 Kg 44.95

Reliable, high capacity 5.25" and 8" Floppy Disks:
Hard-sectored, single-sided 5.25" Floppy Disks. Use with H-17-1 Disk Drives, H-88-1 Disk Controller. Each disk stores up to 100K bytes of data.
HCS-70, Shpg. wt. 1 Kg .... Package of ten, 54.95
Soft-sectored, single-sided, double-density, 48 tpi 5.25" Floppy Disks. Use with H-17-1 or H-17-4 Drive. Requires Z-89-37. 160K bytes per disk.
HCS-66, Shpg. wt. 1 Kg .... Packge of ten, 64.95
Soft-sectored, double-sided, double density, 96 tpi 5.25" Floppy Disks. Require H-17-4 Drive and Z-89-37 Controller. 640K bytes per disk.
HCS-68, Shpg. wt. 1 Kg .... Package of ten, 84.95
Soft-sectored, single-density, single sided 8" Floppy Disks. Use with H/WH-27, H/Z-47, Z-67 and other disk systems. Each disk stores up to 250K bytes of data on 77 tracks, in IBM 3740 format.
HCS-69, Shpg. wt. 1 Kg .... Package of ten, 79.95
Soft-sectored, double density, single-sided 8" Floppy Disks. Use with H/Z-47, Z-67 and other disk systems. Each disk stores up to 500K bytes of data.
HCS-64, Shpg. wt. 1 Kg .... Package of ten, 99.95
Soft-sectored, double-density, double-sided 8" Floppy Disks. Use with H/Z-47, Z-67 and other disk systems. Each disk stores up to 1 megabyte of data.
HCS-65, Shpg. wt. 1 Kg .... Package of ten, 99.95

HUG makes your Heath/Zenith computer even more powerful with its 700-program software library

Get more from your Heath/Zenith computer: A membership in HUG allows you to get the most from your computer. With HUG's 700-program software library, you'll have access to many useful utility and applications programs. With the REMark Magazine subscription, you'll be among the first to learn about Heath/Zenith technological advances. And REMark's interactive forum allows you to participatein an information exchange with other Heath/Zenith computer owners.

 Heath User's Group

- Gain access to over 700 software programs in the HUG Software Library
- Enjoy a one-year subscription to HUG's REMark magazine with your membership
- Participate with other Heath/Zenith owners in REMark's interactive forum

Some of the software programs available from HUG include:

- Memory test programs
- Many disks of CP/M programs
- HDOS-to-CP/M utility
- HDOS device drivers
- Time for HDOS
- Programs for printers
- Modem packages
- Disk dump and dup utilities
- Create-a-program
- File maintenance
- File cruncher
- Editors, text processors
- Sort, cross-reference utilities
- Fixed and floating pt. packages
- Assembly language routines
- Pilot language
- Stock and tax programs
- Home budget maintenance
- Checkbook programs
- Expense report
- Inventory
- Real estate programs
- Time management
- Mailing list
- Educational programs
- Basic letters
- Spelling words
- Vocabulary practice
- Music
- Weather forecasting
- Arithmetic practice
- Calculator
- Metric conversion
- Simultaneous equations
- Graphs
- Plotting
- Solar domes
- Electronic formulas

Latest Additions to the HUG Library

885-1107	HDOS DBMS in BH Basic:	Amateur Radio Logbook and TMS	$40.00
885-1108	HDOS DBMS in MBasic:	Telephone/Mail Info. System	$40.00
885-1109	HDOS DBMS:	Retriever (2 Disks)	$52.00
885-1110	HDOS DBMS:	Autofile	$40.00
885-1115	HDOS DBMS in MBasic:	Aircraft Navigation	$26.00
885-1111	HDOS:	MBasic Graphic Games	$26.00
885-1112	HDOS:	Graphic Games	$26.00
885-1113	HDOS:	Fast Action Games	$26.00
885-1114	HDOS:	Colour Raiders & Goop (HA-8-3)	$26.00
885-1115	HDOS DBMS in MBasic:	Aircraft Navigation	$26.00
885-1214	CP/M DBMS:	Amateur Radio Logbook	$40.00

This software is now available to all HUG members through your local Heathkit Electronic Centre and by mail order. HUG software is available only to HUG Members. When ordering by mail, please use the special order form provided to you by HUG. If purchasing in person at one of our Heathkit Electronic Centres, please present your HUG membership card.

NOT YET A MEMBER? — Drop into any Heathkit Electronic Centre and pick up an application form or send us a note asking that one be sent to you. HUG Membership applications are also included in all Heathkit computer products.

Chapter 13: Buying and Restoration Tips

Retrocomputing

Retrocomputing is the term now widely used for the use of older computer hardware and software. It has increasingly become a popular hobby where enthusiasts collect and restore old computer hardware and software, often for sentimental or nostalgic reasons. The scope includes restoring old computers as well as building replicas and software emulators.

The last few years have even seen some new commercial products offered branded with names like Commodore and Atari as well as entirely new retrocomputing platforms and new programs written such as games.

Many websites and forums exist that are devoted to specific Heathkit computers and can be a great source for exchanging information, finding software, and getting help with restoration and repair. See Appendix A and the bibliography for some of these.

Buying Tips

The surge in demand for old computers has meant that people have dug out old systems (if they weren't thrown out years ago) and put them on the market for sale.

The good news is that auction sites like eBay make it possible to buy just about any conceivable computer from the past. The bad news is that you need to be willing to outbid everyone else worldwide to get it.

Prices continue to go up. A system like an Apple II that was considered almost worthless twenty years ago can today sell for hundreds of dollars and in exceptional cases, thousands.

That said, bargains can still be found at garage sales and local auction sites. You just need to be willing to spend considerable time searching and waiting for what you are looking for to show up at the right price.

When evaluating items, my opinion is that the most important consideration is the cosmetic condition and whether it has issues that cannot be restored by simple cleaning and repairs such as major cracks or severe rust. Missing critical parts like components of the case, circuit boards, cables, power supplies, etc. will make it significantly harder to restore. Look for signs of water damage or burnt circuit boards and indications of major modifications.

Issues of less importance are whether it comes with the original manuals and software (these can usually be obtained from the internet), whether it is known to be working, or if it is missing commonly obtainable parts like resistors, capacitors, and memory chips.

Some units had unique parts like processors with factory ROMs or mechanical parts. In most cases, the only way to get replacements is from another unit. Sometimes it may be necessary to use parts from two or more units to produce one that is complete.

Restoration

The good news with Heathkits is you generally can find full documentation, including assembly instructions.

However, as these were kits, you can't assume they were originally built correctly or were even ever working correctly. It can pay to go through the entire assembly procedure in the manual and confirm all assembly steps were correctly followed. Some kits may have also had minor or major modifications done to them by users over the years. Parts may have been removed and cannibalized for use on other projects.

For the replacement of mechanical parts, 3D printing can sometimes be a solution. I have had success with 3D printing knobs, for example. Generally, you need to have a reference part (even if broken) to measure and make a 3D model. There are also molding techniques that can be used to duplicate small parts.

Unlike, say, vacuum tube radios from the 1940s, the components in computer hardware from the 1970s or later are still usually in good shape, for the most part. An exception can be electrolytic filter capacitors in power supplies that can potentially fail and may need to be replaced.

In most cases, no specialized tools or test equipment is needed. I would recommend buying a low-cost Digital Multimeter (DMM) for making basic electrical measurements and obtaining a good quality temperature-controlled soldering iron. Other tools needed would include pliers and screwdrivers of various types. More expensive equipment like an oscilloscope can be needed to troubleshoot complex issues, but only if you have the expertise to know how to use it and interpret the results.

Be aware of, and if necessary read up on, some basic electrical safety. Most computer equipment operates on low voltages, but high voltages are present in AC line-operated power supply circuitry. Computer monitors with cathode-ray tubes contain very high voltages when operating and have the potential for an implosion of broken glasses if mishandled, and require special safety precautions.

Use common sense. Avoid, whenever possible, working on equipment when powered on. Have a single easy to reach switch to cut off all power. Don't work when tired.

Don't be in a rush to turn on old equipment, as doing so could damage it. Before powering it up you should make a visual inspection for missing, broken, burnt components, wires, fuses, etc. and address anything that looks wrong. Do at least minimal cleaning to remove dust and dirt.

If the unit is AC line operated, test the power supply circuitry before fully powering up the unit, if feasible. Check the power supply voltages and watch (and smell) for any overheating or burning on the initial power up.

Take lots of pictures with a phone or digital camera before any disassembly or modifications are done so you can remember how it was originally put together.

Make detailed notes on issues observed and repairs or modifications made. Take your time and enjoy the process of restoration and troubleshooting any problems.

Where To Get Information

As mentioned, unlike most consumer electronics products, Heathkits have the advantage (at least for items offered as kits) of having full assembly manuals with parts lists and schematic diagrams and usually theory of operation and troubleshooting tips. You will want to obtain manuals for your equipment, which can often be found as free downloads or purchased as hard copies.

In most cases, Heathkit used parts that are still available and can be replaced with only basic soldering skills (unlike modern electronics that uses many surface mount technology components).

Media like floppy disks are still available from various sources, although some like 8-inch floppies or paper tape will be hard to find.

There are websites, forums, and groups dedicated to specific products like Heathkit H-8 or H-11 computers. See Appendix A for a few resources.

Final Thoughts

Collecting and restoring old computers can be fun, relaxing, and rewarding. It can also become addictive!

Once up and running, a vintage computer can continue to provide many hours of entertainment, especially if you write your own programs. You are only limited by your imagination and ability. I encourage you to share your experiences on online forums, social media, blog posts, and YouTube videos.

Good Luck!

(this page intentionally left blank)

Appendix A: References and Resources

Listed here are some general resources on Heathkit computers. Also see the items referenced in the text and listed in the bibliography.

Books

Heath Nostalgia, by Terry A. Perdue.
Paperback 1992, 124 pages. ISBN 978-0963762702
A book on the history of Heathkit that was written by someone who worked as a design engineer at Heath for 18 years. Out of print, but can be found on the used market, both in paperback as well as a CD-ROM version.

Collectible Microcomputers, by Michael Nadeau.
Paperback, 2002, 160 pages. ISBN 0-7643-1600-1
A comprehensive listing of vintage computer manufacturers, it has some coverage of Heathkit and Zenith models.

Heathkit Test Equipment Products, by Chuck Penson.
Paperback, 2014, 200 pages. ISBN 978-0-615-99133-7
While a book on test equipment[5], chapter 22 has some coverage of the Heathkit Analog Computers.

Websites, Forums, and Social Media

https://heathkit.garlanger.com
A site dedicated to preserving the history of the original Heathkit computers run by Mark Garlanger who owns a large amount of Heathkit-related equipment, documentation, and software.

https://www.theoldrobots.com
A website with resources on many robots. Has information and manual downloads for Heathkit robots.

https://www.robotworkshop.com
Has information and resources on robots, including some products and software for Heathkit HERO robots.

http://dunfield.classiccmp.org
Dave's Old Computers website. Has information and manuals for the ET-3400 trainer and H-8 and H-89 computers and related peripherals.

https://www.facebook.com/groups/heathkitcomputers
A Facebook group for Heathkit/Zenith vintage computer users.

---

5   If you are interested Heathkit test equipment, you may want to check out my book *Classic Heathkit Electronic Test Equipment*, available from lulu.com, Amazon, and other sources.

https://groups.io/g/hero-owners
https://groups.io/g/herobots
Two groups.io mailing lists for Heathkit robot users.

http://www.vintagecalculators.com
A good website on vintage calculators, including some Heathkit models.

https://hero.dsavage.net/robots/Hero_FAQ.html
A detailed Frequently Asked Questions (FAQ) list about Heathkit HERO robots.

http://www.classiccmp.org
A web resource for enthusiasts of classic computer hardware, software, and documentation, including Heathkit products.

https://technikum29.de/en/computer/analog
A website dedicated to analog computers, including the Heathkit models.

Appendix B – Combined Product Listing

The table below is a list of Heathkit products related to calculators, robots, computers, and related peripherals and accessories. It was obtained by reviewing a number of old Heathkit catalogs and is not a complete list of all the products ever offered. It does not include some items that were only sold by Heathkit Educational Systems after Heathkit left the kit market. Prices are in US dollars. In some cases, prices were changing rapidly and catalogs listed the price as "Call".

Figure 26: Combined Product Listing

Model	Category	Series	Kit	Description	First Year	Last Year	Lowest Price	Highest Price
830-35	Accessory	H-11	Y	Line Time Clock Switch Modification Kit	1980	1982	$53.50	$93.50
EC-1	Computer	EC-1	Y	Educational Analog Computer Kit	1961	1971	$199.95	$243.95
ECP-3801	Accessory	H-8	N	Heath-recommended cassette recorder for use with H-8	1978	1978	$69.95	$69.95
ECP-3802	Accessory	H-8	N	Heath-recommended audio recording tape (3 pack)	1978	1978	$8.95	$8.95
EE-1800	Robot	HERO 1	N	Robotics Course	1984	1984	$99.95	$99.95
EE-1812	Robot	HERO 1	N	Robot Applications Course	1984	1984	$99.95	$99.95
EE-3404	Accessory	n/a	N	6809 Programming Course, includes 6809 adapter for ET-3400 or ET-3400A.	1984	1984	$99.95	$99.95
ES-1	Computer	H-1	Y	Amplifier power supply kit	1956	1956		
ES-100	Computer	H-1	Y	Initial condition power supply kit	1956	1964	$19.95	$19.95
ES-151	Computer	H-1	Y	Relay power supply kit	1956	1964	$11.95	$11.95
ES-2	Computer	H-1	Y	Amplifier power supply kit	1956	1964	$132.95	$132.95
ES-200	Computer	H-1	Y	Amplifier	1956	1956		
ES-201	Computer	H-1	Y	Operational amplifier kit	1956	1964	$14.95	$14.95
ES-400	Computer	H-1	Y	Cabinet kit	1956	1964	$247.95	$247.95
ES-401	Computer	H-1	Y	Voltage regulator transformer kit	1956	1964	$96.95	$96.95
ES-405	Computer	H-1	Y	Patch cord kit (contains 12 patch cords)	1956	1964	$16.95	$16.95
ES-447	Computer	H-1	Y	Coefficient potentiometer kit	1956	1964	$26.95	$26.95
ES-450	Computer	H-1	Y	Auxiliary coefficient potentiometer kit	1956	1964	$36.95	$36.95
ES-50	Computer	H-1	Y	Reference power supply kit	1956	1964	$22.95	$22.95
ES-505	Computer	H-1	Y	Repetitive oscillator kit	1956	1964	$16.95	$16.95
ES-600	Computer	H-1	Y	Function generator	1956	1964	$69.95	$69.95
ET-100	Trainer	n/a	Y	Basic Learning Computer	1956	1984	$799.95	$799.95
ET-1000	Trainer	n/a	Y	Analog/Digital Circuit Design Trainer	1984	1992	$199.95	$229.95
ET-1000-1	Accessory	ET-1000	N	Extra Removable Breadboard Accessory	1984	1984	$29.95	$29.95
ET-18	Robot	HERO 1	Y	Basic HERO 1 Robot (less arm, voice)	1983	1984	$799.95	$999.95
ET-18-1	Robot	HERO 1	N	HERO 1's Arm (Arm and Gripper Mechanism)	1983	1984	$349.95	$399.95

Model	Category	Series	Kit	Description	First Year	Last Year	Lowest Price	Highest Price
ET-18-2	Robot	HERO 1	N	HERO 1's Voice (Phoneme Speech Synthesizer)	1983	1984	$99.95	$149.95
ET-18-4	Robot	HERO 1	N	Demo ROM	1984	1984	$49.95	$49.95
ET-18-5	Robot	HERO 1	N	Monitor ROM Listing	1984	1984	$39.95	$39.95
ET-18-7	Robot	HERO 1	N	Automatic Mode ROM	1984	1984	$29.95	$29.95
ET-19	Robot	HERO 2000	Y	HERO 2000	1986	1986	$1,999.95	$1,099.95
ET-19-14	Accessory	HERO 2000	Y	Experimenter Board	1986	1986	$89.95	$89.95
ET-19-51	Accessory	HERO 2000	Y	Demonstration ROM	1986	1986	$29.95	$29.95
ET-3100	Trainer	n/a	Y	Trainer, Electronic Design Experimenter	1976	1980	$59.95	$92.95
ET-3100A	Trainer	n/a	Y	Trainer, Electronic Design Experimenter	1981	1982	$79.95	$149.95
ET-3100AS	Trainer	n/a	Y	Trainer, Electronic Design Experimenter, with Spanish manual	1981	1981	$79.95	$79.95
ET-3100B	Trainer	n/a	Y	Trainer, Electronic Design Experimenter	1983	1984	$89.95	$89.95
ET-3100S	Trainer	n/a	Y	Trainer, Electronic Design Experimenter, with Spanish manual	1980	1980	$79.95	$79.95
ET-3200	Trainer	n/a	Y	Trainer, Digital Techniques	1976	1980	$69.95	$89.95
ET-3200A	Trainer	n/a	Y	Trainer, Digital Techniques	1981	1983	$89.95	$99.95
ET-3200B	Trainer	n/a	Y	Trainer, Digital Techniques	1984	1984	$99.95	$99.95
ET-3300	Trainer	n/a	Y	Laboratory Breadboard	1976	1981	$79.95	$94.95
ET-3300A	Trainer	n/a	Y	Laboratory Breadboard	1982	1983	$199.95	$199.95
ET-3300B	Trainer	n/a	Y	Laboratory Breadboard	1983	1984	$99.95	$99.95
ET-3400	Trainer	n/a	Y	Trainer, Microprocessor, 6808 CPU, 256 bytes RAM, 1K ROM	1978	1981	$199.95	$224.95
ET-3400-AE	Trainer	n/a	Y	Trainer, Microprocessor, 6808 CPU, 512 bytes RAM, 1K ROM, 240VAC 50 Hz	1983	1984	$249.95	$249.95
ET-3400A	Trainer	n/a	Y	Trainer, Microprocessor, 6808 CPU, 512 bytes RAM, 1K ROM	1982	1992	$229.95	$229.95
ET-3600	Trainer	n/a	Y	Analog trainer	1992	1992	$139.95	$139.95
ET-3700	Trainer	n/a	Y	Digital trainer	1992	1992	$139.95	$139.95
ET-6800	Accessory	n/a	N	Trainer, 6800 CPU, 1K ROM	1980	1983	$99.95	$129.95
ETA-100	Accessory	ET-100	Y	Expansion Accessory	1984	1984	$1,299.95	$1,299.95
ETA-100-1	Accessory	ET-100	N	Extra Removable Breadboard	1984	1984	$29.95	$29.95
ETA-100-2	Accessory	ET-100	N	Channel 4 Modulator, use with TVs	1984	1984	$39.95	$39.95
ETA-100-3	Accessory	ET-100	N	Channel 3 Modulator, use with TVs	1984	1984	$39.95	$39.95
ETA-19-15	Accessory	HERO 2000	Y	64K RAM Chip Set	1986	1986	$49.95	$49.95
ETA-3400	Accessory	ET-3400A	Y	Microprocessor Trainer Accessory	1980	1984	$150.00	$175.00
ETA-3400-1	Accessory	ET-3400A	N	Optional 3K Chip Set	1981	1984	$47.00	$49.95
ETA-3600-1	Accessory	ET-3600	N	Extra breadboard block for ET-3600/ETW-3600	1992	1992	$19.95	$19.95
ETS-100	Trainer	ET-100	Y	ET-100 and ETA-100	1984	1984	$1,999.00	$1,999.00

Model	Category	Series	Kit	Description	First Year	Last Year	Lowest Price	Highest Price
ETS-18	Robot	HERO 1	Y	Complete HERO 1 Robot (with arm and voice)	1983	1984	$1,199.85	$1,499.95
ETS-19	Robot	HERO 2000	Y	HERO 2000 Robot with Arm	1986	1986	$2,499.95	$2,499.95
ETS-19-1	Accessory	HERO 2000	Y	HERO 2000 Arm with Controller Card	1986	1986	$699.95	$699.95
ETS-19-32	Robot	n/a	Y	Robot Arm Trainer				
ETS-19-35	Accessory	HERO 2000	Y	Remote Keyboard Control 75.43 MHz	1986	1986	$499.95	$499.95
ETS-19-36	Accessory	HERO 2000	Y	Remote Keyboard Control 75.67 MHz	1986	1986	$499.95	$499.95
ETW-100	Trainer	n/a	N	Basic Learning Computer	1984	1984	$1,095.00	$1,095.00
ETW-1000	Trainer	n/a	N	Analog/Digital Circuit Design Trainer	1984	1984	$349.95	$349.95
ETW-18	Robot	HERO 1	N	Assembled Robot (with arm, voice)	1983	1984	$2,199.95	$2,499.95
ETW-19-15	Accessory	HERO 2000	Y	192K Static RAM Expansion Board	1986	1986	$99.95	$99.95
ETW-19-32	Robot	n/a	N	Robot Arm Trainer				
ETW-3100	Trainer	n/a	N	Trainer, Electronic Design Experimenter	1980	1980	$134.95	$134.95
ETW-3100A	Trainer	n/a	N	Trainer, Electronic Design Experimenter	1981	1982	$139.95	$269.95
ETW-3100B	Trainer	n/a	N	Trainer, Electronic Design Experimenter	1983	1984	$159.95	$159.95
ETW-3200	Trainer	n/a	N	Trainer, Digital Techniques	1980	1980	$149.95	$149.95
ETW-3200A	Trainer	n/a	N	Trainer, Digital Techniques	1981	1983	$159.95	$169.95
ETW-3200B	Trainer	n/a	N	Trainer, Digital Techniques	1984	1984	$179.95	$179.95
ETW-3300	Trainer	n/a	N	Laboratory Breadboard	1980	1981	$149.95	$159.95
ETW-3300A	Trainer	n/a	N	Laboratory Breadboard	1982	1983	$199.95	$199.95
ETW-3300B	Trainer	n/a	N	Laboratory Breadboard	1983	1984	$179.95	$179.95
ETW-3400A	Trainer	n/a	N	Trainer, Microprocessor, 6808 CPU, 256 bytes RAM, 1K ROM	1980	1980	$279.00	$279.00
ETW-3400A	Trainer	n/a	N	Trainer, Microprocessor, 6808 CPU, 256 bytes RAM, 1K ROM	1981	1981	$299.95	$299.95
ETW-3400A	Trainer	n/a	N	Trainer, Microprocessor, 6808 CPU, 512 bytes RAM, 1K ROM	1983	1992	$329.95	$329.95
ETW-3600	Trainer	n/a	N	Analog trainer	1992	1992	$229.95	$229.95
ETW-3700	Trainer	n/a	N	Digital trainer	1992	1992	$229.95	$229.95
EWA-100-A	Trainer	ET-100	N	Basic Learning Computer	1984	1984	$1,650.00	$1,650.00
EWA-3400	Trainer	ET-3400A	N	Microprocessor Trainer Accessory	1980	1984	$250.00	$275.00
EWA-3400-1	Accessory	ETA-3400	N	Optional 3K Chip Set	1980	1980	$47.00	$47.00
EWS-100A	Trainer	ET-100	N	ET-100 and ETA-100	1984	1984	$2,750.00	$2,750.00
EWS-19-35	Robot	HERO 2000	N	Assembled HERO 2000 Robot, Arm, and Remote Control with two 75.43 MHz frequency modules	1986	1986	$4,499.95	$4,499.95
EWS-19-36	Robot	HERO 2000	N	Assembled HERO 2000 Robot, Arm, and Remote Control with two 75.67 MHz frequency modules	1986	1986	$4,499.95	$4,499.95
GDC-11	Modem	n/a	N	Acoustic Modem	1982	1983	$199.95	$260.00
GDC-21	Terminal	n/a	N	LEX-21 Portable Terminal	1982	1982	$1,795.00	$1,795.00

Model	Category	Series	Kit	Description	First Year	Last Year	Lowest Price	Highest Price
GDC-21-1	Accessory	GDC-21	N	Acoustic Cup for coupling LEX-21 to telephone	1982	1982	$69.95	$69.95
GDZ-1320	Monitor	n/a	N	Color Video Display for computers, VCRs, cameras	1980	1983	$399.95	$659.95
H-1	Computer	H-1	Y	Analog Computer, Basic Component Group A	1956	1959	$495.00	$520.00
H-1	Computer	H-1	Y	Analog Computer, Full Component Group C	1956	1964	$945.00	$1,445.00
H-1	Computer	H-1	Y	Analog Computer, Medium Component Group B	1956	1959	$760.00	$775.00
H-10	Accessory	H-8/H-11	Y	Paper Tape Reader/Punch	1978	1978	$499.95	$499.95
H-10-2	Accessory	H-10	N	Three Rolls Blank paper tape	1978	1978	$15.95	$15.95
H-10-3	Accessory	H-10	N	Three Boxes Fan-Fold Paper Tape	1978	1978	$15.95	$15.95
H-11	Computer	H-11	Y	Digital H-11 Computer	1978	1978	$2,195.00	$2,195.00
H-11-1	Accessory	H-11	Y	4K Memory Expansion Module	1978	1982	$275.00	$275.00
H-11-10	Accessory	H-11	N	Wire Wrapping Board	1981	1981	$35.00	$35.00
H-11-19	Accessory	H-11	Y	Wire Wrapping Board	1982	1982	$44.95	$44.95
H-11-2	Accessory	H-11	Y	Parallel Interface	1978	1981	$95.00	$130.00
H-11-2	Accessory	H-11	Y	Parallel Interface	1982	1982	$95.00	$95.00
H-11-5	Accessory	H-11	Y	Serial Interface	1980	1981	$105.00	$135.00
H-11-5	Accessory	H-11	Y	Serial Interface	1978	1982	$95.00	$95.00
H-11-6	Accessory	H-11	N	Extended Arithmetic Chip	1978	1981	$190.00	$190.00
H-11-6	Accessory	H-11	Y	Extended Arithmetic Chip	1982	1982	$159.00	$159.00
H-11A	Computer	H-11	Y	DEC-compatible 16-Bit Computer	1980	1982	$1,195.00	$2,195.00
H-125	Printer	n/a	Y	Dot Matrix Printer	1983	1984	$899.00	$899.00
H-14	Printer	n/a	Y	Dot Matrix Printer	1980	1982	$495.00	$595.00
H-17	Disk	H-8	Y	Floppy Disk System	1980	1982	$575.00	$975.00
H-17-1	Disk	H-89	N	Single-Sided Floppy Disk Drive for H-77/Z-77 Disk Systems	1978	1984	$295.00	$425.00
H-17-2	Accessory	WH17	N	5 5.25" Diskettes	1978	1978	$34.95	$34.95
H-17-3	Accessory	H-8	Y	Three Drive Modification Kit	1981	1982	$85.00	$139.95
H-17-4	Disk	H-89	N	Single-Sided Floppy Disk Drive for H-37/Z-37 Disk Systems	1982	1983	$550.00	$795.00
H-17-5	Disk	H-89	N	Double-Sided Floppy Disk Drive for H-77/Z-77 Disk Systems	1984	1984	$550.00	$550.00
H-19	Terminal	H-19	Y	Professional Video Terminal	1980	1980	$675.00	$675.00
H-19-1	Accessory	H-19	N	Source Listings for ROM of H-19 and H-19A Terminals	1981	1983	$25.00	$30.00
H-19-2	Accessory	H-19	Y	Conversion kit, convert H-19 to H-88 All-In-One Computer	1981	1982	$695.00	$995.00
H-19-3	Accessory	H-19	Y	Conversion kit, convert H-19A to H-88 All-In-One Computer	1982	1982	$995.00	$995.00

Model	Category	Series	Kit	Description	First Year	Last Year	Lowest Price	Highest Price
H-25	Printer	n/a	Y	Dot Matrix Printer	1982	1983	$1,695.00	$1,850.00
H-27	Disk	H-11	Y	8" Disk System Kit with 2 drives	1980	1981	$1,995.00	$2,195.00
H-27-2	Accessory	H-27	N	Package of 5 Blank 8-inch Floppy Disks	1980	1980	$25.00	$25.00
H-29	Terminal	n/a	Y	Video Display Terminal	1983	1985	$449.00	$599.00
H-36	Terminal	H-8/H-11	N	LA36 DEC Writer II keyboard Printer Terminal	1978	1978	$2,195.00	$2,195.00
H-36-1	Accessory	H-36	N	Fan-fold Paper for H-36	1978	1978	$44.95	$44.95
H-36-2	Accessory	H-36	N	EIA RS-232C interface	1978	1978	$149.95	$149.95
H-36-3	Accessory	H-36	N	Acoustic Coupler	1978	1978	$339.95	$339.95
H-47	Disk	H-8	Y	8-Inch Dual-Drive Floppy Disk System	1981	1981	$2,995.00	$2,995.00
H-77	Disk	H-88	Y	One 5.25" disk drive	1980	1981	$595.00	$625.00
H-8	Computer	H-8	Y	H-8 Computer	1978	1983	$299.00	$559.95
H-8-1	Accessory	H-8	N	8K Memory Board, includes 4K	1978	1978	$249.95	$249.95
H-8-10	Accessory	H-8	Y	Wire Wrapping Board	1980	1983	$29.95	$49.95
H-8-13	Accessory	H-8	N	Extended Benton Harbor BASIC (1200 baud audio cassette)	1978	1978	$13.95	$13.95
H-8-14	Accessory	H-8	N	Extended Benton Harbor BASIC (fan fold paper tape)	1978	1978	$13.95	$13.95
H-8-15	Accessory	H-8	N	H-8 Systems Software on Paper Tape	1978	1978	$26.95	$26.95
H-8-19	Accessory	H-8	N	Z80 Replacement ROM and Front Panel Key Caps	1983	1983	$20.00	$20.00
H-8-2	Accessory	H-8	Y	Parallel Interface	1978	1982	$150.00	$249.95
H-8-3	Accessory	H-8	N	4K Memory Expansion Chip Set	1978	1978	$179.95	$179.95
H-8-4	Accessory	H-8	Y	4-Port RS-232C Serial Interface	1981	1983	$195.00	$279.95
H-8-5	Accessory	H-8	Y	Serial Cassette Interface	1978	1983	$95.00	$169.95
H-8-7	Accessory	H-8	Y	Circuit Design Breadboard Card	1980	1983	$79.00	$169.95
H-8-9	Accessory	H-8	Y	PAMGO ROM, Allows 1 or 3-button boot-up instead of 10	1980	1983	$20.00	$29.95
H-87	Disk	H-88	Y	Two 5.25" disk drives	1981	1981	$895.00	$895.00
H-88	Computer	H-88	Y	All-In-One Computer, without floppy, includes H-88-5 audio cassette interface	1980	1980	$1,295.00	$1,295.00
H-88-1	Accessory	H-89	N	Hard-Sectored Disk Controller Board for H/Z-89 Computers	1982	1984	$150.00	$229.95
H-88-10	Accessory	H-89	N	Wire Wrapping Board with Bus Connectors	1980	1984	$30.00	$49.00
H-88-18	Accessory	H-89	N	All-In-One Cassette Operating System	1982	1982	$40.00	$40.00
H-88-2	Accessory	H-89	N	16K Random Access Memory (RAM) Expansion Set	1980	1983	$29.00	$95.00
H-88-3	Accessory	H-89	N	3-Port Serial Interface for Older H-89s	1980	1984	$100.00	$150.00
H-88-4	Accessory	H-88	N	Floppy Disk Drive and Controller for H-88	1980	1981	$450.00	$490.00
H-88-5	Accessory	H-89	N	Cassette Interface (not used with CP/M)	1980	1984	$49.00	$165.00

Model	Category	Series	Kit	Description	First Year	Last Year	Lowest Price	Highest Price
H-88-6	Accessory	H-89	N	Backplate Modification Kit	1980	1982	$50.00	$79.50
H-88-7	Accessory	H-89	Y	Replacement ROM Kit	1981	1981	$55.00	$55.00
H-88-9	Accessory	H-89	N	High Capacity Drive Installation Kit	1984	1984	$50.00	$50.00
H-89	Computer	n/a	Y	All-In-One Computer, 16K RAM, floppy	1980	1980	$1,695.00	$1,695.00
H-9	Terminal	H-8/H-11	Y	Serial Terminal	1977	1977	$299.95	$530.00
HA-108	Accessory	H-100	Y	8 MHz and 256K RAM Conversion Kit for H-100	1985	1985	$249.95	$249.95
HA-8-1	Accessory	H-8	N	Extender Board	1980	1982	$40.00	$69.95
HA-8-16	Accessory	H-8	N	16K Byte RAM Chip Expansion Set for WH-8-64	1982	1983	$89.95	$89.95
HA-8-2	Accessory	H-8	N	Music Synthesizer System	1980	1983	$159.00	$295.00
HA-8-3	Accessory	H-8	N	Color Graphics Board	1981	1983	$295.00	$799.95
HA-8-6	Accessory	H-8	N	Z80 CPU Card for H-8	1981	1983	$199.00	$269.95
HA-8-8	Accessory	H-8	N	Extended Configuration Option	1981	1983	$65.00	$99.95
HA-88-3	Accessory	H-89	N	3-Port Serial Interface for older H-89s	1981	1984	$120.00	$165.00
HBT-40-1	Accessory	IBM PC	N	40MB DC2000 tape cartridge	1992	1992	$14.95	$14.95
HBT-40-AT	Accessory	IBM PC	Y	40MB streaming tape drive	1992	1992	$99.95	$99.95
HCA-1	Accessory	n/a	N	Bi-Directional Tractor Feed Accessory for WH-44K/Diablo 1640 KSR and WH-54 Printers	1980	1982	$259.00	$479.95
HCA-10	Accessory	MX-80A	N	Male-to-Male RS-232C Cable	1983	1983	$20.00	$20.00
HCA-11	Accessory	WH-53	N	RS-232 Computer-Modem Cable	1983	1983	$20.00	$29.95
HCA-13	Accessory	WH-12	N	Custom RS-232 Cable to connect WH-12 to H-8 and H/Z-89	1982	1983	$20.00	$29.95
HCA-14	Accessory	MX-80A	N	Parallel Cable	1983	1983	$25.00	$25.00
HCA-2	Accessory	WH-55	N	Printer Stand for WH-55 Printer	1980	1984	$99.00	$99.00
HCA-3	Accessory	H-89	N	Plastic Anti-Glare Filter, Clear	1980	1981	$8.95	$12.95
HCA-4	Accessory	H-19	N	Black Fabric Anti-Glare CRT Filter for H-19/H-19A	1980	1983	$19.95	$19.95
HCA-5-14	Accessory	H-14	N	Dust Cover for H/WH-14	1981	1982	$14.00	$19.95
HCA-5-17	Accessory	H-17	N	Dust Cover for H-17 Floppy Disk System	1981	1982	$14.00	$19.95
HCA-5-77	Accessory	Z/Z-90,Z-90	N	Dust Cover for H-37,H-77,Z-87	1981	1984	$14.00	$19.95
HCA-5-8	Accessory	H-8	N	Dust Cover for H-8	1981	1983	$14.00	$19.95
HCA-5-80	Accessory	MX-80A	N	Protective Dust Cover for MX-80/MX-80A	1982	1983	$14.00	$14.00
HCA-5-89	Accessory	H-19	N	Dust Cover for H-19 and H-19A	1981	1984	$14.00	$14.00
HCA-5-89	Accessory	H-89	N	Dust Cover for H/Z-89, Z-90, H/Z-19	1982	1984	$14.00	$24.95
HCA-6	Accessory	H-89	Y	Wire Wrapping Kit	1980	1983	$12.95	$21.95
HCA-7	Accessory	H-89	N	Wire Wrapping Socket Kit	1980	1984	$29.95	$49.95
HCA-9	Accessory	H/Z-125	N	Printer Stand for Z/Z-125 Printer	1981	1984	$99.00	$99.00
HDC-100	Accessory	H-100	N	Dust Cover for Low-Profile Computer	1983	1985	$16.00	$16.00

Model	Category	Series	Kit	Description	First Year	Last Year	Lowest Price	Highest Price
HDC-120	Accessory	H-100	N	Dust Cover for All-In-One Computer	1983	1985	$16.00	$16.00
HDC-125	Accessory	H/Z-125	N	Dust Cover for H/Z-125 Printer	1983	1984	$16.00	$16.00
HDC-207	Accessory	H-100	N	Dust Cover for the HS/Z-207	1984	1984	$16.00	$16.00
HE-Robot	Robot	n/a	N	HE-RObot (became PC-BOT)	2012	2012	$8,000.00	$8,000.00
HFM-9600	Modem	n/a	N	Internal fax/modem, 9600/2400 bps, for Heathkit laptops and ZDS equivalents.	1992	1992	$149.00	$149.00
HKS-11	Computer	H-11	N	Complete H-11A 16-Bit Microcomputer System	1981	1982	$3,995.00	$5,494.90
HKS-82	Computer	H-8	N	Complete Advanced H-8 Computer System	1980	1980	$1,995.00	$1,995.00
HKS-89-1	Computer	H-89	Y	H-89 All-In-One Computer with non-glare white CRT, floppy drive	1981	1981	$1,725.00	$1,725.00
HKS-89-2	Computer	H-89	Y	H-89 All-In-One Computer with non-glare green CRT, floppy drive	1981	1981	$1,725.00	$1,725.00
HKS-89-3	Computer	H-89	Y	H-89 All-In-One Computer with standard white CRT, floppy drive	1981	1981	$1,695.00	$1,695.00
HM-1100	Accessory	H-11	N	H11 Manual Set	1978	1981	$25.00	$30.00
HM-800	Accessory	H-8	N	H-8 Manual Set	1978	1981	$30.00	$30.00
HS-100-21	Computer	Z-100	Y	Low Profile, monochrome graphics, 128 KB RAM, one 5.25" drive	1983	1983	$2,199.00	$3,299.95
HS-11	Computer	H-11	N	H11 Computer System with 8K, parallel interface, serial interface, paper tape reader/punch, DEC Writer terminal	1978	1978	$3,350.00	$3,350.00
HS-1100-21	Computer	H-100	Y	Low-Profile Computer, Monochrome graphics, 128KB RAM, one 320KB 5.25" floppy	1983	1983	$1,999.00	$1,999.00
HS-1101-21	Computer	H-100	Y	Low Profile, monochrome graphics, 128 KB RAM, one 320 KB 5.25" drive, Z-DOS	1984	1984	$1,999.00	$1,999.00
HS-1101-22	Computer	H-100	Y	Low Profile, monochrome graphics, 128 KB RAM, two 320 KB 5.25" drives, Z-DOS	1984	1984	$2,299.00	$2,299.00
HS-1108-41	Computer	H-100	Y	H-100 Low-Profile Computer, 256K RAM, MS-DOS	1986	1986	$999.00	$999.00
HS-1108-41	Computer	H-100	Y	Low-Profile with 256K RAM, one 5.25" drive, 8 MHz operation, and MS-DOS	1985	1985	$1,599.00	$1,599.00
HS-1108-42	Computer	H-100	Y	Low-Profile with 256K RAM, two 5.25" drives, 8 MHz operation, and MS-DOS	1985	1985	$1,799.00	$1,799.00
HS-1151-21	Computer	HS-151	Y	Low-Profile Personal Computer, 128K RAM, one 5.25" disk drive with 360KB storage	1985	1985	$1,299.00	$1,299.00
HS-1151-22	Computer	HS-151	Y	Low-Profile Personal Computer, 128K RAM, two 5.25" disk drives with 720KB storage	1985	1985	$1,499.00	$1,499.00
HS-148-41	Computer	H-148	Y	Compact Personal Computer with one 5.25" disk drive	1985	1985	$999.00	$999.00

Model	Category	Series	Kit	Description	First Year	Last Year	Lowest Price	Highest Price
HS-151-21	Computer	HS-151	Y	Low-Profile Personal Computer, 128K RAM, one 5.25" disk drive with 360KB storage	1984	1984	$1,899.00	$1,899.00
HS-151-22	Computer	HS-151	Y	Low-Profile Personal Computer, 128K RAM, two 5.25" disk drives with 720KB storage	1984	1984	$2,199.00	$2,199.00
HS-158-41	Computer	H-158	Y	Expandable Personal Computer with one 5.25" disk drive	1985	1985	$1,599.00	$1,599.00
HS-158-42	Computer	H-158	Y	Expandable Personal Computer with two 5.25" disk drives	1985	1985	$1,799.00	$1,799.00
HS-161-21	Computer	HS-161	Y	Portable Personal Computer with non-glare 9" amber CRT, 128 KB RAM, 4 open IBM compatible expansion slots, one 5.25" disk drive, with 360 KB of storage	1984	1984	$1,699.00	$1,699.00
HS-161-22	Computer	HS-161	Y	Portable Personal Computer with non-glare 9" amber CRT, 128 KB RAM, 4 open IBM compatible expansion slots, two 5.25" disk drives, with 720 KB of storage	1984	1984	$1,999.00	$1,999.00
HS-19-1	Terminal	H-19	Y	Professional Video Terminal with anti-glare white CRT	1981	1982	$725.00	$1,035.00
HS-19-10	Computer	H/Z-19	N	H/Z-19 Conversion System to convert to H-89 All-In-One Computer	1983	1983	$995.00	$995.00
HS-19-2	Terminal	H-19	Y	Professional Video Terminal with anti-glare green CRT	1981	1983	$549.00	$899.95
HS-19-3	Terminal	H-19	Y	Professional Video Terminal with standard white CRT	1981	1983	$549.00	$899.95
HS-207-41	Disk	H-100	Y	Eight-inch Floppy Disk System with one disk drive and capable of storing 1.25 megabytes (MB) of data on a double-sided double-density 8" diskette	1984	1984	$999.00	$999.00
HS-207-42	Disk	H-100	Y	Eight-inch Floppy Disk System with two 8" disk drives, 2.5MB of data storage	1984	1984	$1,599.00	$1,599.00
HS-217	Disk	H-100	Y	Winchester upgrade kit for H-100, for models with full-height drives	1984	1985	$999.00	$1,799.00
HS-217A	Disk	H-100	Y	Winchester upgrade kit for H-100, for models with half-height drives	1984	1985	$999.00	$1,799.00
HS-248	Computer	n/a	Y	IBM compatible, 286, 512KB RAM, one 5.25" floppy	1986	1986	$2,499.00	$2,499.00
HS-2526	Computer	IBM PC	Y	IBM compatible, 286 processor, 12 MHz CPU, 1MB RAM, one 3.5" floppy drive	1988	1988	$2,199.00	$2,199.00
HS-2526-A	Computer	IBM PC	Y	IBM compatible, 286 processor, 12 MHz CPU, 1MB RAM, one 3.5" floppy drive	1989	1989	$1,899.00	$1,899.00
HS-2860	Computer	IBM PC	Y	Laptop, 286 CPU, 1MB RAM, one 3.5" floppy drive	1988	1989	$2,599.00	$2,999.00

Model	Category	Series	Kit	Description	First Year	Last Year	Lowest Price	Highest Price
HS-2862	Computer	IBM PC	Y	IBM compatible laptop, 286, 1MB RAM, one 3.5" floppy	1990	1990	Call	Call
HS-2862-A	Computer	IBM PC	Y	IBM compatible laptop, 286, 1MB RAM, 20MB hard drive, 640x480 video.	1992	1992	$999.00	$1,449.00
HS-3286	Computer	n/a	Y	IBM compatible laptop, 16 MHz 386SX CPU, 3 MB RAM	1990	1990	Call	Call
HS-3629	Computer	n/a	Y	IBM compatible, 386, 2MB RAM, one 3.5" floppy	1989	1989	$3,999.00	$3,999.00
HS-3629-A	Computer	IBM PC	Y	IBM compatible, 386, 2MB RAM	1990	1990	Call	Call
HS-3629-B	Computer	IBM PC	Y	IBM compatible, 386, 2MB RAM, 2x40MB hard drive, 3.5" floppy	1992	1992	$1,795.00	$2,393.00
HS-37-1	Disk	H/Z-89, Z-90	Y	Floppy drive, 5.25", single-sided, external, single	1982	1984	$795.00	$1,195.00
HS-37-2	Disk	H/Z-89, Z-90	Y	Floppy drive, 5.25", single-sided, external, dual	1982	1984	$1,295.00	$1,895.00
HS-386-A	Computer	IBM PC	Y	16 MHz 386 Desktop Computer, 1MB RAM, 5.25" floppy drive	1987	1987	$3,349.95	$3,349.95
HS-386-C	Computer	IBM PC	Y	16 MHz 386 Desktop Computer, 1MB RAM, 3.5" floppy drive	1988	1989	$2,699.00	$3,349.00
HS-3860	Computer	IBM PC	Y	IBM compatible laptop, 386, 2MB RAM, one 3.5" floppy, 40MB hard drive	1989	1989	$4,369.00	$4,369.00
HS-40	Computer	IBM PC	Y	IBM compatible, 8 MHz 286, 1MB RAM, two 3.5" floppies	1988	1988	$1,699.00	$1,699.00
HS-40A	Computer	IBM PC	Y	IBM compatible, 8 MHz 286, 1MB RAM, two 3.5" floppies	1989	1989	$1,599.00	$1,599.00
HS-42	Computer	IBM PC	Y	IBM compatible, 12 MHz 286, 1MB RAM, two 3.5" floppies	1989	1989	$1,799.00	$1,799.00
HS-5100	Computer	IBM PC	Y	IBM compatible, 1MB RAM	1990	1990	Call	Call
HS-5100-A	Computer	IBM PC	Y	IBM compatible, 1MB RAM, 286 processor	1990	1990	Call	Call
HS-5100-SX	Computer	IBM PC	Y	IBM compatible, 386SX, 1MB RAM, 3.5" floppy, 40MB hard drive, Zenith FTM VGA monitor.	1992	1992	$1,299.00	$3,304.00
HS-5100-X	Computer	IBM PC	Y	IBM compatible, 1MB RAM, 386SX processor	1990	1990	Call	Call
HS-77-1	Disk	H/Z-89, Z-90	Y	Floppy drive, 5.25", single-sided, external, single	1982	1984	$499.00	$825.00
HS-77-2	Disk	H/Z-89, Z-90	Y	Floppy drive, 5.25", single-sided, external, dual	1982	1984	$769.00	$1,125.00
HS-88-1	Computer	H-88	Y	H-89 All-In-One Computer with non-glare white CRT, no floppy drive	1981	1981	$1,325.00	$1,325.00
HS-88-2	Computer	H-88	Y	H-89 All-In-One Computer with non-glare green CRT, no floppy drive	1981	1981	$1,325.00	$1,325.00
HS-88-3	Computer	H-88	Y	H-89 All-In-One Computer with standard white CRT, no floppy drive	1981	1981	$1,295.00	$1,295.00

Model	Category	Series	Kit	Description	First Year	Last Year	Lowest Price	Highest Price
HS-89-1	Computer	H-89	Y	All-In-One Computer with anti-glare white CRT	1982	1982	$2,795.00	$2,795.00
HS-89-2	Computer	H-89	Y	All-In-One Computer with anti-glare green CRT	1983	1984	$1,049.95	$2,795.00
HS-89-3	Computer	H-89	Y	All-In-One Computer with standard white CRT	1983	1984	$999.95	$2,750.00
HSA-1120-21	Computer	H-100	Y	All-In-One Z/Z-100 series computer, non-glare amber CRT	1983	1983	$2,149.00	$3,499.95
HSA-1121-21	Computer	H-100	Y	Monochrome graphics, non-glare amber CRT, 128 KB RAM, one 320 KB 5.25" drive, Z-DOS	1984	1984	$2,149.00	$2,149.00
HSA-1121-22	Computer	H-100	Y	Monochrome graphics, non-glare amber CRT, 128 KB RAM, two 320 KB 5.25" drives, Z-DOS	1984	1984	$2,449.00	$2,449.00
HSA-1128-41	Computer	H-100	Y	All-In-One with monochrome graphics, non-glare amber CRT, 256K RAM, one 5.25" drive, 8 MHz operation, and MS-DOS	1985	1985	$1,699.00	$1,699.00
HSA-1128-42	Computer	H-100	Y	All-In-One with monochrome graphics, non-glare amber CRT, 256K RAM, two 5.25" drives, 8 MHz operation, and MS-DOS	1985	1985	$1,899.00	$1,899.00
HSA-2161-21	Computer	HS-161	Y	Portable PC with amber CRT and single 5.25" disk drive	1985	1985	$1,299.00	$1,299.00
HSA-2161-22	Computer	HS-161	Y	Portable PC with amber CRT and dual 5.25" disk drives	1985	1985	$1,499.00	$1,499.00
HSG-1120-21	Computer	H-100	Y	Monochrome graphics, non-glare green CRT, 128 KB RAM, one 320 KB 5.25" drive, Z-DOS	1984	1984	$2,149.00	$2,149.00
HSG-1121-21	Computer	H-100	Y	Monochrome graphics, non-glare green CRT, 128 KB RAM, one 320 KB 5.25" drive, Z-DOS	1984	1984	$2,149.00	$2,149.00
HSG-1121-22	Computer	H-100	Y	Monochrome graphics, non-glare green CRT, 128 KB RAM, two 320 KB 5.25" drives, Z-DOS	1984	1984	$2,449.00	$2,449.00
HSG-1128-41	Computer	H-100	Y	All-In-One with monochrome graphics, non-glare green CRT, 256K RAM, one 5.25" drive, 8 MHz operation, and MS-DOS	1985	1985	$1,699.00	$1,699.00
HSG-1128-42	Computer	H-100	Y	All-In-One with monochrome graphics, non-glare green CRT, 256K RAM, two 5.25" drives, 8 MHz operation, and MS-DOS	1985	1985	$1,899.00	$1,899.00
HSG-120-21	Computer	H-100	Y	All-In-One Z/Z-100 series computer, non-glare green CRT	1983	1983	$2,349.00	$3,499.95
HSG-2161-21	Computer	HS-161	Y	Portable PC with green CRT and single 5.25" disk drive	1985	1985	$1,299.00	$1,299.00

Model	Category	Series	Kit	Description	First Year	Last Year	Lowest Price	Highest Price
HSG-2161-22	Computer	HS-161	Y	Portable PC with green CRT and dual 5.25" disk drives	1985	1985	$1,499.00	$1,499.00
HSW-1120-21	Computer	H-100	Y	Monochrome graphics, non-glare white CRT, 128 KB RAM, one 320 KB 5.25" drive, Z-DOS	1983	1983	$2,149.00	$2,149.00
HSW-1121-21	Computer	H-100	Y	Monochrome graphics, non-glare white CRT, 128 KB RAM, one 320 KB 5.25" drive, Z-DOS	1984	1984	$2,149.00	$2,149.00
HSW-1121-22	Computer	H-100	Y	Monochrome graphics, non-glare white CRT, 128 KB RAM, two 320 KB 5.25" drives, Z-DOS	1984	1984	$2,449.00	$2,449.00
HSW-1128-41	Computer	H-100	Y	All-In-One with monochrome graphics, non-glare white CRT, 256K RAM, one 5.25" drive, 8 MHz operation, and MS-DOS	1985	1985	$1,699.00	$1,699.00
HSW-1128-42	Computer	H-100	Y	All-In-One with monochrome graphics, non-glare white CRT, 256K RAM, two 5.25" drives, 8 MHz operation, and MS-DOS	1985	1985	$1,899.00	$1,899.00
HSW-120-21	Computer	H-100	Y	All-In-One Z/Z-100 series computer, non-glare white CRT	1983	1983	$2,349.00	$3,499.95
HT-10	Terminal	n/a	Y	Video Display Terminal, includes ZVM-121 video monitor without modem	1983	1985	$399.00	$399.00
HT-1011	Terminal	n/a	Y	Video Display Terminal, includes ZVM-121 video display monitor, RS-232C port and 300 baud modem	1983	1985	$449.00	$449.00
HT-11	Software	H-11	N	BASIC Interpreter	1981	1982	$350.00	$490.00
HT-11-1	Software	H-11	N	FORTRAN Language	1981	1982	$250.00	$350.00
HTX-10	Terminal	n/a	Y	Video Display Terminal, less video display monitor and without modem	1983	1985	$279.00	$279.00
HTX-10-1	Modem	n/a	N	Auto-dial and auto-answer 300 baud modem for use only with HTX and ZTX model terminals	1983	1985	$69.95	$69.95
HVM-1220A	Monitor	n/a	Y	Economical 12" Monochrome Monitor	1986	1987	$59.95	$89.95
HVM-122A	Monitor	n/a	N	Video display	1984	1984	$89.95	$109.95
IC-2006	Calculator	n/a	Y	Four-function pocket calculator kit. 1/8" high LED 8-digit display. 9V battery. Optional GRA-43-1 AC adapter.	1973	1976	$29.95	$69.95
IC-2008	Calculator	n/a	Y	Desktop calculator kit. 8-digit gas discharge display 4-function plus constant. Fixed and floating point modes.	1972	1972	$139.95	$139.95
IC-2008A	Calculator	n/a	Y	Desktop calculator kit. 8-digit gas discharge display. 4-function plus constant. Fixed and floating point modes. Replaced IC-2008.	1973	1973	$139.95	$139.95

Model	Category	Series	Kit	Description	First Year	Last Year	Lowest Price	Highest Price
IC-2009	Calculator	n/a	Y	Four-function pocket calculator kit. 8-digit LED display. Auto power-off. Internal rechargeable NiCd batteries. Optional desk set with charger, pen and pad holder. Optional carrying case.	1973	1974	$74.95	$99.50
IC-2100	Calculator	n/a	Y	Electronic Slide Rule Desktop calculator kit. 4 function plus square, square root, log and trig functions in degrees and radians. 1/2" 8-digit gas discharge display. Memory register. Line powered.	1974	1976	$79.95	$119.95
IC-2108	Calculator	n/a	Y	Desktop calculator kit. 4-function plus constant. Fixed and floating point modes. 1/2" 8-digit gas discharge display. Line powered.	1973	1976	$29.95	$69.95
ICA-2009-1	Accessory	IC-2009	N	Carrying Case for IC-2009 Calculator	1974	1974	$3.95	$3.95
ICL-2009	Calculator	n/a	Y	IC-2009 calculator with carrying case and desk set	1974	1976	$49.95	$74.95
MPI-150	Printer	n/a	N	Impact Matrix Printer	1984	1984	$995.00	$995.00
MPI-99	Printer	n/a	N	Impact Matrix Printer	1984	1984	$599.00	$599.00
MX-100	Printer	n/a	N	Epson MX-100 printer	1983	1983	$1,199.00	$1,199.00
MX-80	Printer	n/a	N	Epson MX-80 printer	1982	1982	$899.00	$899.00
MX-80-2	Accessory	MX-80	N	Serial interface for MX-80 Printer	1982	1982	$110.00	$110.00
MX-80-3	Accessory	MX-80A	N	Buffered RS-232C Serial Interface	1983	1983	$135.00	$199.95
MX-80-4	Accessory	MX-80A	N	ROM Set to add extended graphics set to MX-80s	1983	1983	$60.00	$99.95
MX-80A	Printer	n/a	N	Epson MX-80A Dot Matrix Printer	1983	1983	$499.00	$899.95
OC-1401	Calculator	n/a	Y	OC-1401 Aircraft Navigation Computer. Flight calculations based on air speed, wind triangle, VOR, up to 9 flight legs. Internal rechargeable batteries. Optional hard and soft carrying cases.	1978	1981	$99.95	$169.95
OCW-1401	Calculator	n/a	Y	Assembled version of OC-1401	1978	1981	$149.95	$199.95
PBS-101	Computer	IBM PC	Y	Portable Workstation,laptop, 20MB hard drive, printer	1988	1988	$3,399.00	$3,399.00
PBS-202	Computer	IBM PC	Y	High-Performance Compact Workstation, two 3.5" floppies, 20MB hard drive, monitor, printer, software	1988	1988	$2,799.00	$2,799.00
PBS-4	Computer	IBM PC	N	Affordable Student Workstation, 20MB hard drive, printer	1988	1988	$999.00	$999.00
PBS-502	Computer	IBM PC	Y	Desktop Publishing Workstation, 1 3.5" floppy drive, 20 MB hard drive, laser printer, mouse, UPS	1988	1988	$5,599.00	$5,599.00
PBS-602	Computer	IBM PC	Y	Complete Office Manager Workstation, 2 3.5" floppy drives, 20MB hard drive, printer, fax machine	1988	1988	$6,299.00	$6,299.00

Model	Category	Series	Kit	Description	First Year	Last Year	Lowest Price	Highest Price
PBS-702	Computer	IBM PC	Y	Computer-Aided Design Workstation, 386 CPU, 387 processor, 80MB hard drive	1988	1988	$13,499.00	$13,499.00
PBS-801	Computer	IBM PC	N	Computer-Based Instrument Workstation, 286 CPU, digital scope, industrial monitor, printer, UPS	1988	1988	$5,999.00	$5,999.00
RT-1	Robot	HERO JR.	Y	HERO JR.	1984	1984	$599.95	$599.95
RTA-1-1	Accessory	HERO JR.	N	Infrared Motion Detector	1984	1984	$119.95	$119.95
RTA-1-2	Accessory	HERO JR.	N	Remote Control Accessory	1984	1984	$179.95	$179.95
RTA-1-3	Accessory	HERO JR.	N	RS-232 Accessory	1984	1984	$49.95	$49.95
RTA-1-4	Accessory	HERO JR.	N	Two extra batteries	1984	1984	$59.95	$59.95
RTA-1-5	Accessory	HERO JR.	N	Cartridge Adapter	1984	1984	$49.95	$49.95
RTC-1-2	Accessory	HERO JR.	N	Preprogrammed Cartridge: Songs, Phrases and Rhymes #1	1984	1984	$19.95	$19.95
RTC-1-3	Accessory	HERO JR.	N	Preprogrammed Cartridge: Animals, Blackjack and TicTacToe	1984	1984	$39.95	$39.95
RTC-1-4	Accessory	HERO JR.	N	Preprogrammed Cartridge: Special Occasions	1984	1984	$19.95	$19.95
RTC-1-5	Accessory	HERO JR.	N	Preprogrammed Cartridge: Math Master	1984	1984	$24.95	$24.95
RTC-1-6	Accessory	HERO JR.	N	Preprogrammed Cartridge: Riddle Robot/Tongue Twister	1984	1984	$24.95	$24.95
RTC-1-8	Accessory	HERO JR.	N	Preprogrammed Cartridge: BASIC	1984	1984	$49.95	$49.95
RTR-1-1	Robot	HERO JR.	Y	HERO HR. with RS-232 and Cartridge Adapter Accessories	1984	1984	$649.95	$649.95
RTR-1-2	Robot	HERO JR.	Y	HERO HR. with Infrared Motion Detector, Remote Control, RS-232, and Cartridge Adapter Accessories	1984	1984	$849.95	$849.95
SK-203	Accessory	n/a	Y	Printer Buffer, serial and parallel interfaces	1987	1987	$199.95	$199.95
TM-100	Accessory	H-100	N	H/Z-100 Technical Manuals	1983	1985	$55.00	$110.00
TM-240	Accessory	Z-200	N	Technical Manual for the Z-200	1985	1985	$49.00	$49.00
WH-11-1	Accessory	H-11	N	Assembled 4K Memory Expansion Module	1980	1980	$95.00	$95.00
WH-11-2	Accessory	H-11	N	Parallel Interface	1980	1981	$150.00	$160.00
WH-11-5	Accessory	H-11	N	Serial Interface	1980	1981	$150.00	$160.00
WH-11-51	Accessory	H-11	N	Adapter Cable for H-11-5 Serial Interface	1980	1981	$15.00	$15.00
WH-11-UL	Computer	H-11	N	Assembled/UL-approved Computer	1981	1981	$2,100.00	$2,100.00
WH-11A	Computer	H-11	N	Assembled H-11A Computer	1980	1982	$1,995.00	$2,995.00
WH-12	Accessory	n/a	N	Votrax Type 'N' Talk Speech Synthesizer	1982	1984	$299.00	$599.95
WH-13	Accessory	H-8	N	Acoustic Modem	1980	1980	$175.00	$175.00
WH-14	Printer	n/a	N	Assembled H-14 line printer	1980	1982	$595.00	$795.00
WH-17	Disk	H-8	N	Floppy Disk System	1978	1982	$645.00	$1,095.00
WH-19	Terminal	H-19	N	Factory Assembled and Tested H-19 Video Terminal	1980	1980	$995.00	$995.00

Model	Category	Series	Kit	Description	First Year	Last Year	Lowest Price	Highest Price
WH-23	Modem	n/a	N	Modem, LEX-11 acoustic, 300 bps	1981	1984	$139.00	$159.00
WH-24-1	Printer	n/a	N	TI-810 Doc Matrix Printer	1980	1981	$1,695.00	$1,695.00
WH-27	Disk	H-11	N	Assembled H-27 Dual-Drive Floppy Disk System	1980	1982	$2,595.00	$3,995.00
WH-33	Modem	n/a	N	Direct-Connect Modem	1981	1982	$195.00	$295.00
WH-34	Printer	n/a	N	DECwriter Teleprinter	1980	1981	$1,095.00	$1,095.00
WH-42	Accessory	n/a	N	Hayes Chronograph	1983	1984	$199.00	$199.00
WH-43	Modem	n/a	N	Modem, Hayes Smartmodem 300	1982	1984	$279.00	$499.95
WH-44K	Printer	n/a	N	Assembled and Tested Diablo 1640 RO Printer	1980	1980	$2,995.00	$2,995.00
WH-44K	Printer	n/a	N	Letter Quality Printer/Terminal for Word Processing	1980	1981	$2,995.00	$3,295.00
WH-53	Modem	n/a	N	Modem, Hayes Smartmodem 1200	1983	1984	$695.00	$1,199.95
WH-54	Printer	n/a	N	Diablo Daisy-wheel printer	1981	1983	$2,295.00	$3,995.00
WH-54B	Printer	n/a	N	Diablo Daisy-wheel printer	1984	1984	$1,999.00	$1,999.00
WH-55	Printer	n/a	N	Diablo Daisy-wheel printer	1984	1984	$1,199.00	$1,199.00
WH-63	Modem	n/a	N	Modem, Muraphone MM-100 300 bps direct connect	1983	1984	$99.00	$99.00
WH-8	Computer	H-8	N	Factory Assembled and Tested H-8 Computer	1980	1980	$399.00	$399.00
WH-8-16	Accessory	H-8	N	16K RAM Wired Memory Board	1980	1981	$299.00	$299.00
WH-8-37	Accessory	H-8	N	Soft-Sectored Floppy Disk Controller Board	1983	1983	$249.00	$395.00
WH-8-4	Accessory	H-8	N	4-Port RS-232C Serial Interface	1980	1981	$250.00	$250.00
WH-8-41	Accessory	H-8	N	Serial adapter cable	1980	1983	$15.00	$31.95
WH-8-47	Disk	H-8	N	Wired H-8 to H-47 Interface, with two RS-232C Serial Ports	1981	1981	$235.00	$235.00
WH-8-5	Accessory	H-8	Y	Serial Cassette Interface	1980	1981	$20.00	$145.00
WH-8-51	Accessory	H-8	N	Serial adapter cable	1980	1983	$15.00	$32.95
WH-8-64	Accessory	H-8	N	64K Wired Memory Board	1982	1983	$599.95	$599.95
WH-87	Disk	H-89	N	Assembled Dual-Drive Floppy Disk System	1980	1980	$1,195.00	$1,195.00
WH-88-16	Accessory	H-89	N	64K RAM Expansion Kit	1981	1984	$115.00	$174.95
WH-88-47	Accessory	H-8	N	Wired All-In-One to H-47 Interface	1981	1981	$195.00	$195.00
WH-89-CA	Computer	H-89	N	Fully Assembled All-In-One Computer, 48K RAM, floppy, serial i/o	1980	1980	$2,895.00	$2,895.00
WH-9-1	Terminal	H-9	N	Interface Adapter Cable	1980	1980	$15.00	$15.00
WH-9121	Printer	n/a	N	Daisy Wheel Printer/Electronic Typewriter	1982	1983	$1,995.00	$2,695.00
WHA-11-16	Accessory	H-11	N	32K Byte (16K Word) Memory Expansion Module	1981	1981	$495.00	$495.00
WHA-11-5	Accessory	H-11	N	Printer to H-11A Serial Interface Board	1980	1981	$150.00	$150.00

Model	Category	Series	Kit	Description	First Year	Last Year	Lowest Price	Highest Price
WHA-11-6	Accessory	H-11	N	16K Word (32K Byte) Memory Expansion Module	1980	1982	$480.00	$795.00
WHA-34-2	Accessory	n/a	N	Tractor Feed for WH-34	1980	1981	$179.00	$179.00
Z-125	Printer	n/a	N	Dot Matrix Printer	1983	1984	$1,499.00	$2,495.00
Z-19	Terminal	H-19	N	Assembled version of H-19	1981	1983	$995.00	$1,395.00
Z-204	Accessory	H-100	N	Assembled H/Z-100 Multiport Input/Output Card (serial and parallel)	1985	1985	$395.00	$395.00
Z-205	Accessory	H-100	N	256 KB RAM Upgrade Circuit Board	1983	1985	$599.00	$999.00
Z-205-1	Accessory	H-100	N	64 KB RAM Memory Expansion Set	1983	1985	$79.99	$180.00
Z-205-4	Accessory	Z-200	N	256K RAM Chip Set	1985	1985	$199.00	$199.00
Z-205-4	Accessory	H-100	N	256K RAM Chip Set	1985	1985	$199.00	$199.00
Z-207-3	Disk	H-100	N	Second Disk Drive for kits and ZF-100-21	1983	1983	$99.95	$395.00
Z-207-41	Disk	H-100	N	Assembled and tested Eight-inch Floppy Disk System with one disk drive and 1.25MB storage	1983	1984	$1,599.00	$1,599.00
Z-207-42	Disk	H-100	N	Assembled and tested Eight-inch Floppy Disk System with two disk drives and 2.5MB storage	1983	1984	$2,299.00	$2,299.00
Z-207-6	Disk	H-100	N	Assembled and tested second Half-Height Eight-Inch Disk Drive, 1.25MB double-sided, double-density storage	1984	1984	$699.00	$699.00
Z-207-7	Accessory	Z-200	N	5.25" 360K Floppy Disk Drive	1985	1985	$250.00	$250.00
Z-216-8	Accessory	H-100	N	8087 Numeric Coprocessor for H/Z-100 Computers	1985	1985	$429.00	$429.00
Z-219-1	Accessory	H-100	N	Color Video RAM Chip Set	1983	1985	$74.99	$160.00
Z-22	Terminal	n/a	N	Economical user user-friendly terminal	1985	1985	$649.00	$649.00
Z-25	Printer	n/a	N	Dot Matrix Printer	1981	1982	$1,595.00	$2,495.00
Z-29	Terminal	n/a	N	Video Display Terminal	1983	1984	$849.00	$849.00
Z-29-1	Accessory	Z-29	N	Palm Rest Accessory	1983	1985	$15.00	$15.00
Z-29-2	Accessory	Z-29	N	ROM Source Listing	1984	1985	$25.00	$25.00
Z-329	Accessory	Z-200	N	High-Resolution Monochrome Video Card	1985	1985	$200.00	$200.00
Z-37	Disk	Z-89	N	Dual-Sided Floppy Disk System	1982	1983	$2,495.00	$2,495.00
Z-39	Terminal	n/a	N	Terminal	1985	1985	$749.00	$749.00
Z-405	Accessory	Z-200	N	1.5MB Memory Board, 128K installed	1985	1985	$399.00	$399.00
Z-409	Accessory	Z-200	N	Standard Video Card with monochrome and RGB outputs, 320x200 pixel resolution	1985	1985	$239.00	$239.00
Z-416	Accessory	Z-200	N	80287 Numeric Co-Processor	1985	1985	Call	Call
Z-47-BA	Disk	Z-89	N	Dual 8" Floppy Drive	1981	1981	$3,500.00	$3,500.00
Z-49	Terminal	n/a	N	Video Display Terminal	1984	1985	$1,099.00	$1,099.00
Z-49-G	Terminal	n/a	N	Video Display Terminal with green CRT	1984	1984	$1,099.00	$1,099.00

Model	Category	Series	Kit	Description	First Year	Last Year	Lowest Price	Highest Price
Z-67	Disk	Z-89	N	10.782 Megabyte Commercial Winchester Disk System	1981	1982	$5,800.00	$8,995.00
Z-87	Disk	Z-89	N	Single-Sided Floppy Disk System	1981	1983	$1,195.00	$1,695.00
Z-87-89	Disk	H/Z-89	N	Floppy drive, 5.25", single-sided, external, dual	1984	1984	$769.00	$769.00
Z-87-90	Disk	Z-90	N	Floppy drive, 5.25", single-sided, external, dual	1983	1984	$769.00	$999.00
Z-89-11	Accessory	H-89	N	Multi-Mode Interface Card	1982	1982	$225.00	$225.00
Z-89-37	Accessory	H-89	N	Soft-Sectored Disk Controller Board for H/Z-89 Computers	1982	1984	$299.00	$495.00
Z-89-67	Accessory	H-89	N	Interface, Required to interface Z-67 to H/Z-89 All-In-One Computer	1981	1982	$195.00	$255.00
Z-89-81	Computer	H-89	N	Assembled and tested H-89 with 48K bytes of RAM, built-in floppy disk drive 100K bytes of data storage and three serial I/O ports	1982	1983	$3,745.00	$3,995.00
Z-89-FA	Computer	Z-89	N	Assembled Z-89 Computer with 48K RAM, 5.25" Floppy	1981	1981	$2,895.00	$2,895.00
Z-90-80	Computer	H-89	N	Assembled with 64K bytes of RAM, Z-89-37 Double-Density Disk Controller Board, no internal disk storage and three serial I/O ports	1982	1983	$3,745.00	$3,995.00
Z-90-82	Computer	H-89	N	Assembled with 64K bytes of RAM, the Z-89-37 Controller Board, built-in floppy disk drive for 160K bytes of data storage and three serial I/O ports	1982	1983	$4,145.00	$4,395.00
Z-90-90	Computer	H-89	N	Assembled and tested H-89 with Z-89-37 Controller Board, 64K RAM, less disk drive	1984	1984	$2,499.00	$2,499.00
Z-90-92	Computer	H-89	N	Assembled and tested H-89 with Z-89-37 Controller Board, 64K RAM, 48 TPI disk drive	1984	1984	$2,799.00	$2,799.00
ZA-100-4	Accessory	H-100	N	S-100 Extender Board, allows easy maintenance and troubleshooting of accessory boards that fit into S-100 slots	1984	1985	$59.00	$79.00
ZA-138-42	Computer	n/a	N	Z-138 Portable Computer, IBM PC compatible	1985	1986	$1,999.00	$1,999.00
ZC-37	Disk	H/Z-90, Z-90	N	Floppy drive, 5.25", double-sided, external, dual	1984	1984	$1,699.00	$1,699.00
ZCM-1390	Monitor	n/a	N	13" Diagonal Color Monitor	1987	1987	$699.00	$699.00
ZCM-1490	Monitor	n/a	N	14" Diagonal Flat Technology Monitor	1987	1987	$999.00	$999.00
ZCM-1492	Monitor	n/a	N	14" Diagonal Flat Technology Monitor	1990	1990	Call	Call
ZD-12	Disk	Z-200	N	5.25" 1.2MB Floppy Disk Drive	1985	1985	$599.00	$599.00
ZD-200	Disk	Z-200	N	20MB Winchester Disk Drive	1985	1985	$1,499.00	$1,499.00
ZD-400	Disk	Z-200	N	40MB Winchester Disk Drive	1985	1985	$2,499.00	$2,499.00

Model	Category	Series	Kit	Description	First Year	Last Year	Lowest Price	Highest Price
ZDH-1211-DE	Computer	IBM PC	N	Z-159 Model 2 Computer with 640K RAM, two 5.25" floppies	1988	1988	$1,599.00	$1,599.00
ZDH-1217-DE	Computer	IBM PC	N	Z-159 Model 2 Computer with 640K RAM, one 5.25" floppy, one 20MB hard drive	1988	1988	$2,199.00	$2,199.00
ZF-100-21	Computer	Z-100	N	Assembled Low-Profile Computer with monochrome graphics and one 5.25" floppy disk drive	1982	1983	$2,899.00	$4,895.00
ZF-101-31	Computer	Z-100	N	Assembled, Low Profile, monochrome graphics, 192 KB RAM, one 320 KB 5.25" drive, Z-DOS	1984	1984	$3,029.00	$3,029.00
ZF-110-22	Computer	Z-100	N	Assembled Low-Profile Computer with color graphics capability and two 5.25" floppy disk drives	1982	1985	$3,499.00	$5,995.00
ZF-111-22	Computer	Z-100	N	Assembled, Low Profile, color graphics, 192 KB RAM, two 320 KB 5.25" drives, Z-DOS	1984	1984	$3,499.00	$3,499.00
ZF-118-42	Computer	H-100	N	Assembled Low-Profile with monochrome graphics, 256K RAM, two 5.25" drives, 8 MHz operation, MS-DOS and LOTUS 1-2-3	1985	1985	$2,399.00	$2,399.00
ZF-120-22	Computer	Z-100	N	Assembled All-In-One H-100, 12" green CRT, 128 KB RAM, two 320 KB 5.25" drives	1983	1985	$3,499.95	$4,099.00
ZF-148-41	Computer	H-148	N	Assembled Compact Personal Computer with one 5.25" disk drive	1985	1985	$1,499.00	$1,499.00
ZF-148-42	Computer	H-148	N	Assembled Compact Personal Computer with two 5.25" disk drives	1985	1985	$1,799.00	$1,799.00
ZF-151-21	Computer	HS-151	N	Assembled Low-Profile Personal Computer, 128K RAM, one 5.25" disk drive with 360 KB storage	1984	1984	$2,699.00	$2,699.00
ZF-151-22	Computer	HS-151	N	Assembled Low-Profile Personal Computer, 128K RAM, two 5.25" disk drives with 720 KB storage	1984	1984	$3,099.00	$3,099.00
ZF-158-41	Computer	H-158	N	Assembled Expandable Personal Computer with one 5.25" disk drive	1985	1985	$2,199.00	$2,199.00
ZF-158-42	Computer	H-158	N	Assembled Expandable Personal Computer with two 5.25" disk drives	1985	1985	$2,499.00	$2,499.00
ZF-171-42	Computer	n/a	N	Z-171 Portable PC, 256K RAM, two 5.25" floppy drives	1985	1986	$2,399.00	$2,699.00
ZF-241-81	Computer	Z-200	N	Assembled Z-200 with 512K RAM and one 1.2MB floppy drive	1985	1985	$3,999.00	$3,999.00
ZFA-161-21	Computer	IBM PC	N	Assembled Portable Personal Computer with non-glare 9" amber CRT, 128 KB RAM, 4 open IBM compatible expansion slots, one 5.25" disk drive, with 360 KB of storage	1984	1985	$2,150.00	$2,799.00

Model	Category	Series	Kit	Description	First Year	Last Year	Lowest Price	Highest Price
ZFA-161-25	Computer	IBM PC	N	Assembled Portable Personal Computer with non-glare 9" amber CRT, 128 KB RAM, 4 open IBM compatible expansion slots, two 5.25" disk drives, with 720 KB of storage	1984	1985	$2,599.00	$3,199.00
ZFG-121-32	Computer	H-100	N	Assembled H-100 with non-glare green CRT, 192K RAM, two 5.25" drives, 8 MHz operation, MS-DOS and LOTUS 1-2-3	1985	1985	$2,499.00	$2,499.00
ZFL-171-42	Computer	IBM PC	N	Assembled Portable Z-171 Computer with 256K RAM, two 5.25" drives, LCD display	1986	1986	$2,699.00	$2,699.00
ZFL-181-92	Computer	IBM PC	N	Z-180 Laptop, 640K RAM, two 3.5" floppies	1986	1986	$2,399.00	$2,399.00
ZFL-181-93	Computer	IBM PC	N	Z-181 Laptop, 640K RAM, two 3.5" floppies	1987	1987	$2,399.00	$2,399.00
ZMM-1470-G	Monitor	n/a	N	14" Diagonal Monochrome Monitor	1986	1987	$299.00	$299.00
ZMM-149-A	Monitor	n/a	N	14-inch Diagonal Monochrome Monitor, amber	1987	1987	$299.00	$299.00
ZMM-149-P	Monitor	n/a	N	14-inch Diagonal Monochrome Monitor, white	1987	1990	$299.00	$299.00
ZP-150	Computer	IBM PC	N	Z-150 Laptop, Microsoft Works in ROM	1985	1986	$699.00	$699.00
ZSS-184-1	Computer	IBM PC	N	SupersPort Model 2 Laptop with two 3.5" floppy drives	1988	1988	$2,399.00	$2,399.00
ZSW-184-2	Computer	IBM PC	N	SupersPort Model 20 Laptop one 3.5" floppy drive and 20MB hard disk	1988	1988	$3,599.00	$3,599.00
ZT-1	Terminal	ZT-1	N	Low-Cost Personal Terminal, with one-button access to CompuServe, with monitor	1983	1983	$569.00	$1,089.00
ZT-1-2	Accessory	ZT-1	N	Terminal Carrying Case	1983	1985	$24.99	$24.99
ZT-1-3	Terminal	n/a	N	Universal ROM set for upgrading older ZT-1s into programmable one-key access models	1984	1985	$49.95	$49.95
ZT-1-U	Terminal	n/a	N	Assembled and tested Terminal with monitor and modem less RS-232C serial port	1983	1984	$549.00	$549.00
ZT-1-UZ	Terminal	n/a	N	Assembled and tested Terminal with monitor and modem less RS-232C serial port	1985	1985	$549.00	$549.00
ZT-10	Terminal	n/a	N	Assembled and tested Terminal, includes video display monitor without modem	1983	1985	$499.00	$499.00
ZT-11	Terminal	n/a	N	Assembled and tested HT-1011 with video display, RS-232C port and modem	1983	1984	$579.00	$579.00
ZT-11-Z	Terminal	n/a	N	Assembled and tested HT-1011 with video display, RS-232C port, 300 baud modem	1985	1985	$579.00	$579.00

Model	Category	Series	Kit	Description	First Year	Last Year	Lowest Price	Highest Price
ZT-1A	Terminal	n/a	N	Low-Cost Personal Terminal, with one-button access to The Source, with monitor	1983	1983	$569.00	$1,089.00
ZT-1A	Terminal	n/a	N	Low-Cost Personal Terminal, with one-button access to The Source, with monitor	1983	1983	$569.00	$569.00
ZTA-1-1	Accessory	n/a	N	Parallel Cable	1983	1985	$25.00	$25.00
ZTC-3034-EB	Computer	IBM PC	N	TurbosPort 386 Model 40 Computer with 2MB RAM, one 3.5" floppy, 40MB hard drive, MS-DOS	1995	1995	$7,999.00	$7,999.00
ZTC-3034-MO	Computer	IBM PC	N	TurbosPort 386 Model 40 Computer with 2MB RAM, one 3.5" floppy, 40MB hard drive, modem, MS-DOS	1995	1995	$8,499.00	$8,499.00
ZTX-1	Terminal	n/a	N	Low-Cost Personal Terminal, with one-button access to CompuServe, needs video monitor	1983	1983	$449.00	$449.00
ZTX-1-U	Terminal	n/a	N	Assembled and tested Terminal with modem less monitor, RS-232C serial port	1983	1984	$449.00	$449.00
ZTX-1-UZ	Terminal	n/a	N	Assembled and tested Terminal with model less monitor and RS-232C serial port	1985	1985	$449.00	$449.00
ZTX-10	Terminal	n/a	N	Assembled and tested Terminal less video monitor and without modem	1983	1985	$399.00	$399.00
ZTX-11	Terminal	n/a	N	Assembled and tested HT-1011 with modem RS-232C port less video display monitor	1983	1984	$479.00	$479.00
ZTX-11-Z	Terminal	n/a	N	Assembled and tested HT-1011 with RS-232C port, 300 baud modem, less video display monitor	1985	1985	$479.00	$479.00
ZTX-1A	Terminal	n/a	N	Low-Cost Personal Terminal, with one-button access to The Source, needs video monitor	1983	1983	$449.00	$449.00
ZVM-121	Monitor	n/a	N	Monochrome Video Display	1982	1984	$139.95	$199.95
ZVM-121-1	Accessory	n/a	N	Cable to connect HVM/ZVM-121/12/123, to IBM	1984	1984	$5.00	$5.00
ZVM-121-1	Monitor	Z-100	N	Monochrome Video Display, Orchard Tan	1983	1983	$139.95	$139.95
ZVM-121-1	Monitor	n/a	N	Optional Monochrome Video Display, for use with HTX and ZTX terminals	1984	1984	$139.95	$139.95
ZVM-121-2	Accessory	n/a	N	Cable to connect HVM/ZVM-121/12/123, to Atari 1200	1984	1984	$15.00	$15.00
ZVM-121-Z	Monitor	Z-100	N	Monochrome Video Display, Earthtone color	1983	1985	$139.95	$199.95
ZVM-1220-A	Monitor	n/a	N	12" Diagonal Monochrome Monitor, amber	1986	1987	$119.95	$119.95
ZVM-122A	Monitor	n/a	N	Assembled and tested monitor with amber CRT	1983	1984	$139.95	$169.95
ZVM-123	Monitor	n/a	N	Assembled and tested monitor with green CRT	1983	1983	$139.95	$139.95

Model	Category	Series	Kit	Description	First Year	Last Year	Lowest Price	Highest Price
ZVM-123-2	Accessory	n/a	N	Tilt Base for HVM/ZVM-122/123	1984	1984	$15.00	$15.00
ZVM-1230-A	Monitor	n/a	N	12" Diagonal Monochrome Monitor, green	1986	1987	$119.95	$119.95
ZVM-123A	Monitor	n/a	N	Assembled and tested monitor with green CRT	1984	1984	$139.95	$139.95
ZVM-124	Monitor	n/a	N	Assembled monitor for use with IBM-PC and PC compatible computer systems, amber CRT needs monochrome printer adapter card	1984	1984	$199.00	$199.00
ZVM-1240	Monitor	n/a	N	12" Diagonal Monochrome Monitor, amber, TTL compatible	1986	1987	$169.95	$169.95
ZVM-131	Monitor	n/a	N	Assembled medium-resolution monitor	1983	1984	$379.00	$379.00
ZVM-133	Monitor	n/a	N	Assembled high-resolution RGB-only monitor	1984	1984	$559.00	$559.00
ZVM-1330	Monitor	n/a	N	13" Diagonal Color Monitor	1987	1987	$649.00	$649.00
ZVM-1330	Monitor	n/a	N	13" Diagonal Color Monitor	1986	1986	$649.00	$649.00
ZVM-134	Monitor	n/a	N	Assembled High-resolution color video display	1983	1983	$699.00	$1,099.00
ZVM-134-1	Accessory	ZVM-134	N	Cable to connect ZVM-134 to Z-100 Computer	1983	1983	$20.00	$34.95
ZVM-134-2	Accessory	ZVM-134	N	Cable to connect ZVM-134 to IBM Personal Computer	1983	1983	$34.95	$34.95
ZVM-134-21	Accessory	ZVM-134	N	ZVM-134 to IBM PC 16-Color Cable	1983	1983	$20.00	$20.00
ZVM-135	Monitor	n/a	N	Assembled high-resolution monitor	1983	1986	$599.00	$599.00
ZVM-136	Monitor	n/a	N	Assembled long-persistence RGB-only monitor	1984	1984	$799.00	$799.00
ZVM-1360	Monitor	n/a	N	13" Diagonal Color Monitor, long persistence	1986	1986	$799.00	$799.00
ZVM-1380	Monitor	n/a	N	13" Diagonal Color Monitor	1986	1986	Call	Call
ZVM-1380-C	Monitor	n/a	N	13" Diagonal Color Monitor	1987	1987	$799.00	$799.00
ZW-110-32	Computer	Z-100	N	Assembled Low-Profile Computer with color graphics capability, 192KB RAM, one 320KB 5.25" floppy disk drive and an internal 11MB Winchester disk drive	1983	1983	$5,499.00	$5,799.00
ZW-111-32	Computer	Z-100	N	Assembled and tested Low-Profile Desktop Computer with internal 11 MB Winchester disk drive, one 320 kilobyte 5.25-inch floppy disk drive, 192 kilobytes of RAM, color graphics capability	1984	1984	$5,499.00	$5,499.00
ZW-118-42	Computer	H-100	N	Assembled Low-Profile with internal 11MB Winchester, one 5.25" drive, 256K RAM, 8 MHz operation, MS-DOS and LOTUS 1-2-3	1985	1985	$3,399.00	$3,399.00

Model	Category	Series	Kit	Description	First Year	Last Year	Lowest Price	Highest Price
ZW-120-32	Computer	Z-100	N	Assembled and tested Low-Profile Desktop Computer with non-glare green CRT, 192 KB RAM, one 320 KB 5.25" disk drive and an internal 11 MB Winchester disk drive	1983	1983	$5,599.00	$5,899.00
ZW-121-32	Computer	Z-100	N	Assembled and tested All-In-One Desktop Computer with internal 11 MB Winchester disk drive, one 320 kilobyte 5.25-inch floppy disk drive, 192 kilobytes of RAM, non-glare green CRT	1984	1984	$5,599.00	$5,599.00
ZW-151-22	Computer	HS-151	N	Assembled Low-Profile Personal Computer, 128K RAM, 10.68 MB 5.25" rigid disk, one 5.25" disk drive with 360 KB total storage	1984	1984	$4,799.00	$4,799.00
ZW-158-42	Computer	H-158	N	Assembled Expandable Personal Computer with 10.6MB Winchester hard disk and one 5.25" disk drive	1985	1985	$3,699.00	$3,699.00
ZWG-121-32	Computer	H-100	N	Assembled All-In-One with internal 11MB Winchester, one 5.25" drive, 192K RAM, 5 MHz operation, MS-DOS and LOTUS 1-2-3	1985	1985	$3,499.00	$3,499.00
ZWL-183-92	Computer	IBM PC	N	Z-183 Laptop, 640K RAM, 3.5" floppy, 10MB hard drive	1987	1987	$3,499.00	$3,499.00
ZWL-200-2	Computer	IBM PC	N	Laptop, 286 CPU, 1MB RAM, one 3.5" floppy drive, 20MB hard drive	1988	1988	$4,999.00	$4,999.00

(this page intentionally left blank)

Bibliography

1: Robert Scharff, *The How and Why Wonder Book of Robots and Electronic Brains*, 1963, ISBN 978-0-5528657-2-2.

2: Jeff Tranter, *Letters from India: The Chronicles of a Canadian Family Living in India from 1970 to 1972*, 2023, ISBN 978-0-9921382-1-9.

3: Wikipedia, CARDboard Illustrative Aid to Computation, https://en.wikipedia.org/wiki/CARDboard_Illustrative_Aid_to_Computation

4: Briel Computers website (no longer in business), http://brielcomputers.com

5: ReActiveMicro website, sells Briel's Replica 1 and other products, https://www.reactivemicro.com/product/replica-1-plus-from-briel-computers

6: Mike Willegal's website: Apple, Scelbi, and other vintage computers, https://www.willegal.net

7: My YouTube Channel, http://www.youtube.com/user/jefftranter

8: Lulu Press website, http://lulu.com

9: Website for this book with errata, updates, etc., https://github.com/jefftranter/misc/tree/main/HeathkitComputersBook

10: Current Heathkit website, http://www.heathkit.com

11: Andrew S. Cromarty, Jacob H. Neugass, Jasen Levoy, *Electronics enclosure systems and methods*, United States patent application #20170086339 , 2017.

12: Andrew Scott Cromarty, Jacob H. Neugass, Jasen Levoy, William Charles Calhoun, *Radio-related telecommunications systems and methods*, United States patent application #20170033430 , 2017.

13: Mark Garlanger's JavaScript H89 Emulator, https://heathkit.garlanger.com/emulator/jsH89

14: Wikipedia, PDP-11, https://en.wikipedia.org/wiki/PDP-11

Bibliography

(this page intentionally left blank)

Table of Figures

Table of Figures

(this page intentionally left blank)

Alphabetical Index

About the Author

Jeff Tranter built his first Heathkit in 1974 and has a collection of Heathkits that he has described in over 100 YouTube videos. With a lifelong interest in computers, he has owned or used many of the early microcomputers, and more recently has acquired old computers and replicas as part of the retrocomputing movement. He previously published the book *Classic Heathkit Test Equipment*. A licensed amateur radio operator since 1976, he holds a degree in Electrical Engineering and has worked as a test engineer, software developer, consultant, and manager. He lives with his wife in Ottawa, Canada.